1990

The Arabic Role in
Medieval Literary History

University of Pennsylvania Press

Middle Ages Series

Edited by EDWARD PETERS

*Henry Charles Lea Professor
of Medieval History
University of Pennsylvania*

*A complete listing of the books
in this series appears
at the back of this volume*

THE ARABIC ROLE IN MEDIEVAL LITERARY HISTORY

A Forgotten Heritage

MARIA ROSA MENOCAL

uɦɦ University of Pennsylvania Press
Philadelphia

Library of Congress Cataloging-in-Publication Data

Menocal, María Rosa.
    The Arabic role in medieval literary history.

    (The Middle Ages)
    Bibliography: p.
    Includes index.
    1. Literature, Medieval—Arab influences.
2. Romance literature—Arab influences.
3. Literature, Medieval—Research.   4. Romance
literature—Research.   I. Title.   II. Series.
PN682.A67M46   1987   809'.894   87-5011
ISBN 0-8122-8056-3 (cloth)
ISBN 0-8122-1324-6 (paperback)

Designed by Adrianne Onderdonk Dudden

"But now tell me," William was saying, "why? Why did you want to shield this book more than so many others. . . . Why did this one fill you with such fear?" "Because it was by the Philosopher. Every book by that man has destroyed a part of the learning that Christianity had accumulated over the centuries. The fathers had said everything that needed to be known about the power of the Word, but then Boethius had only to gloss the Philosopher and the divine mystery of the Word was transformed into a human parody of categories and syllogisms. The Book of Genesis says what has to be known about the composition of the cosmos, but it sufficed to rediscover the Physics *of the Philosopher to have the universe conceived in terms of dull and slimy matter, and the Arab Averroes almost convinced everyone of the eternity of the world."*

—*Umberto Eco,* The Name of the Rose

Contents

Preface

Les étymologies arabes assignées par M. Ribera aux mots *troubadour* . . . ne convaincront certainement personne. (Alfred Jeanroy, *La poésie lyrique des troubadours*, 1934)

Accident and coincidence play as prominent a role in directing and shaping an individual's work as do perspicacity and good sense, perhaps a larger one. In the case of my own interest in how western scholarship has structured its view of the medieval past, both accident and an aging Lady Philology played critical roles. The story bears telling because it is preliminary to the discussion that follows, and as a narrative of detection and discovery, I believe it to be typical of the often-blindfolded search for parts of the literary ancestry of medieval Europe that many others have undertaken.

I began to study classical Arabic when well along in my graduate study in Romance philology, largely as a lark. I was fortunate enough to find the justification and encouragement for the venture from a professor of medieval Spanish who, as a former student of Américo Castro, was more prone to see the potential value of such an enterprise than most. But what I had assumed to be a somewhat pedantic fling became considerably more engaging, because the verb *ṭaraba*—meaning "to sing," among other things—happened to be on the vocabulary list of the first-year Arabic course I was taking.[1] Moreover, one day the Arabist who was teaching the course mentioned matter-of-factly that this *ṭaraba* was the root of the European word *troubadour*.

I was surprised both by the facility of the pronouncement and by its apparent status of established fact in the world of oriental studies, since in Romance philology nothing could be more remote than such certainty about the origins of the word *troubadour*. I knew even then that among Romance scholars it was a cause célèbre, its origins unknown and disputed, a textbook etymological riddle still assigned in Romance philology courses. I also knew that any intimations or suspicions that it was Arabic in derivation must be largely subterranean, not part of what was presented in the standard course. I thus demurred, saying only that it did not seem to me that this was the accepted etymon. The professor then suggested I might look it up and deliver confirmation or denial. I did indeed look it up, and I subsequently spent years sorting out the pieces of the puzzle, uncovering the tracks of an almost obsessive etymological search that had engaged countless linguistic and literary historians before me.

Few other etymologies, in fact, have provoked and sustained the interest of Romance scholars as that of *trobar* and *troubadour,* both because it has seemed to be *introuvable* (as Spitzer would pun when he added his name to the list of those succumbing to the lure of the mystery) and because it is emblematic and symbolic of an even greater and more obsessive mystery of origins, that of the troubadours' poetry itself. The sign may be arbitrary, but the ties it has to its object are formidable. Medievalists of all stripes have never succeeded in dismantling or avoiding the maze of disputes over the origins of troubadour poetry and "courtly love," and philologists have been hardly more successful in their efforts to establish the roots of *trobar,* or even its meaning. Before the divorce of historical linguistics from literary studies, the same individuals would address the origins of the two phenomena, the word and the poetry, in the same breath; after it, the phenomena might be addressed separately but hardly less vigorously.

Thus, as a relative innocent I found myself in the middle of what are among the most hotly debated topics in Romance studies, and I faced a trajectory of scholarship I could not explain in rational terms, for in looking into the etymology of *trobar* I had discovered what other philologists knew so well, that this bête noire and touchstone of Romance philology had produced staggering amounts of scholarship and had been debated from virtually every possible viewpoint. Indeed, from Diez's and Schuchardt's somewhat fanciful (but no less vigorously defended) notion that it came from *tŭrbāre,* as in *tŭrbāre aquam,* "to disturb the water," to the Neogrammarian plea for a reconstructed (and unattested) **tropāre,* few stones had been left unturned, few arguments left unargued. But "virtually" and "few" turn out to be key qualifiers. One argument—that it came from an Arabic word—was not only *not* favorably received, but worse, it was not even deemed worthy of heated and acrimonious discussion. The Arabic etymon was apparently destined never to figure as one of the *OED*'s list of possible solutions of an unresolved etymological mystery.

I did ultimately find the source for the Arabic etymon, the view accepted as patent truth by many Arabists. It turned out that in 1928, when this etymology was very much a riveting feature of the intellectual preoccupations of Romance scholars and when there seemed to be an unresolvable impasse among the different proposals that had been circulating since Diez's time, the eminent Spanish Arabist Julián Ribera had suggested that *trobar* may have come from the Arabic *ṭaraba*. It was a simple proposal, based on the hypothesis that the interaction of Romance and Arabic cultures in northern Spain and Provence had been substantial, especially in the musical and musical-poetic spheres. The evidence for his view existed in numerous historical sources and, more suggestively, in other related etyma, such as those pertaining to musical instruments. Aware of the linguistic difficulties of the solutions debated among Romance scholars, Ribera also pointed out that the proposed Arabic derivation was, relatively speaking, almost completely problem-free. It presented neither the semantic nor the phonetic difficulties of *tŭrbāre* and *tropāre*. *Ṭaraba* meant "to sing" and sing poetry; *ṭarab* meant "song," and in the spoken Arabic of the Iberian peninsula it would have come to be pronounced *trob;* the formation of the Romance verb through addition of the *-ar* suffix would have been standard. He was right on all counts, and his case was effortlessly documentable.[2]

After reading through the morass of disputes, lacerating contradictions, and fanciful speculations that characterized Romanists' arguments over the word's origins from halfway into the nineteenth century until past the quarter mark of the twentieth, and then reading Ribera's proposal, it occurred to me that the latter might well have been received as a welcome newcomer in the sweepstakes, a fruitful new path to explore, something new to fight about. As a novice and a naive student of the vicissitudes of Romance scholarship, it even occurred to me that philologists might have been enthusiastic about finding an unexpected solution to such a tenacious problem. But what I discovered in reading post-Ribera notes and articles on the subject, was that nothing could have been further from the truth. In fact, if today's philology student does not encounter this proposal under circumstances rather unusual for a Romanist (such as being in an Arabic class) it is still quite possible to remain completely ignorant of the fact that the Arabic etymon was ever proposed.

Ribera's etymon was never considered by Romanists. There is not a single etymological dictionary of English or a Romance language that gives the Arabic etymon as even a possibility, although the question is usually noted as "unresolved." While Romance scholars were aware of this new proposal, their attitude and the seriousness with which they dealt with it were neatly summarized by Jeanroy in the single sentence I have used above as an epigraph: It is an argument not worth arguing, because it could not convince anyone. Jeanroy's position is far from the exception; it is the norm.

Why had a plausible, straightforward, and not overtly irrational etymon for a highly problematic word in Romance been utterly rejected, cast into the oblivion of half-forgotten curiosities? Was it merely because it was Arabic? And why, when I turned to the parallel discussion of the origins of the poetry of *trobar,* did I encounter an analogous situation, one in which belief in the "Arabist theory" (a nebulous term that covers any number of different and often conflicting theories) was considered at best idiosyncratic?[3]

Whatever attitudes lay behind such wholesale rejection suddenly seemed to me considerably more intriguing than the original, clearly illusory, possibility of finding or establishing the truth about the origins of the word itself, let alone the poetry. From my perspective, the greater mystery lay in the configuration of a discipline within which the possibility that the answer to the riddle was an Arabic one produced either highly negative reactions or no reactions at all. The very possibility of an Arabic solution was shunned as taboo. For me, the question became not whether this word or that image came from the language, poetry, or philosophy of al-Andalus, as the Arabic-speaking Europeans called their Iberian homeland, but why discussions of such possibilities had such a different cast from others that concerned the medieval period and its cultural milieu—assuming that such discussions took place at all. This book is the result of my exploration of that question.

The number of books and articles on some aspect or other of the Arabist question is much greater than most Romance scholars might assume. It is a subject that, perhaps paradoxically, has engendered many studies over many years. The earliest were written in the eighteenth century. From that vantage point, in fact, the earliest theory of the origins of Romance vernacular love poetry is Arabist. But as I began to read in this extensive body of scholarship, I noticed that most works have several things in common. The first is that almost all begin or end with the observation that acceptance of the apparent facts or tendered theories they present is difficult, that Westerners—Europeans—have great difficulty in considering the possibility that they are in some way seriously indebted to the Arab world, or that the Arabs were central to the making of medieval Europe. A second shared feature of such studies is that they do not explore such observations further and go forward with the explicit or implicit assumption that whatever the nature of those blinders or the cause of the neurosis, the weight of the truth, reasonable argument, or unarguable fact that they proceed to disclose will win out.[4]

But the third feature they have in common is that fate and the reception of Europeanists have proven this assumption to be illusory: The powers of "reason" and "fact" in this sphere (at least as they have seemed to many) have not succeeded in altering the assumptions that shape the view of the Middle Ages held by most medievalists. The power of the general view remains considerably stronger. It rarely allows for the acceptance of specific studies, the canonization of specific texts, or the integration of specific bits of knowledge into our working body of information about the period. I became increasingly convinced that those scholars who pointed out the blinders of the West in this regard were no less blocked from the field of vision of most of their colleagues for having done so.

The present study is thus based on the premise, and derived from the conviction, that no specific study of any of the theories called "Arabist" can be successful so long as the most general views we have of the medieval period are as hostile to the notions of such influence and interaction as they currently are. Obviously, the hypothesis or the fact of an Arabic etymon for *trobar,* for example, is unintelligible and ultimately undiscussable, at least productively, if a considerable number of Romance scholars find it unimaginable—and thus unresearchable and unproveable. And many do. Thus, part of this study is an exploration of that observation that has remained, by and large, just an observation: that European scholarship has an a priori view of, and set of assumptions about, its medieval past that is far from conducive to viewing its Semitic components as formative and central. The aim is to explore the causes and configurations, as well as the inadequacies and shortcomings, of such views and to set out what different views of the period might emerge if we are able to strip ourselves of some of our cherished notions of "Westernness," notions we cling to quite strongly at times. The rest of the book is an attempt to reveal some of the different views of the literature of the medieval period that might emerge if such general views were revised as I suggest; if the myth of our literary heritage, in other words, were written differently. It attempts to glimpse what some of the configurations of medieval literary history and historiography would be if Arabist studies were not always unimaginable and thus usually marginal and on the defensive. That is, what would our study and recounting of that history be, for example, if all studies on this or that medieval Arabic "borrowing" were not so heavily shackled by the constraints of proving what is a priori unproveable to its readers and unreadable for the rest? What would our perceptions of medieval narrative be if the *Disciplina clericalis* and the *Thousand and One Nights* were part of the curriculum? Or our appreciation of the lyric of the twelfth century if our anthologies included the Hispano- and Siculo-Arab poets? What would it be if we did not have a simplistic notion, in this regard, of the complex phenomena of problematic cultural interaction and influence?

Thus I am reversing the priorities and emphases of my own predecessors. Rather than mention in passing that our views of the medieval period are hostile to a specific case of influence and then emphasize the proof that the influence is there all the same, I believe it is of primary importance to shift some of the emphasis to an exploration of the proposition that our view *is* hostile, to explore its deficiencies and inadequacies, and to consider the distortions it has created. Only then can one note, with any hope of being heard, that certain examples of influence seem to exist, for they will exist only if a different perspective has molded our appraisals. It is the vision of the period, the assumptions we hold, that must be explored first, for it is within such parameters that facts seem provable, theories logical, influence reasonable.

I undertake this study with the assumption that neither the case of *trobar* nor that of troubadour poetry is idiosyncratic. Moreover, literary historians have recently been coming to grips with the implications and effects of ideology on the telling of history, and it seems to me that the time is ripe for an exploration of some of the problematic aspects of medieval European literary history. I also undertake this enterprise in the hope that it may in some measure vindicate and return from exile some of the work of many others before me whose research I use gratefully, extensively, and unabashedly but who, I believe, overvalued the power of evidence and underestimated the power of the standards by which it is judged. I have made no great discoveries of undeniable links, constructed no new "proofs," or found heretofore lost manuscripts showing the West's indebtedness to medieval Arabic culture. I recount no facts that have been unknown or have remained unadduced by many in previous discussions. I will attempt merely to show why the texts, facts, and discoveries of others have seemed negligible or ignorable to so many Romance literary historians and to sketch out a perspective that would render them significant, that would bring them in from the cold and the oblivion to which they have so long been relegated.

This study, finally, is written in the belief that *ṭaraba* is as logical an etymon for *trobar* as *tŭrbāre* or **tropāre*, as worthy of a place in our interminable discussions and of an entry in the *OED,* only if we assume it to be thinkable in the first place. For Julián Ribera *was* wrong, and his theory quite naturally dismissable, in terms of the prevalent view of the medieval period. The question is whether that view is adequate, whether we wish to continue to spin such an ancestral myth.

Although writing a book is by and large a solitary exercise, it eventually seems to entangle any number of other people in the enterprise. Fortunately, prefatory acknowledgments allow us to release them from the snares (and all responsibility) and to thank them for having played their part. I happily acknowledge, first of all, the indirect but crucial role in the writing of this book played by the friends and colleagues whose unflagging moral support of my work in general, especially in difficult moments, made a greater difference than they perhaps realize. To pretend to name them all would be to invite some inadvertent omission, but I cannot fail to mention Victoria Kirkham, whose intellectual and personal generosity over the years has been decisive.

I am particularly endebted to those who have patiently read and reread any number of versions of this book, beginning with the doctoral dissertation from which it evolved into its present radically altered form. Without the criticisms, as well as the encouragement, of George Calhoun, Alan Deyermond, and James Monroe, it is unlikely that I would have had either the gumption to scrap what I started out with or the perseverance to devote the time and energy necessary for this project. My debt to Clifton Cherpack, who now knows far more about the matter of Araby in medieval Romance than any *dix-huitiémiste* alive—and far more than he bargained for—is not repayable. With everything from his unrelenting criticism of my style to his unflappable sense of humor that helped banish discouragement, he made this book possible. I hope he can live with that burden.

Some years before I was born, a young undergraduate at Princeton went to spend a summer in Cuba, in part to learn Spanish. As fate would have it, he was a guest in my grandparents' home. Several years ago he recounted to me how my grandfather, a generous and kind soul, helped him practice his numbers in Spanish by sitting with him at the family *finca* out in the country and patiently making him read aloud his own students' scores on exams he was correcting. The young man who profited by his love of teaching, in whatever shape it might take, would go back to Princeton and eventually become one of Américo Castro's most gifted and accomplished students and, coming full circle, my own unstintingly generous teacher and mentor. Without Samuel Armistead, without the inspiration he has always provided and his magnificent, multifaceted teaching, I would not be in this field today. The anecdote he recounted about learning how to count in Spanish from my grandfather was touching, in part because it made me realize how much the older and the younger man were alike in their wonderful and limitless dedication to learning. I count myself very lucky to have benefited so abundantly from those characteristics of Sam Armistead, as have, I know, all the others who have studied and worked with him.

It has always been a source of considerable regret for me that my grandfather, a scholar and professor himself, did not live long enough for me to know him better than I could as a child. He would be pleased, I believe, to see this book, and even more pleased, no doubt, to know how fully his own minuscule but gracious act of instruction had been repaid a thousand times over. This book is thus dedicated to the memory of my grandfather, Juán Manuel Menocal, and to Samuel Gordon Armistead, my teacher.

Notes

1. There are a number of problems involved in rendering Arabic words and names into English, and I do not pretend to resolve these in this book. When using Arabic words that are commonly used in English, I have used the form that is most commonly used, even if it may not provide the most accurate rendering of the Arabic: Koran rather than Qurʾān, Islam rather than Islām, and so forth. Less commonly used words and names that are generally unfamiliar I have transcribed using the most commonly used system in English. The word *muwashshaḥa* has an Arabic plural, *muwashshaḥāt*, but it has been discussed so frequently in English in recent years as to have acquired an English plural form, *muwashshaḥas*. I have used both, being guided by the extent to which my discussion is technical in nature.

2. For a detailed exploration of all the proposals concerning the etymology of *trobar* and documentation of the history of research on this word, see Menocal 1982. Menocal 1984 contains, in addition, an exploration of two other etymological discussions where the proposed Arabic etyma have been neglected: those of *matar* and *usted*.

3. More detailed accounts of the shunning of the Arabist theory in the discussion of the origins of troubadour poetry are found in Menocal 1979 and 1981.

4. Among dozens of examples, see two of the most recent: Watt 1972 and 1974. The latter, a talk in Italian that Watt considers a summary of his earlier book-length study on the influence of Islam on medieval Europe, includes a pointed comment: "La ragione di questa

mancata coscienza o trascuratezza del debito europeo verso gli arabi non si deve al caso né all'ignoranza: proprio come un nevrotico rimuove i fatti spiacevoli del suo passato così l'Europa ha cancellato dalla sua coscienza il suo debito al mondo arabo; perché, in altre parole, le da fastidio riconsocere il valore di un popolo che considera inferiore a sé:" (Watt 1974:81). See also the opening pages of Makdisi 1974 and 1976, where the author notes the difficulties encountered in such scholarship and quotes others in that regard. Chejne 1980 recounts the reaction of a Hispanist colleague to his work on al-Andalus and its impact on medieval Europe by saying he must just be another one like Asín and Ribera, one of those prone to see *moros* ("Moors") everywhere. A striking—and to this writer perplexing—exception to this role is Boase (1976), whose positive appraisal of the Arabist theory, among others concerning the origins question he surveys (and it is a remarkably comprehensive and evenhanded survey; see Cummins' 1978 review) is presented as if no obstacles had been encountered by the proponents of that theory.

CHAPTER ONE

The Myth of Westernness in Medieval Literary Historiography

Leave to us, in Heaven's name, Pythagoras, Plato and Aristotle, and keep your Omar, your Alchabitius, your Aben Zoar, your Abenragel.

—Pico della Mirandola

Modern civilization's myriad pretensions to objectivity have unfortunately tended to obscure the fact that much of our writing of history is as much a myth-making activity as that of more primitive societies. We often regard tribal histories or ancient myths that do not cloak themselves in such pretensions as less objective than our own. We are prone to forget that history is written by the victors and serves to ratify and glorify their ascendancy—and we forget how many tracks are covered in that process. The writing of literary history, the close and often indispensable ancillary of general history, is preoccupied with the myths of our intellectual and artistic heredity, and it, too, tells those stories we want to hear, chooses the most illustrious parentage possible, and canonizes family trees that mesh with the most cherished notions we hold about our parentage.

The most general, and in many ways the most influential and pervasive, image or construct we have is that of ourselves and our culture, an entity we have dubbed "Western," a clearly comparative title. Whether it is spoken or unspoken, named or unnamed, we are governed by the notion that there is a distinctive cultural history that can be characterized as

Western, and that it is in distinctive, necessary, and fundamental opposition to non-Western culture and cultural history. Few of us, even less as laymen than as scholars, have conceived of developments or tackled specific problems in the literary and cultural history of western Europe assuming anything other than that this is an appropriate model.

While the value and accuracy of such a characterization for the modern (that is, usually the Renaissance and post-Renaissance) period is for others to decide, and while it has recently been the object of intense criticism,[1] its relevance for those whose scholarly domain is further back in time, namely Europe's medieval period, has been less carefully examined. In fact, the continued relatively routine acceptance of the clichéd East-West dichotomy for the medieval period is particularly noteworthy because medievalists have for some time been attempting to overthrow a series of other clichés and simplistic perceptions of the Middle Ages.

But this particular aspect of the myth of our past appears to be so fundamental that questioning it is not part of the various programs for the reorientation and revival of medieval studies, and its precepts continue to be part of the foundation of most studies, including many viewed as new, even revolutionary, in their approaches. What many consider to be the ravages of the new criticism have left at least this part of our old-fashioned notions intact.[2]

The irony is that while the Kiplingesque dichotomy, with its tacit presupposition of the superiority of West over East, had its grounding in the visible particularism of Europe and the irrefutable dominance of European empires over their colonies in more recent periods, the medieval situation has been characterized by many, with ample documentation, as something more resembling the reverse. A surprising number of historians of various fields, nationalities, and vested interests have described the relationship in the medieval world as one in which it was al-Andalus (as Muslim Spain was called by the Arabs) and its ancestry and progeny that were ascendant, and ultimately dominant, in the medieval period. It has been variously characterized as the age of Averroes, as an Oriental period of Western history, a period in which Western culture grew in the shadows of Arabic and Arabic-manipulated learning, the "European Awakening," with the prince, a speaker of Arabic, bestowing the kiss of delivery from centuries of deep sleep. For a considerable number of historians, the "renaissance of the twelfth century" is a phrase that in part masks a revolution instigated and propagated by Andalusians and their cultural achievements.[3]

Remarkably little of the information and few of the hypotheses that have informed these views have passed into the realm of common knowledge, however. Even less so has this story—or its beginnings, the beginnings of a cultural history different from the one we are more used to nurturing—penetrated the ranks of the literary historians of medieval Europe.[4] The resistance to a consideration of this different story of our parentage, of a displacement of our conception of our fundamental cultural lineage, is quite deep-seated. The tenor of some of the responses to the suggestion that this Arab-centered vision might be a more viable historical reconstruction for the West has occasionally been reminiscent of the reactions once provoked by Darwin's suggestion (for so was the theory of evolution construed) that we were "descended from monkeys." It is time to scrutinize such responses more closely and critically than we have in the past.[5]

A preconceived and long-established, even canonized, image has a great impact on research on the literary and cultural history of a period. It would hardly be revolutionary to note that its import is enormous. We operate with a repository of assumptions, and knowledge based on those assumptions, that govern what concepts, propositions, and hypotheses we find tenable. The images we have of certain periods and cultures, the intellectual baggage we carry, is an inescapable determinant and shaper of what we are able to see in or imagine for those cultures or periods of time. Those images also determine what facts we include in our histories and what texts we canonize in our literary histories, although we then use those same facts and canons to justify and enhance the history they tell. The images and paradigms that thus govern or dictate our views, the parameters of our research, are not free of political and ideological factors or cultural prejudices, although the notion that there is such a thing as value-free, objective scholarship persists in many quarters to this day, particularly in literary scholarship.[6]

But the veil of supposed objectivity is not limited to the older, explicitly historicizing philological period of our literary studies. One of the effects of the advent and popularity of American new criticism, with its emphasis on the primacy of the "text itself" was to give greater vigor to that myth of the possibility of objectivity, the possibility of considering a text with very limited or no interference from external, and possibly distorting, considerations. There is some irony in the fact that while previous historically based literary studies may have explicitly tied texts to a cultural and historical paradigm that served to explicate the text, the new criticism in most instances succeeded merely in masking the effects that such an image had on the readings of the texts. While making believe that they had somehow miraculously been eliminated from the literary world-view of the scholar, the structuralist analysis of much literature, in fact, further cemented and canonized the historicocultural images and parameters that an earlier period of criticism had felt obliged to reestablish in each piece of scholarship.

At least in principle, the older procedure could lead to a questioning and criticism of the proffered cultural views and assumptions. There is little question, of course, of the benefits wrought by that shift in our perspective, of the value of many of the precepts of a supposedly purer and self-referential analysis of literary texts. It succeeded in restoring a notion of the special qualities of literature qua literature and corrected many of the deficiencies of previous scholarship.

But the silence of much of structuralism on issues such as the relevant sociohistorical background for a self-referential and supposedly purely synchronic analysis of a medieval text only ratified, for students as well as fellow scholars, the validity of the Europeanist diachrony and social milieu that clearly informed the semantic fields of such analysis.[7] Thus, the appearance of possible objectivity masked but did not eliminate the problem of a regnant ideological image in certain branches of literary historiography. Its dominance in literary criticism over the past thirty years has helped to preclude any direct examination of what images and paradigms we operate with and what their value and/or accuracy might be. Or it may be that it is merely coincidental that the effects of the shift away from a historical perspective in literary studies have been strongest in the precise period in which many historians and their textual discoveries (such as that of the *kharjas*) were suggesting that it was timely to revise our image of the past. In either case, the turning of the tide or the apparent end of a cycle makes it more critically acceptable to address the issue of our conceptual and imaginative paradigm of medieval history.

The notion that there are paradigms that govern both periods of history and bodies and periods of scholarship and that these paradigms undergo periodic revolutions has become so commonplace since the appearance of Thomas Kuhn's proposal as to make it redundant to quote Kuhn himself on the subject. It has become part of the common parlance of scholarly discourse in many areas to consider the nature and effects of such paradigms and, when they are perceived to exist, the shiftings of paradigms that signal major changes or revolutions of a "world view" or an "image."

The paradigm that to such a great extent established our own notions of what constituted the Middle Ages was partially formed in the immediate postmedieval period, which viewed itself as a renaissance—a rebirth, if we accept the implications of the terminology—following that moribund period. The definitions of "self" and "other" that emerge during this period commonly regarded as primarily modern, both chronologically and for its formative influence, focus in great measure on the nature of its relationship with preceding periods, the classical and the medieval. It was in and through the Renaissance that the dominant position of the classical Greek and Latin worlds emerged. The concept of self, and ultimately of the Western self, would be strongly affected, in many cases completely dominated, by the emerging relationship between the modern and the classical worlds, a relationship viewed as ancestral. Out of this relationship there was derived, ultimately, the critical notion, which remains strong today, of the essential continuity and unity of Western civilization from the Greeks through fifteenth-century Italy, having survived the lull of the Dark Ages, and thence through the rest of Europe and European history. It is a notion of history formulated as much to deny the medieval past and its heritage as to establish a new and more worthy ancestry.[8]

But in this view of the world that preceded the Renaissance, the world from whose shadow it emerged, the paradigm of the Renaissance is necessarily paradoxical. A delicate balance must be maintained between sameness, in which the medievals were part of a continuum, and change, in which they were different and inferior. The depiction of the medieval world as a dark age during which the real knowledge and legitimate pursuits of Western man (those which had flourished and reached their zenith in Greece and Rome) were temporarily in hiatus, moribund, dormant, stifled, or nonexistent, became so fundamental a part of the general perception of history that it is still operative in many spheres to this day. Although certain aspects of that paradigm, primarily the impression of a formidable primitivism due to the medieval world's divorce from the classical heritage, have been debunked (though only very recently), other vestiges of it are clearly part of the working assumptions of many scholars.[9]

Arguably, the notion clung to most tenaciously is a variation of what in Spanish literary historiography is succinctly called *estado latente:* Despite the overt darkness and significant breaks in the continuity with classical ancestors, the medievals were still fundamentally, if covertly, Western. It may have been a relatively dormant period, but it was nonetheless a link with those whose accomplishments did more clearly define Western culture.

Several logical corollaries are implicit in this image of the Renaissance and of how it is at once a period set apart from the medieval period, allied as it was with the Greeks and Romans in their golden age, and a period that saw the beginnings of modern western Europe. The first is the partial or complete omission of a recognition that the medieval world had included centers of learning and revival where men were conversant with the Greek heritage that was to be "rediscovered" in the Renaissance. Nor was it likely, within the limits of this conceptual framework, that one would imagine that one of the characteristics of the earlier, darker period could have been the existence of a secular humanism in open struggle with the forces of dogmatic faith. The admission of the existence of such phenomena would not only have robbed the later period of its claims to being a renascence, at least in any dramatic and absolute way, but it would also have deprived it (and us, since in great measure we continue to cling to that particular historical dialectic) of that clear-cut distinction between the two periods that is dominant in modern European historical mythology.

But the remainder of the myth, the crystallization of the concept of Europeanness and its ancestry, was largely spun out in the nineteenth century, and it played a critical role at this moment of high-pitched awareness of the particularity and superiority of Europe that came with the imperial and colonial experience and the post-Romantic experience with the Orient. This experience certainly helped sharpen the perception not only of European community and continuity but also its difference from others, or from the Other. It was an Other (and the Arab world was one of its principal manifestations) that Europe was by its own standards bringing out of the darkness and civilizing, at least as far as that was possible for those who were not European in the first place.

Thus was eliminated the possibility that the Middle Ages might be portrayed as a historical period in which a substantial part of culture and learning was based in a radically different foreign culture. To view an Arabic-Islamic component, even in its European manifestations, as positive and essential would have been unimaginable, and it would remain so as long as the views and scholarship molded in that period continued to inform our education. The proposition that the Arab world had played a critical role in the making of the modern West, from the vantage point of the late nineteenth century and the better part of this century, is in clear and flagrant contradiction of cultural ideology. It is unimaginable in the context of the readily observable phenomenon that was institutionalized as an essential element of European ideology and that has remained so in many instances to this day: cultural supremacy over the Arab world.

It is, consequently, altogether logical that part of the vision of the Middle Ages, that part that saw it as relatively backward, ignorant, and unenlightened, has by and large been eliminated, or at least substantially modified, while the structurally balancing notion of its fundamental sameness, its place in a largely unbroken continuum of what constitutes Westernness is, if anything, more elaborately developed and more deeply entrenched. It is in the context of the nineteenth and twentieth centuries, the period during which modern philology (as it was once called) became an academic discipline and an intellectual field, that the major additions to the general cultural paradigms for the medieval period have emerged and been codified.

The earliest addition, which was clearly marked by the imprint of Romanticism, was the bringing into focus and prominence of the "primitive" European or folkloristic constituent elements of medieval culture, raising to a level of respectable analysis the inquiry into such things as the Celtic or Germanic influences on the culture and literature of the early Romance world. The other, not so much an innovation as a rigid codification of earlier notions about the "Age of Faith," is the elevation of scripture and scriptural exegesis as the most potent, usually the overwhelming, cultural component of the Middle Ages. In its most extreme form, this view of the power of Christian faith and its institutions is strong enough to completely eliminate most other possible cultural factors. The image was to attain its most exacting articulation in the scholarship of D. W. Robertson and the Robertsonians.[10]

The first of these major additions to or refinements of our notions of the nature of medieval culture highlights and enhances nonclassical but unmistakably European elements. It weaves the contributions of the cultural substratum into the story of the making of Europe and ratifies the legitimacy of that heritage as an integral part of the West. The second image, in turn, codifies Christianity, the triumphant religion of the West, as its dominant and shaping cultural force, an essential, rather than incidental, component of our cultural ancestry. Both the non-Roman substratum and the Christian superstratum are (not by accident, one might guess) elements peculiarly and characteristically European, essential ingredients in what sets the West apart from everywhere else.

While most individual medievalists have more complex and variegated views of the period on which they work than any of these simple paradigms, the paradigms are nonetheless there, and they are formative factors. To spell them out is to delimit and understand the parameters of the medieval cultural factors that are normally considered and that are normally accepted as reasonable. Thus if one's study is grounded in the

pre-Latin substratum—its mythology, folklore, or literature—or if it re-
lies on a close reading of the Latin sermons, the Church fathers, or the
Latin "foundation," then it falls within those acceptable and canonized
limits. It does not challenge the boundaries of the image of the medieval
period but instead adds to the evidence for the validity of that image.
Even more important, perhaps, a study that falls within the limits of
those possible narratives of European history needs neither justification
(as to why one would bring such texts or presumed sociocultural conditions to bear on the study) nor external, nontextual proof that the writer
in question was specifically aware of the texts or other material adduced.
Such studies need no apologies.

Within such contexts our paradigmatic views of the medieval period
have not readily expanded to include the possibility of greater cultural
polymorphism. Indeed, given the historical circumstances and cultural
ambience of the formative period of our discipline, such a move would
have been surprising and uncharacteristic. Nineteenth and early twentieth
century medievalists could, without having radically to alter their view of
themselves and their world, proceed to redefine the extent to which the
medieval world was not as backward as it might previously have seemed
to be. But a reappraisal of the role played by an essentially alien, Semitic
world in the creation of the basic features of that same period would have
involved dangerous and ultimately untenable modifications of the paradigms governing their view of themselves. While cultural ideology may
often remain unarticulated—its very unconsciousness being one of its essential traits—it is no less powerful for being unspoken, and it would be
naive to argue that the cultural unconscious does not play a formative role
in any variety of cultural studies. An individual, even a scholar, can
scarcely operate outside its bounds.[11]

The relative paucity of material wealth, the perceived cultural inferiority, and the demonstrable powerlessness of the Arab world in the
period in which modern medieval scholarship was carefully delimiting its
parameters could hardly have suggested or encouraged a dramatically different view of relations between East and West. Contemporary views
generated by the relative positions of the two cultures—with one eclips-
ing and dominating, literally shaping, the other—could not have escaped
being factors in the elaboration of an image of the Arab world, even in an
earlier period, that could have been, at most, marginal in the formation of
our own culture and civilization. It is fruitless and somewhat misguided
to be sanctimonious about such matters, to judge or condemn others by
moral and ethical standards that did not exist in their own universes. But

it is equally misguided to ignore the fact that such ideologies have existed or to suppose that intellectual enterprises have remained unaffected by their tenets.

Within this context, then, how surprising can it be that in the relatively short history of our discipline, not only has there been no addition to the medieval paradigm of an important Semitic or Arabic role, but also that whatever intimations of such a role had survived from earlier periods or have been introduced more recently have largely been discarded or put aside.[12] The untenability of such a notion lies not so much in the difficulty of revising our view of an earlier period of history. In and of itself, that is relatively easy to do, and historical revisionism is one of the most popular of academic pastimes. The key to the unimaginability of this particular bit of revisionism is that it would have challenged and ultimately belied the regnant worldview, requiring the reversal of an ideologically conditioned sense of the communal Western self. It requires the ability not only to imagine but to accept as plausible and admissible an image of our own civilization, at one of its formative moments, as critically indebted to and dependent on a culture that was for some time generally regarded as inferior and, by some lights, as the quintessence of the foreign and the Other.

And yet, in the past one hundred and fifty years or so there have been numerous suggestions within the scholarly community that one of the critical components in the making of the Middle Ages was Arabic and/or Semitic. The critical literature exploring and detailing such views is in fact copious. But although a certain group of historians, and the odd literary historian, has stated or reiterated the view, or some aspect of it, that one or more basic features of our medieval world was directly or indirectly dependent on the medieval Arabic European world, such perspectives have never become part of the mainstream within the community of scholars who regularly deal with medieval European studies, particularly literary studies.[13] The Arabic component of our paradigmatic view of the Middle Ages has always remained incidental; it has never been systemic. It may perhaps account for a given, usually isolated, feature, but such a feature is literally a world apart from the cultural sets that are perceived to be integral to the general system of medieval European culture.[14]

The two closest approximations to a revision of such views, and what can only be described as their failure, are themselves indicative of the unflagging vitality of the paradigm. On the one hand, there has been a Europeanization, an adaptation and absorption into this paradigm, of the body of information that reveals that Arabic "translations," particularly in the eleventh and twelfth centuries, contributed decisively to the intellectual revival of Europe at that time.[15] The impulse and need to absorb this discovery that otherwise threatened the coherence of Western ideology as imposed on the Middle Ages, was dictated in great measure by the eminence of the European historian who first called the phenomenon to the attention of a wide audience of fellow Europeanists. The mode of its absorption into the existing matrices was suggested by the title of Charles Homer Haskins's own work, *The Renaissance of the Twelfth Century*. The association between this renaissance and the later and atavistically European renaissance was inescapable. In fact, the thrust of Haskins's argument could reasonably be construed as being that the dating of the European Renaissance was off by several centuries, that the European discovery or rediscovery of our ancestral and hereditary culture really began in the twelfth century, and that a general secular cultural revival of considerable proportions followed on its heels. But Haskins was aware of the fact that such translations were almost universally an essential feature of Arabic intellectual life in Europe at the time (both in Sicily and Spain); that many of the most influential "translations" were not at all translations from the Greek as such, but rather translations of Arabic philosophical commentaries on Aristotle, who for some centuries had been one of the philosophical luminaries in the Arabic tradition; and that the propagation and reception of such texts was at least in some measure explicable only in terms of a deeper penetration and knowledge of Arabic intellectual life in Europe, and of its far greater prestige, than had previously been adduced.[16]

Another failure in introducing a paradigmatically meaningful Semitic component to the European view of its own medieval period is considerably more complex and perhaps more accurately described as a success, although one of very mixed blessings and benefits. The only image of the Middle Ages that regularly admits a shaping and globally influential role for Arabs and Jews is that cultivated and perpetuated by many Hispanists and Spaniards, both medievalists and more general historians and philosophers. This exception, as far as it goes, is undoubtedly due to the fact that the seven-century-long Arab "occupation" of large parts of the Iberian peninsula is a historical fact less easily dismissed and ignored by Spaniards than by other Europeans.[17] But, curiously enough, with a handful of very important exceptions, the nature of the molding influence and its effects on subsequent events and tendencies in Spanish culture and history as they are perceived by many generations of Spaniards and Hispanists is a derailing one. It was, in simplified form, a de-

Europeanizing one at best and in most other cases a largely or over-whelmingly negative one.[18] The most popular vision is one that might be represented by citing the eminent historian Sánchez-Albornoz, whose views are succinct, if extreme: "Without Islam, who can guess what our destiny might have been? Without Islam, Spain would have followed the same paths as France, Germany and England; and to judge from what we have achieved over the centuries in spite of Islam, perhaps we would have marched at their head" (translation, Monroe 1970:257). While few other cultural or literary historians have been as vigorous and frank as he, it is difficult to dispute the prevalence and strength of some variety of this ar-gument.[19] This and its many other companion pieces and like opinions reveal once more the firmness of the Europeanist view that the true Eu-rope and Europeanness are not Arabic- or Jewish-influenced. What at first glance is a formative component is more accurately a deforming com-ponent in terms of the rest of Europe, the real Europe. In Sánchez-Albornoz's view (and that of numerous others), Spain's defects—its not being up to the standards of France, England, and Germany—are a result of the misfortune of having been de-Europeanized by Semitic influences. But is this really substantially different from the premise of those literary historians who appear to be writing the history of a country they present as fully a part of the Western tradition, one in which the existence of Mus-lims and Jews and their cultures might never be guessed by the innocent reader?[20] Do not both views express, in different styles, the same prem-ises, that is, that Semiticised Spain is less than the rest of Europe and that Spain with those elements blotted out would be part of the European tra-dition? For other Europeanists, most of whom naturally enough take their cues on matters Hispanic from Hispanists, the result has often been that characterized by the notion of Spain's "cultural belatedness" vis-à-vis the rest of Europe.[21]

Even so, one must know that the question of the effect of the Arab sojourn in Spain is hardly a matter of vital importance to most medi-evalists. Sánchez-Albornoz's preoccupation with the subject is a result of his being a Spaniard, not the natural result of being a Hispanist or a me-dievalist. Most Hispanists and medievalists begin their study of medieval literature with the first texts in Romance and assume Latin, conceivably even Greek, to be the necessary classical languages to be learned. Hebrew and Arabic are normally considered superfluous. Even in the wake of the "discovery" of the Mozarabic *kharjas* nearly forty years ago, when a con-siderable number of Spanish medievalists actually teach these Romance refrains of classical Arabic and Hebrew poems, only a distinct minority of scholars and teachers read them or present them as part of the full poems (written in one or the other of the two classical Semitic languages) of which they are, in fact, a part.[22]

Knowledge of this body of poetry and the expected subsequent awareness of the world from which it came apparently has not affected the traditional canon of Romance literary history. There is no sign of the imminent appearance on required reading lists of Ibn Quzmān, Jehudah ben-Ezra, Maimonides, or Averroes. The signs abound that even in the period after the discovery of the *kharjas* which was once heralded as the beginning of a "new spring" for European lyric studies,[23] only a relative handful of the details of our story have been altered or expanded, few or none of its basic premises have been modified, and its vitality is hardly diminished. Anthologies of medieval European lyric can still be published with a paltry section entitled "Arabic and Other Nonmainstream Poetry," and it may be comprised solely of a fragment of Ibn Ḥazm's *Dove's Neck-Ring*, which would be as if in the section on Provençal lyric there were but a fragment of Andreas Capellanus's treatise.[24] Prominent cutting-edge journals in literary studies can still devote entire issues to the crossroads at which medieval literary studies find themselves and include not the slightest hint that one of the problems to be addressed is that of the cultural biases and boundaries that delimit the field itself, despite the many indications of the inadequacy of the canon and its parameters that have surfaced in the last forty years.[25]

The crossroads, turning points, or moments of crisis that medieval literary studies have faced, and faced up to, in recent years have overwhelmingly been those concerning methods of literary criticism. The choice is most simply presented as being that between the formalist criticism of scholars such as Zumthor and the classicist criticism best exemplified by the still-authoritative work of Curtius. What all this has increasingly boiled down to is the question of whether medieval literary studies, once the vanguard of the discipline of modern literary studies, will remain largely a bastion of old-fashioned, philological, historicizing study, which is increasingly removed from the critical and theoretical avant-garde. Either of the two possible answers to this question raises eyebrows and threatens those parties who have a vested interest in the dominance of one approach or another.

So far, neither answer has implied any necessary reevaluation of the very bases of our definition of the medieval period, its literature, or its salient cultural features and parameters. The compromise between the two extremes, stated both elegantly and succinctly by Poirion, is to see (and therefore presumably to analyze) the literary text as being "situated at the point of connection between the imaginary and the ideological" (Poirion 1979:406). The most reasonable critic, therefore, rejects both the dehistoricization of formalist criticism (and many of its progeny) and the devaluation of the essential literary or imaginative properties of texts, which is peculiar both to very traditional philological studies and to some contemporary new critical analysis.

But the most reasonable critic, of whatever critical stripe, might also wish to question and reevaluate his or her most basic concept of the fundamental historicocultural characteristics of the period, because such a concept ultimately affects in innumerable ways the results of the application of any method. The strength of the model or image with which we start out is paramount; at a minimum, it defines what is and is not possible, what a word or image that we "know" or "recognize" is likely to mean, or not to mean. This is self-evident if the approach used is one of the several classicist variations, since at least one of the principal objectives of such a study is archaeological, to find and establish the historicocultural backdrop of the text at hand. This linguistic, literary, and cultural backdrop informs both the questions asked and the answers given. It determines the probable meaning and origin of a word in the twelfth century, a given author's presumed use of Aquinas or a Bernardine sermon, and the kind of assumptions we make about the relationships between a text and its society. But, as I noted earlier in this chapter, the impact of our model, this background, is scarcely less at the other end of the critical spectrum, in formalist studies.[26]

In both cases such premises are fundamental determinants, and yet, paradoxically, it seems they are also the premises we have least frequently questioned or examined. But, given the many studies that suggest that they may be inadequate, are these not rightly among those most deserving of scrutiny, justification, and validation? One knows, or believes it to be a fair assumption, that an eleventh-century word did not denote "airplane" or "tomato," or "relativity" in the Einsteinian sense of the word. But how have we determined, and is it a reasonable determination, that it is more or less likely that the word *gazel* used in Provençal could have meant what it did for speakers of Hispano-Arabic? How can we still be so certain of our assumption that the basic reading list for a budding medievalist should include Aquinas and Augustine but not Ibn Ḥazm or Avicenna? How revolutionary or revealing can the deconstruction of medieval texts be if the series of social and ideological mores or norms presumably being covertly subverted in such texts have themselves not been carefully scrutinized? The ideologically bound strictures and limits of our "common knowledge" and even "common sense" are not easily by-passed. As Stanley Fish has noted (in a discussion that was hardly concerned with the role of Arabs in medieval Europe):

> I argue that whatever account we have of a work or a period or of the entire canon is an account that is possible or intelligible only within the assumptions embodied in current professional practice. Rather than standing independently of our efforts, works, periods, and canons have the shape they do precisely because of our efforts, and therefore no act of literary criticism, no matter how minimally "descriptive" can be said to "bypass" the network that enables it. (Fish 1983:357)

But even more engaging than the fact that our paradigms govern us *faute de mieux* should be the recognition that many of the most widely discussed critical problems of literary history and even theory, particularly as applied to medieval studies, dovetail well with an explicit exploration and reevaluation of the images we hold of the medieval period and the nature of the canon that derives from it directly or indirectly. It seems only logical that in the resurgent discussion of the dialectic of the sameness versus the alterity of the medieval period and its cultural relics, a discussion that tacitly recognizes the parallel and sometimes overlapping dialectic between self and other, we should more closely and explicitly reevaluate our assumptions and knowledge of the often-hidden Other—the Arab, the Semite, the Averroes—who stands silently behind Aristotle in the thirteenth century. Perhaps more to the point, we might ask in this context whether he really was so silent in the thirteenth and fourteenth centuries or whether it is not instead our postrenascentist views and parlance of the period that have made him so, giving his place to others whose ancestry we find more illustrious and thus shielding ourselves from a recognition that strikes at the heart of certain beliefs about ourselves. And is the dialectic that governed the Middle Ages really or exclusively that between pagan and Christian, and between classical and modern, or is this, too, a legacy of the Renaissance view of that period and an ancillary to the colonial and postcolonial view of ourselves?

The theoretical questions of the nature of meaning, of whether it is created or received, and of the covert and self-subverting meanings of both literary and nonliterary texts, can obviously be carried out with no wider or more revolutionary a concept of the cultural and literary mores than those we already have, those explicitly canonized and triumphant in Western literary historiography. But should not the more revealing exploration of such questions be correlated with an investigation into the mores that were discarded or subsumed, damned explicitly or tacitly by the authorities of the time and the cleansing historians of later periods? Can we as medievalists afford to continue to believe that because an eleventh-century duke of Aquitaine was Christian and "European" his poetic lexicon was delimited by the official Christian and "European" ideologies of his time? Can we speak authoritatively about the repressions and subversions of his poetry if we begin by accepting as valid parameters for his universe what has emerged as legitimate and Catholic in subsequent periods of time? And are there not patent and often ironic gaps in discussions of the "anxiety of influence" that are informed only by possible influences that were and have been canonized?

Revisionism, in literary history as well as in other fields, is often unpopular. It can seem to involve the ritualized murder of cherished ancestry. This is the case no matter whether it is described in the oedipal terminology of Bloom, in the context of the notions of historical relativism and storytelling of White, or in terms that follow the concepts of discourse of Foucault.

But at this juncture it is important to clarify several issues that may make the particular literary-historical revision that I will suggest seem less dramatic and more reasonable. First, I am scarcely suggesting that the prevailing image and canon we have needs to be discarded in toto. In fact, I do not believe any segment of the canon need be discarded at all. Rather, my analysis of the ideological factors that have shaped our images leads me to believe that it is the existing canon and image that have unjustifiably discarded important figures and texts or have undervalued them or euphemized them to the point that they have lost much of the power and impact many believe they had for their contemporaries—and that in turn informed texts that we *have* canonized. The suggestion is not that Aquinas be removed or replaced. On the contrary, it is that we add the tradition of Averroes to it, and perhaps then begin to see the extent to which Aquinas is a response to other, Averroean texts.

In other words, I believe that the selective process of history and literary history has, in the natural course of telling the story of the victors, deprived us of an appreciation of many critical subtexts, and has in great measure eliminated or simplified and distorted beyond recognition many of the cultural forces that were catalytic in the medieval period. Thus the part of the image that I propose should be discarded is that part that has eliminated the possibility of seeing in the Andalusian world the impetus for change and that part that cannot imagine that a cultural force now seemingly alien to our own was once a part of its foundation.

My own casting of this period of cultural and literary history is itself selective, of course, and as much constrained to pick and choose facts and texts as any other. I have few delusions that it is any less a myth than those I am attempting to modify in the process, but I think it is a myth that has several advantages. The first is that it does not shy away from the concept of a mixed ancestry for western Europe that until recently has seemed largely unimaginable and insupportable. The second is that I believe that it enriches rather than impoverishes the recounting of the story we already work with, the readings of texts we have already agreed on. Thus my criticism of the existing myth is, as I have just noted, that it is insufficiently variegated to account for the medieval period and its considerably different historicopolitical circumstances, and that it is too much shaped by cultural prejudices of an era in Western ideology that although just now in its death throes in some areas is still quite powerful in the realm of literary historiography. It can perhaps now be fruitfully discarded there as well.

Notes

1. See primarily Said 1978 and some of the extended criticism and further considerations engendered by his book. Three reviews are of particular interest: Lewis 1982, whose highly negative reaction reflects much of the response of the traditional "Orientalist" academic community; Beard 1979, whose favorable reaction raises the question, among others, of the expansion of Said's model to other areas of academic scholarship; and Brombert 1979, which is valuable because of its detachment from the Orientalist scene and the issues of general academic interest it explores. The salient points made by Said that are relevant to my discussion (and that are, incidentally, those least contradicted, even by his staunchest critics) are found in the introduction (1–28) and can be summarized as follows: that the formation of the image of the West is contrapuntal to the formation of the image of the Orient; that the dominant discourse is one of superiority "reiterating European superiority over Oriental backwardness, usually overriding the possibility that a more independent, or more skeptical, thinker might have had different views on the matter" (7); that the distinction between "pure" and "political" knowledge is not an absolute and clear one and that the liberal consensus that knowledge is fundamentally apolitical "obscures the highly if obscurely organized political circumstances obtaining when knowledge is produced" (10); that literary studies in particular have assiduously avoided discussion of the issue of political ideology shaping the structures of knowledge and have generally "avoided the effort of seriously bridging the gap between the superstructural and the base levels in textual, historical scholarship." (13)

2. For two recent examples of collections of articles devoted to the pressing critical problems in medieval studies, see *New Literary History* 10 (1979) and *L'esprit créateur* 18 (1978) and 23 (1983).

3. Makdisi 1974 includes both his own statement about the "European awakening" and pertinent quotes from some of his predecessors (Lombard and Dawson are among the most important). For this perspective on the history of medicine specifically, see Sarton 1951, and from the point of view of the history of science in general, see Haskins 1924.

Haskins 1927, the widely read and cited *Renaissance of the Twelfth Century,* is also revealing. Roughly the last half of the book deals with aspects of that renaissance that were explicitly Arabic-derived. In the area of the history of philosophy, few have underestimated the importance of Averroes. Even Kristeller, who is primarily concerned with the Latin tradition, makes serious concessions to the importance of the Arabic tradition: "As is well known, the Aristotelianism of the Arabs, and especially that of Averroes, exercised a powerful influence upon the Jewish thought of the later Middle Ages . . . and strongly affected the philosophy of the Christian West" (Kristeller 1961:28–29). He is nevertheless able to follow such an observation with this one: "If we want to understand the history of thought and learning in the Western Latin Middle Ages we must first of all realize that it had its foundations in Roman, not Greek, antiquity" (Kristeller 1961:29).

4. These generalizations about the attitudes among Romance medievalists are just that, generalizations, and they are hardly exempt from the enumeration of any number of exceptions. But even a cursory glance at the structures of our academic departments, the standard medieval canon, the sorts of courses that are (and are not) taught, requirements for degrees, general bibliographies, literary anthologies and literary histories, and so forth, all will confirm that as a rule such generalizations are accurate. It is curious that although there is widespread acceptance of the general endebtedness of the West to Arabic sciences and some branches of philosophy, this appears to be generally ignored when we construe the background of our literary history, although Latin-based developments in the sciences and philosophy—many of them dependent on the Arabic tradition—are almost invariably accounted for. Studies that recognize the centrality of the Arabic tradition in some other cultural sphere or its importance in terms of political history often proceed to discuss the literary problem as if those other instances of interaction were irrelevant. Thus, Bonner (1972) notes both that there was substantial interaction between Provence and al-Andalus, and between Provence and the rest of the Arab world (because of the crusades), and even that intellectual, cultural, and material developments in those areas far outstripped those of the rest of Europe. Yet, not only does he then go on to discuss these new developments in Provence as if none of this had been the case, but the map he presents for the world of the Provençal troubadours cuts off at the Pyrenees—as graphic a representation as one can imagine of how irrelevant that world seems to be. Other explicitly contradictory analyses include Frank 1955a, which details the extent to which Arabic courtly poetry and song were a fact of everyday life at the court of Alfonso II, the rallying point of both Catalan and Provençal troubadours, but then says that, nevertheless, all of this in no way influenced that poetry, apparently assuming that such influence must be expressly and directly acknowledged in the poetic texts themselves, presumably in Arabic. A comparable position is found in Rizzitano and Giunta 1967 (see further discussion in Chapter 4). Sutherland 1956, a refutation of Denomy's work on the influence of Arabic thought on the troubadours, includes the comment that the influence was "diffuse" and thus is not to be found in the poetry—assuming, presumably, that poetic influence is not diffuse. Bezzola (1940) asserts that one cannot continue categorically to exclude the possibility of any Arabic influence on the first troubadours, and he then proceeds to do just that through his lack of any further discussion of the influence that is in fact implicit in his presentation of the historical background of William IX. In Van Cleve 1972 the chapter on the Italian lyric is presented as if no hint of Arabic culture, poetry, or song existed there, although that chapter immediately follows one on the intellectual life at the court, which he presents as completely Arabized. A distinction is made between poetry and other intellectual life that is difficult to reconcile with the unity of such traditions in virtually every other sphere of literary study, medieval or not. This split between the general historical background and literature is also reflected in the fact that while so much medieval literature elaborates or alludes to imaginary visions of the Arab world and characters—Saladin, for example—who are clearly identified as being a part of that world, relatively few of the critical discussions of these literary phenomena are

concerned with either the extent to which they might reflect (and thus be understood in terms of) an influential view of that world and those people. See Paris 1895 for an early example that is not altogether outdated in its basic approach to the subject. Even studies on the French epic (so much of which is explicitly concerned with dealings with the Arab enemy) do not characteristically discuss the relationship with the Arab world as complex and problematic, nor do they regularly adopt any more sophisticated a view of the situation than that which is depicted at the surface level of the poems. (Notable exceptions to this are Galmés de Fuentes 1972 and 1978.) Even studies on *Aucassin and Nicolette*—a work clearly concerned with the question of dialogue, alterity, and juxtapositions and no less clearly allusive to the Arabic world conjured up by Aucassin's name and Nicolette's birth—can completely bypass the issue of the Arabic world in the *chante-fable*. See Calin 1966 for an example of the former, even in a critically sophisticated study. See Vance 1980 for a recent example of the latter.

5. The problem is perhaps best exemplified in cases where a scholar does comparative work and/or breaches the presumed demarcations of Arabic and European scholarship. One of the most noteworthy cases of this, an extreme case but far from a unique one, is certainly that of María Rosa Lida's work on the *Libro de buen amor* and its Semitic antecedents (Lida 1940 and 1959). She was severely taken to task by the respected and influential Spanish historian Sánchez-Albornoz (1979:258–75). Although few other scholars are as vitriolic as he, this specific case is worth mentioning precisely because his attack on Lida's work makes explicit those attitudes that are in other cases covert, although no less powerful, and because it reflects certain premises that are characteristic of a considerable number of scholars working in an area that is not only marginalized but, it would seem, protective of its marginalization. Lida's work, according to Sánchez-Albornoz, is deficient because she is not an Arabist (a Spanish Arabist, it almost goes without saying) and consequently incapable a priori of sound knowledge of the Arabic and Hebrew texts she is discussing. Lida's impeccable scholarly credentials show just how exaggerated such a territorial attitude is, since it implies that this area is so special that others not of the same school and training have no business dealing with it at all and are incapable of working on it competently. Why is an otherwise competent scholar and reader of literary texts rendered incompetent when faced with a decent edition and/or translation of an Arabic or Hebrew text written and/or circulated in Spain or Sicily in the Middle Ages? And if we are working with deficient editions or translations, which is sometimes adduced, or if we have incomplete knowledge of the historicocultural background of such texts, why is such a situation not remedied by those who in the same breath are staking this out as their territory? Such attitudes, coming as they often do from those concerned with Arabic studies, can only contribute in equal measure with the Europeanist's attitude of neglect perpetuating the isolation of the field.

But the criticism of Lida's work voiced by Sánchez-Albornoz goes a step further and in some measure sheds light on the nature of the other criticism he has made. He fails to comprehend her attempt to link the Hebrew (and thus Arabic) texts of medieval Spain with a Christian, truly "Spanish" text, which in his opinion can only be understood "dentro del cuadro de la literatura occidental" (Sánchez-Albornoz 1979:264). He sees her work, in fact, as the result of her "natural devoción . . . hacia los hombres y las empresas de su raza" (Sánchez-Albornoz 1979:259). This unmistakable allusion to her Jewish background is more than casual or incidental anti-Semitism, and that is why I have adduced it here. It is a reflection of the extent to which scholars who *do* work on the medieval European Semitic traditions, both Arabic and Hebrew, have been no more exempt from the prejudices of cultural ideology than the medievalist community as a whole. It would be fallacious to assume that those whose work is devoted to the study of those traditions necessarily have any more positive an attitude toward the object of their study than those who reflect the prejudices of our cultural ideology in their unwillingness to recognize the existence of those texts and cultural traditions in the first place. Most important, the reader should know that such attitudes are neither obsolete relics nor views restricted to Spaniards obsessed with the Semitic elements of their own past. The reader who glances at any of the issues of the last several years of the journal *Al-Andalus* (before its demise and rebirth as *Al-Qanṭara*), at García Gómez's prologue to the second edition of *Las jarchas romances de la serie árabe,* or at his lecture on the occasion of the fiftieth anniversary of the Escuela de estudios árabes de Madrid, can hardly come away with the impression that either acute territorialism or thinly veiled prejudice are things of the past in this field. Not only would one find there articles by a certain Angel Ramírez Calvente (whose identity is otherwise unknown, so this is probably a nom de plume) embodying a less-than-professional attack on Samuel Stern, who is Jewish, but also from García Gómez himself, paterfamilias of Hispano-Arabic literary studies, invectives clearly directed at Monroe, who is dealt with as an *innominato*. Dismissals of those who are simply "norteamericanos," "anfibios," "pseudo-especialistas," or "ajenos . . . a nuestra familia" stake out the boundary lines quite clearly—and they should serve as a warning that an attempt to cross them would not be welcome, or even tolerable.

The most recently published polemics between Jones and Hitchcock on one side and Armistead and Monroe on the other serve to show, among other things, the extent to which Jones rejects arguments made by Armistead and Monroe simply because neither are bona fide Arabists according to his definition of the term (see Jones 1980, 1981, and 1983; Hitchcock 1984; Armistead 1982 and 1986; Monroe 1982; and Armistead and Monroe 1983 and 1985). Consequently Jones considers Armistead and Monroe incapable of understanding why the *kharjas* can only be understood as part of the classical Arabic tradition (and by Arabic classicists). Leaving aside for the moment the substance of the argument, Jones's approach is reminiscent of the kind of argument Sánchez-Albornoz makes when Jones questions Armistead's competence in dealing with an Arabic text ("I have a problem," Jones states, "which Professor Armistead possibly does not share. . . . On principle I do not work on the Arabic texts on the basis of translations" [1983:51]). It is not difficult to understand, when reading Jones's works, that it all boils down to the belief that the lines that have been drawn between the Arabist's domain and the Romance scholar's domain are appropriate ones and that hybridization is unhealthy and produces bad scholarship (even, ironically, when one is dealing with clearly hybrid poetry.) Moreover, there is here an intellectual condescension that evokes memories of Sánchez-Albornoz's attitude toward Lida's "meddling." This is manifest in comments such as that cited above but even more so in Jones's adducing the authority of "most Arabs and Arabists" to back his views, although his principal cited sources for the view that the poetry is a part of the classical Arabic tradition exclusively could hardly be considered authoritative or up-to-date on the subject of Hispano-Arabic poetry: Nicholson 1907, and Watt and Cachia 1965 (the latter of which devotes all of eight pages to the poetry of Spain but includes a paragraph-long rebuttal of the work of the major historian and critic of Andalusian poetry, Pérès.) The fact that Pérès and Monroe are the two scholars who have devoted the most attention specifically to Hispano-Arabic Andalusian poetry (Pérès 1953 and Monroe 1974 being the essential handbooks on the subject) apparently counts for less than being a mainstream Arabist who has not altered his views by attempting to understand that poetry in terms of al-Andalus as a hybrid society and in the context of Romance as well as Arabic traditions. And Jones's condescension is such that, even in citing Watt and Cachia, he fails to cite their full opinions, as expressed in the concluding paragraph of those twelve pages: "So it was that in Spain, alone among Muslim lands, the vigorous spirit of the common people breached the wall of convention erected by the classicists" (Watt and Cachia 1965:121).

In a different sphere, it is revealing to note that the most hostile attacks on Gittes's 1983 article on "The *Canterbury Tales* and the Arabic Frame Tradition" are by individuals who take her to task for incomplete and faulty knowledge when she speaks of the Arabic tradition. These letters are, in fact, primarily concerned with the accuracy of sources in *pre*-Arabic traditions, which Gittes has identified using the handful of sources accessible to a nonspecialist and which, in any case, as she points out, are not directly relevant to the fate of the narrative tradition *within* Europe.

6. Since Aristotle, the notion that ideology affects all historical writing has been an important feature of the criticism of historiography and discussions of the inherent problems in distinguishing between history and poetry. For a recent exchange and discussion of the effect of ideology on literary studies and the effect it is currently having on the profession (though in general terms rather than on the medieval sphere specifically), see Said 1983, Fish 1983, and Bate 1983. Other recent contributions to the subject are Said 1982 and especially White 1982. White makes a series of observations that are particularly pertinent to our study: Hegel "was convinced . . . that you could learn a great deal, of both practical and theoretical worth, from the study of the study of history. And one of the things you learn from the study of the study of history is that such study is never innocent, ideologically or otherwise, whether launched from the political perspective of the Left, Right, or Center" (White 1982:137).

7. Ellis 1974 gives a succinct view of the application of structuralism to medieval studies and maintains that the only difference is that of learning a different language, which is just like learning any foreign language (of which one need learn only the synchronic state and need not know any of its history). Two of the most striking and revealing cases of the pitfalls of this approach are found in Guiraud 1971 and 1978. Guiraud's first study of the etymological structures of *trobar* is explicitly synchronic, but the author is hardly free either from the problems of the enigmatic history of the word or, more significantly, from what diachronic studies of that history have told him. In fact, at a certain juncture he faces the fact that his synchronic analysis of what the word means is somewhat at odds with the range of possibilities provided by the diachronic studies he is aware of, and these exclude Ribera's proposal. In his reworking of this material in the later publication, Guiraud takes into account the possible Arabic etyma for Provençal *joi* and *jovens* in Chapter 6. (This is Denomy's proposal [Denomy 1949], but clearly Guiraud is only familiar with Lazar's 1964 presentation of that material.) However, still unfamiliar in 1978 with the suggested Arabic derivation of *trobar,* he is elusive about the problem of the apparent disjunction between synchronic and diachronic analyses, and following on the heels of his presentation of the case of *jovens,* this seems all the more ironic. It is also a very explicit case of how illusory it is to attempt to separate the two areas of study so neatly. For further discussion of this general issue, see note 26 below, and for different perspectives on the dehistoricization of medieval texts and studies of them, see Bloomfield 1979 and Nichols 1983. Jauss 1979 and Calin 1983 tackle the problem from the perspective of the "otherness" of the medieval period and its dialectical relationship with the modern one.

8. It is revealing to take Petrarch, as many scholars do, as one of the first explicit advocates of such an analysis of history. His role as one of the first humanists has been discussed by many, and his views on the primacy of classical studies, on the darkness of the Dark Ages, and on that entire constellation of notions are widely known and cited. It is revealing to note, and this is less often referred to, that such views were accompanied by quite virulent anti-Arabism. For a presentation and analysis of this phenomenon, see Gabrieli 1977. Hays 1968 is also helpful for understanding the relative modernity of our concept of what constitutes Europe.

9. The debunking of the myth of the darkness of the Middle Ages is certainly best exemplified by Haskins 1927, but Pernoud 1977 indicates that many of those views have never been completely eradicated, and why in her view they ought to be. Among general literary historians there is surprisingly often a notion of the primitivism of the medievals relative to the modern period, and prominent critics (see Bloom 1973) can still regard everything before the Renaissance as antediluvian. Even among medievalists, similar views are not unknown. Zumthor (1975), to take one example, is able to characterize the period and its men as incapable of autobiographical writing. A recent nonacademic perspective on

the surge of interest in medieval studies and what this implies for our general perceptions of the period is Murphy 1984. See also Jauss 1979 and Calin 1983.

10. For a succinct history and extensive bibliography of the development of these views as reflected in scholarship dealing with troubadour lyrics, see Boase 1976.

11. Prévost (1972:18), inspired by Althusser, notes that people "use" ideology, but "sont également produits et mis en mouvement par l'idéologie, par ce qui fonctionne comme un véritable *inconscient culturel*" (emphasis mine). Evidence of the institutionalization of these general views surrounds us. General anthologies of European medieval literature do not, as a matter of course, include examples of literature written in Arabic or Hebrew, nor do they even, in many cases, acknowledge or discuss its existence as part of the general historical background. Courses on medieval literature, with few exceptions, perform the same excision. Even the very definition of what is "Spanish" literature that is implicit in the structure of courses and histories and anthologies of the literature systematically excludes what was written in Arabic and Hebrew at the same time as what was written in the Romance vernaculars. The definition of a Hispanist has rarely included knowledge of Islamic Spain from any but a rudimentary *fronterizo* point of view. In the often daunting inventory of languages deemed necessary tools for a medievalist, Arabic rarely figures. The respective bodies of literature are shelved in different sections of our libraries, are studied by different scholars, and are taught in different departments, even though in some cases they may come from the same place and time. A familiarity with the works of Dante, Boccaccio, and Petrarch is considered necessary for the truly competent French or Spanish medievalist, but even rudimentary information on the translations of Arabic and Hebrew works commissioned by Frederick II or of the Arabic poetry dedicated to his grandfather Roger is rare even in an Italian medievalist. Augustine and Aquinas are *de rigueur;* Averroes and Maimonides are obscure figures at best. To argue that there are and have been exceptions to such rules would hardly contradict the validity of this rudimentary outline of the general system. It is more telling that we are easily able to name the exceptions, whereas an enumeration of the instances of conformity to such norms would be a daunting task.

12. Curiously, much of the resistance to such a change in our appreciation of the Arabic role in medieval Europe comes from the area of Arabic studies as well, as indicated above in note 5. The only comprehensive and critical study of the historiography of Arabic Europe, Monroe 1970, confirms what even casual observation might well reveal: The conceptual schism between East and West (Arabic and Romance) has in turn resulted in the creation of fundamentally separate fields of inquiry, the setting up of a field that falls between two stools. (No adequate equivalent of Monroe 1970 exists for Siculo-Arabic studies, but see Bausani [1957] 1977, Gabrieli 1957, and Ahmad 1975.) The study of Arabic culture as it existed in Europe is a poor and regularly neglected relation. While often there is a certain amount of lip service paid to the heights of the cultural glory of Córdoba, little recognition of the centrality of al-Andalus in the overall contours of Arabic history can be measured through institutional yardsticks. In fact, it is noteworthy that traditionally the scholars who have studied Arabic culture in Spain have been Spaniards, and those who have been students of Siculo-Arabic matters, Italian. Further confirmation of how far from the Orientalist mainstream this area of study and its scholars are may also be found where one might least expect it. Curiously enough, it is virtually completely ignored in Said's *Orientalism.* It is telling that in that wide-ranging and usually unsparingly critical review of the discourse of Orientalism, there is a virtually complete omission of both the phenomenon and the subsequent study of the history and culture of the Arabs in medieval Europe. One cannot but be struck by, and perhaps relieved at, this ignoring of the discourse of Orientalism when it has addressed the question of the Arab on European soil—let alone the further question of why scholarship in those instances has assumed that, despite seven hundred years there, the Arab never became a European and even that the territory he occupied was thus not part of Europe for that period of time! There is clearly some irony in this, in that Said would have

found even more convincing grist for his polemical mill in the annals of Spanish Arabism than he found in the writings of Arabists who worked in more traditional areas of Islamic studies, areas that do not address, for example, the question of how the Arabs actually de-Europeanized a group of otherwise legitimate Europeans under their control. There is further irony in the extent to which this reveals that even Said, critic par excellence of the Orientalist discourse, is not altogether immune to what is certainly a part of that discourse—its segregation of Arabic or Arabized Europe. Part of the myth that he is attempting to demolish is ratified in his choice of texts and scholars, and his choice reflects the view that the real Europe is a Europe almost completely unaffected by hundreds of years of Arab domination, that the only real Orientalism, or Arabism, is that practiced solely by those who have always been the colonizers of the Arabs, not those who were transformed by Arabic colonization and who have had to come to grips with that fact in themselves. But even without going this far, without dissecting *Orientalism* from the same vantage point from which it dissects that field, one can certainly note that this most widely read and influential discussion of the marginalizing approach to the study of the Arabs outside of Europe itself very much reflects the segregation of the study of European Arab culture and history and just how marginal the scholarship on the Arabs in medieval Europe really is.

13. Even traditional Orientalists of the sort severely criticized in Said 1978 have noted the Orientalism of scholarship on the medieval period. See note 4 of the preface, above. In Watt 1972, one finds a statement that might have been made by Said himself: "In this post-Freudian world men realize that the darkness ascribed to one's enemies is a projection of the darkness in oneself that is not fully admitted. In this way the distorted vision of Islam is to be regarded as a projection of the shadow-side of European man" (83). Daniel 1960 is the most extensive exploration of the misconceptions of Europeans concerning Islam, and it is remarkable that many of his observations about the ignorance and prejudice that are part of this view are relevant not only for the medieval period. See also Southern 1962. A recent study of the crusades concludes with the succinct observation that "modern Western European Christians seem in general to be as ignorant of the fundamentals of Islam as their twelfth-century predecessors" (Finucane 1983:211). To fully realize how acceptable, even expected, much racial prejudice was until very recently, one need only read any of the social histories of the twentieth century or biographies of some of the individuals whose lives and views have spanned the period of vastly altered attitudes. It is enlightening, for example, to read of the matter-of-factness as well as the depth of anti-Indian and anti-Arab feelings among the British upper classes in Manchester's biography of Churchill. Or, on this side of the Atlantic, the overt racism and anti-Semitism that is considered unspeakable today but that until recently was not only not shocking but was expected of the educated classes are both described in some detail in Lash's biography of Eleanor Roosevelt.

14. Hitchcock 1977 is a good indication of the studies dedicated to the *kharjas* alone, and a considerable number of those studies have discussed direct or ancillary questions of possible Arabic borrowings. Even more telling, perhaps, would be a glance at Cantarino 1965, which includes a full bibliography of studies on Dante and on the possible influence of Arabic texts on the *Commedia*. One is struck both by the quantity of such studies (there are eighty-one entries in his bibliography) and by the fact that so very few of them are by mainstream Italianists. Cantarino himself notes that "Asín Palacio's theory, although rejected almost unanimously and without any qualifications by Dante critics, did not fail to leave a deep influence on subsequent research *of which, however, Dante scholars have not always been fully aware*" (182, emphasis mine). Cantarino's survey of this scholarship and of the extent to which it has been ignored by Dante scholars led him to conclusions much like my own. In noting the impasse in the pseudodebate over Dante's indebtedness to Arabic sources, he concludes that it "shows rather to what extent the controversy has ceased to be a problem which can be restricted only to the study of Dante's sources. The controversy has become a problem to be solved only with a reinterpretation of our understanding of the European

Middle Ages as a time in which Arabic and Jewish cultural elements as well are given the place they deserve as components of the so-called "Western" tradition. In this light the 'influence' of a specific work on any particular author is only an episode" (191).

15. The term "translation" is here used in quotation marks because, although it is the term normally used, it can be seriously misleading. For a fuller discussion, see Chapter 2.

16. For examples of this Europeanist absorption of Haskins's work, see Southern 1953, Wolff 1968, and Benson, Constable, and Lanham 1982. The centrality of the Arabic tradition is apparent even in studies that do not explicitly acknowledge it and that may seem to be saying something quite different. See note 3 above for Haskins's and Kristeller's indirect revelations. For explicit and detailed explorations of the centrality of Averroes, his own relationship with Aristotle, and the different translations available in Europe, see both Peters 1968 and Lemay 1963a.

17. I use the term "occupation" in quotation marks partially because its accuracy is questionable when one is dealing with a seven-hundred-year period and most of all because the use of such terms is so often among the best indicators of current attitudes we have about the presence of Arabs in Europe. I can think of few other seven-hundred-year long "occupations," and it would seem that this usage, so often reflexive, is indicative of the general image of the entire phenomenon as something quite removed from Europe, a temporary (long but still transient) interlude. The terms "Western" and "occidental," to make another example, are often used as if they were geographical notions but at the same time in explicit juxtaposition to Islamic Spain without further explanation of how or why the Iberian peninsula comes to be relegated to the East. Clearly, geographical terminology has been reshaped by notions of cultural ideology in such cases. It is still more interesting to note that even studies specifically dedicated to exploring or demonstrating connections between the Arabic and Romance worlds often begin with the assumption of a fundamental separateness that must be "bridged." See, for example, the titles of many works, especially Terrasse 1958, *Islam d'Espagne, une rencontre de l'Orient et de l'Occident,* or Menéndez Pidal 1956 ("Eslabón"), both among the best general sources of information on the admixture, rather than separation, of culture in medieval Spain. (Interestingly enough, it is the word for "bridge" in Arabic, *al-Qanṭara,* that was chosen as the name for the journal that has replaced *Al-Andalus.* See its first issue, in 1890, for a discussion.) Thus the name of a conference to explore the issue is "Islam and the Medieval West," with an intimation of the separateness of those two entities, and the title of the 1965 Spoleto conference, "L'Occidente e l'Islam nell'alto Medioevo," conveys a similar impression. No less so Makdisi's 1976 "Interaction between Islam and the West" or Jean Richard's 1966 "La Vogue de l'Orient dans la littérature occidentale du moyen âge." Even Menéndez Pidal's 1955 *Poesía árabe y poesía europea,* one of the best essays on the subject of the close and vital interrelations between the two poetries, has a title that might well create a quite different impression: that the Arabic tradition (and he is, of course, speaking of the Andalusian one) is *not* European. The same notions impinge on concepts of nationality. As I note in several other places in this book, the very use of the title "Spaniard" is implicitly defined in racial and religious terms. The Cid is a Spaniard, but Ibn Ḥazm and Maimonides are not; they are an Arab and a Jew respectively.

18. Monroe 1970, which is both comprehensive and analytically acute, is undoubtedly the best source of the two closely related issues discussed here, covering both how the Arabs and Islam have been studied academically within the Spanish intellectual tradition and how the question of Spain's special character as a part of the European community has been shaped by Spaniards' views on the "Arab question." The now-classic works on the latter issue are Castro (all entries in the bibliography) and Sánchez-Albornoz [1956] 1966. The polemic is far from dead, as Sánchez-Albornoz 1973 indicates. See also Glick 1979, the introduction of which includes a concise summary of the different views on the question. Glick begins his study by noting that "History seems scarcely distinguishable from myth" (3) and goes on to note that, in the realm of dealing with the Spanish past, the problem is

more than usually acute. He notes that "long after the enemy was vanquished, the Jews expelled, and the Inquisition disbanded, the image of the 'Moor' remained as the quintessential stranger, an object to be feared" (3).

19. There are some views that are more explicitly negative on the Arabs than Sánchez-Albornoz's. Bertrand's 1952 comments verge on the unquotable and include observations that Arabs are "enemies of learning" and a "nullity as civilizing elements." Those wishing to read as vitriolic an example as any of anti-Arab prejudice are referred to pp. 82–94 of the English translation.

20. It is important to remember here how closely related were the literary and philosophical traditions of Hebrew and Arabic in Spain. In many instances it is more accurate to recall them as a single reasonably coherent tradition with two different prestige languages than as two completely separate ones. Suffice it to recall that the *kharjas* that Stern deciphered were *kharjas* to Hebrew *muwashshahas*. For the close relationship between those poems in the two different classical languages, see especially Stern 1959 and Millás y Vallicrosa 1967. It is also helpful to recall the admixture of originally Hebrew and Arabic elements in prose narrative as well. See M. J. Lacarra 1979. The melding of those traditions is evident in the text of the *converso* Petrus Alfonsi; see Hermes [1970] 1977, M. J. Lacarra 1980, and Vernet 1972 and 1978. Because of the prestige of Arabic as the language of letters and philosophy, Maimonides was perhaps the most noteworthy, but far from the only, Jewish writer to have used Arabic as his medium. For admixture in the textual history of the philosophical tradition, see Lerner 1974, introduction.

21. Thus, when Curtius writes his brief observations on "Spain's Cultural 'Belatedness'" (Curtius 1953:541–43) he cites Sánchez-Albornoz in support of his views. The short piece by Curtius is worth reading in any case because it reveals much in its three pages about the sort of exclusionary and negative image some of the most important Romance medievalists have had of medieval Arabic culture in Europe.

22. "Discovery," too, is a misleading term. Stern's famous "discovery" of 1948 is much more accurately described as an "identification." The *kharjas* were not lost or unknown—they even existed in published form. It was just that no one knew what they were. The Arabists and Hebraists who had worked on the *muwashshahas* of which they are a part had no idea of what they were, because, of course, they were studying Arabic or Hebrew literature, not Romance, and they did not imagine that the literature they were dealing with, despite its geographical provenance, had anything to do with Romance. Romance scholars, on the other hand, even those Hispanists working on medieval material, would have little if anything to do with material written in Arabic even within their own geographical and chronological sphere of interest, or even, as turned out to be the case here, with texts written in Romance but preserved in either Hebrew or Arabic transliteration and embedded in texts written in one of those two classical languages. The circumstances render Stern's identification and decipherment of these texts far more worthy of the greatest possible respect than any mere "discovery," any serendipitous stumbling on a lost manuscript, would have been. It was not accident or good fortune but rather his accurate understanding of the cultural situation in medieval Spain that made it possible, an understanding few scholars before him had had—or at least had applied. In addition, his success is best honored as a landmark, proof of the failure of our views of and approaches to the culture of al-Andalus, of medieval Spain, to accurately identify or deal with its literature. It is a failure that has not been overcome by Stern's discovery and that affects the study of the *kharjas* and other Hispano-Arabic poetry to this day. Instead, the achievement is popularly reduced to mere discovery, which many, if not most, Europeanists believe to be literally the case.

23. Alonso 1958 (in his essay "Un siglo más para la poesía española") and Alonso 1961 (in "Cancionillas 'de amigo' mozárabes: Primavera temprana de la lírica europea"); also, of course, Menéndez Pidal, especially 1961.

24. O'Donoghue 1982 is the most recent example, but it would be misleading to think

that that editor is particularly negligent. In fact, this anthology is remarkable for having included anything Arabic at all, and O'Donoghue takes some pride in noting what a broadening of the usual range of texts this comprises. He is certainly justified in noting that even this is an improvement.

25. See citations in notes 2 and 7 above. See also Corti 1979 for a discussion of models and antimodels in medieval culture and Bloomfield 1979 on continuities and discontinuities in the medieval world. In neither is there any hint that the Arabic cultural phenomenon might be an important example of an antimodel or that the question of alterity and sameness in the medieval period might be profitably reviewed, taking the Arab other and alterity as an informing concept.

26. To understand and accept the Saussurian dichotomy between diachrony and synchrony as meaning that the two are absolutely separable rather than separable as different focuses of analysis, is as fallacious in literary studies as it is in linguistics. For an extended and lucid discussion of this fallacy in linguistics, see Lehmann 1968. Many of the same kinds of problems explored here also come to light when concepts and terms are displaced from linguistics into literary studies.

CHAPTER TWO

Rethinking the Background

> *If we understand by Averroism the use of Averroes' commentary on Aristotle, then every medieval Aristotelian, including Aquinas, was an Averroist.*
> —Paul Oscar Kristeller, *Renaissance Thought*

WILLIAM, CIRCA 1100

A half dozen years before the birth of William IX, duke of Aquitaine, who was to become one of the most powerful men of his time in both political and cultural affairs, there occurred one of the most famous and well-documented examples of the taking of Arabic cultural "booty" by southern French Christians.[1] This was the taking of Barbastro by Guillaume de Montreuil in 1064, during which he is said to have taken a thousand slave girls, captured women, back to Provence. Even if this were an apocryphal and gross exaggeration serving to emphasize the barbarity of the Christians from the Arab chronicler's point of view, we have little reason to assume that the courts of Provence of the late eleventh century were oblivious to the art of Arabic sung poetry that the captured women would have brought with them.

The world from which these women were abducted was al-Andalus, and they and other refugees and victims of the wars of reconquest were familiar figures in Christian courts on both sides of the Pyrenees. In the tradition of all those throughout history who have been forced from their homeland, they took with them many of the trappings of the world from which they came, and in some small measure they recreated that world. Thus in Narbonne, Béziers, and Montpellier, Jewish and other Andalusian refugees taught some of the learning that already distinguished al-Andalus as an advanced culture, and in the courts of Aquitaine, Andalusian music and songs provided entertainment. After all, both the learning and the music had been essential features of any measure of civilization in the world from which they had fled or been abducted.

The political and cultural vicissitudes of al-Andalus had been many since the successful initial conquest in 711. The emirate had introduced a centralizing principle of government in the eighth century but, at that early moment of political consolidation, relatively little cultural activity that we know of. The creation and coming of age of the great Caliphate of Córdoba began in 929, but the building of the great mosque, the symbol of and monument to that enterprise, had been started in the previous century. It was a period in which the Arabization and even Islamization of the conquered peoples was a source of wonder and chagrin. The prestige of a language and culture, Arabic, that was no longer new or foreign had become indisputable. The transforming effects of that cultural prestige were lamented by Alvarus, bishop of Córdoba, in 854:

> Our Christian young men, with their elegant airs and fluent speech, are showy in their dress and carriage, and are famed for the learning of the gentiles; intoxicated with Arab eloquence they greedily handle, eagerly devour and zealously discuss the books of the Chaldeans [i.e., Muhammadans] and make them known by praising them with every flourish of rhetoric, knowing nothing of the beauty of the Church's literature, and looking with contempt on the streams of the Church that flow forth from Paradise; alas! the Christians are so ignorant of their own law, the Latins pay so little attention to their own language, that in the whole of the Christian flock there is hardly one man in a thousand who can write a letter to inquire after a friend's health intelligibly, while you may find countless rabble of all kinds of them who can learnedly roll out the grandiloquent periods of the Chaldean tongue. They can even make poems, every line ending with the same letter, which display high flights of beauty and more skill in handling meter than the gentiles themselves possess. (Translation, Watt 1965:56).

But it was not, in fact, until the subsequent century, the tenth, that the Andalusian Arabic world of belles-lettres and other arts emerged from the shadow of the East, which it had largely emulated, and came into its own, flourishing and nurturing experimentation and a wide range of poetic forms as it did the same in the plastic arts, as it minted gold coins, and as it introduced a sophistication in many spheres that was unknown in Europe for some centuries. Alvarus's distress had he witnessed, a hundred years later, the cultural prestige and success of the descendants of the Arab invaders and those who had adopted their language and culture would have been even more warranted and more acute. The situation was such that the man who at the millenium was to be Pope Sylvester II, an Aquitainian named Gerbert of Aurillac, had come to Spain in his formative years in quest of knowledge. Gerbert stayed three years in Catalonia studying mathematics and astronomy from the collection at Ripoll, which partook of the riches of Andalusian writings on these subjects, and it is reputed that he managed a visit to the great library of Córdoba itself. A man in many ways far ahead of his compatriots who did not cultivate the knowledge of al-Andalus, Gerbert was the first northern European to see the advantage of the numeral system of the Arabs, one that the Andalusians were still perfecting.

The prestige and luxury, and the distress of the Alvaros, would continue to grow in the subsequent century. The century into which the captives of Barbastro were born, the eleventh, was one characterized, paradoxically, by considerable political upheaval (the dissolution of the caliphate) and great affluence for the literature, the poetry, of that world. The astonishing wealth and growth of the capital, Córdoba, had spilled over to other areas and cities of al-Andalus and had considerably broadened the base of material and cultural well-being. Thus, when central authority collapsed and was replaced politically by the city-states known as the *mulūk aṭ-ṭawāʾif*, the financial and artistic bases for considerable material and cultural prosperity had already been established. The stage was set for the golden age of Hispano-Arabic literature, whose writers included three of the Andalusians destined to be best remembered by posterity: Ibn Shuhaid, Ibn Ḥazm, and Ibn Zaidūn. The first was the author of a trip to the afterlife; the second, of a treatise on love that combines poetry and prose; and the third was the premiere writer of love poetry of his age. Following on the heels of these renowned litterateurs of the last days of the caliphate came many more poets nurtured by the beneficent climate of the *mulūk*, cities in which the cultivation and patronage of the arts and all manner of science and philosophy became a high priority for monarchs themselves. The heads of these small but glowing kingdoms were learned or proficient in at least one specialty (philosophy, poetry) and expected no less from those to whom they offered their hospitality. Their courts vied with each other as hospices for the arts, and for poetry in particular.

But the great poetic form of the period was at first disdained by many of the most renowned poets. It reached its peak of popularity as the Cid Campeador was menacing many of the *mulūk* and while other cities, such as Barbastro, were plagued by incursions from the north. The song was called *muwashshaha*. The reasons for its lack of respect among the paragons of *haute culture,* men such as Ibn Ḥazm, were also the reasons for its success and popularity among those less protective of the canon of Arabic literature. The song embodied the symbiotic culture of al-Andalus rather than its classical Arabic heritage, and it vaunted its uniqueness with something revolutionary: a final verse in Mozarabic, the Romance vernacular of this world. The formal and musical alternations between strophes and refrain in these songs were reiterated and enhanced by the oscillation between classical and vernacular, between the language and poetry of the courts and that of the streets.

Some of the purists may not have liked it, but their disapproval, like the disapproval of many guardians of the old classical ways in every culture and period of history, did little to prevent its spreading popularity. The innovation, in fact, proved widely appealing for numerous generations of Andalusians, and for none more than for those of the eleventh century, whose cultural decadence in the eyes of stricter Muslims was to invite (or at least to serve to justify) the invasion of the fundamentalist Almoravids. It was a fateful invasion for the history of Europe and its culture, one that would provoke the alliance between the Cid and some of the *mulūk* and that would precipitate a long period of orthodox retrenchment that would eventually exile two of the greatest Andalusian philosophers, Maimonides and Averroes.

But in 1064 that period of defense and austerity was still in the unimaginable future, and the status quo in Spain was still one of prolific cultural production, luxurious court life, and the heyday of the revolutionary new song, the *muwashshaḥa*. Contacts between the men of Provence and those whose sphere of influence was still mainly limited to south of the Pyrenees were far from infrequent, and they were varied. Already in the time of William the Great, grandfather of William IX, the export of Andalusian scholarship to other parts of Europe was noteworthy: An astrolabe had been built at Lièges in 1025, and several books on the subject, clearly dependent on the works of the Arabic predecessors who had developed the instrument, were available by the midpoint of the century and were instrumental in the revolution in navigation that followed. The material, intellectual, and artistic riches that escaped al-Andalus in bits and pieces such as these graced the ancestral home of the man who was to be known as the first troubadour. Even as a young man he could hardly have avoided knowing the songs of the women of Barbastro, because the Arabic singing-slaves taken by Guillaume de Montreuil were dutifully presented by that William to his commander in chief, William VI of Poitiers, father of the man whose own songs would for many centuries be known as the first songs of Europe.

Whether or not William of Aquitaine, in his childhood or adolescence, heard the entertainments of the Barbastrian women then serving, through the vicissitudes of history and the Reconquest, in Provence, it is most unlikely that during his lifetime he could have remained ignorant of the salient features of life as it was lived in the Taifa kingdoms of Spain or of the many amenities that world provided for its inhabitants.

In fact, even aside from the particular incident at Barbastro and its ramifications in the life of William, everything we know about the geographic and political ties of what are now southern France and northern Spain (the latter far from completely reconquered or Christianized) shows clearly the extent to which the citizens of the area of Languedoc were in intimate contact with and tied to the *fronterizo* and the still strongly Arabized world of the late eleventh century. During the lifetime of William of Aquitaine the two societies were contiguous, and the interrelations between the two worlds, which we are scarcely justified in seeing as fundamentally separate, were remarkable. A rough sketch of their political history alone tells a story that reveals much. The county of Barcelona, which remained largely in Arab hands until well after the period of the first troubadours, spanned the western Pyrenees to include areas that in modern times separate France from Spain. Saragossa, for example, was not captured until 1118. The kingdom of Aragon was nominally Christian at the turn of the twelfth century, but many of its cities remained Muslim for some time. Even those that were in Christian hands had been so only for a very short period of time. Huesca, for example, had only been recaptured in 1096.

William was thus born and raised in Christian territory more than just randomly or sporadically involved with its Andalusian and semi-Andalusian neighbors. And the record of William's direct ties with the culture of the *muwashshaḥas* and of his own society's life in the limelight of al-Andalus leaves little or no doubt that the birth of Provençal troubadour poetry occurred at a time and place when the Arabic world and its culture were of immediate fascination and importance. Toledo, already an important seat of learning and translation, was conquered in 1085, and what followed in the wake of that Christian military victory was a victory of far greater proportions for Arabic learning, the virtual explosion of cultural material from al-Andalus to all points north.

In 1094, two years before the Aragonese city of Huesca was captured, William had married Philippa of Aragon, and his fascination with the most distinctly Arabized, polyglot and culturally polymorphous society of the reconquered territories was well noted at home—and little to be wondered at, given the tastes and proclivities nurtured earlier in life. It was not the first, nor would it be the last, occasion on which he would enjoy the considerable benefits of the rich court life, the learning, the music and singing that had already made Córdoba a byword for an unimaginable abundance of such wealth and were soon to make Toledo the best-known gateway to at least certain parts of that wealth. William, like his fellow Aquitainian Gerbert before him, had many advantages and previews of what was to come, since his personal ties with the *fronterizo* world were already intimately established when he married the Aragonese princess. One of his sisters had married Pedro I of Aragon, and yet another had married none other than Alfonso VI of Castile, the same Alfonso who had not only captured Toledo but had proclaimed himself "Emperor of Spain and the Two Faiths."

In 1095, the year after his marriage, the First Crusade began. William followed it to the Holy Land in 1100, when Jerusalem had already fallen. He remained there for several years (the years for which there is the clearest documentation of the virtually complete acculturation of the crusaders to Arab ways, though few of them, of course, had the advantages William had had). Back in Europe, a William who is described by his contemporaries as both restless and bored with traditional Christian society, who was twice excommunicated by the Church for ambiguous departures from orthodox Christian behavior, who was reviled by contemporary Christian chroniclers as an enemy of "modesty and goodness," and who was by now as familiar with the prodigious cultural wealth of both Palestinian and Andalusian court life as any Christian monarch of his lifetime could hope to be, this same William began to write the courtly lyric poetry that was to make him the father of the courtly vernacular lyric of Europe.

William interspersed this period of cultural fertility and innovation with a number of crusading excursions to Spain, including one, in 1119, as part of a broad-based alliance that attempted to turn back the fundamentalist Almoravids, who had invaded al-Andalus in 1091. While that campaign was successful (William himself was apparently present in 1120 at the defeat of the Almoravids at Cutanda), the war was ultimately lost and the magnificent library of Córdoba burned.

Such circumstances witnessed the birth, or at least the definitive molding, of the Provençal lyric that was to become the focal point, from a Europeanist's perspective, of the courtly and lyric culture of medieval Europe. And for the next several generations of troubadours, the cultural ambience would be far from removed from the kind of knowledge of Andalusian culture William had had. The courts of Barcelona, Aragon, and

Castile maintained their wealth of Andalusian trappings, reinforced by refugees seeking havens from the fundamentalist reforms taking place in al-Andalus, and these same courts were the often-visited havens of some of the best-remembered troubadours: Guiraut de Borneil, Arnaut Daniel, Peire Vidal, Marcabru, Raimbaut d'Orange, and Peire d'Auvergne. Perhaps, in part, they appealed so to these men for the same reasons that such a world of cultural symbiosis and richness, of artistic diversity and promise, had appealed to the first of their school, William. It was a world described succinctly and affectionately by Raimon Vidal:

> Totas genz, Cristians, Jusievas e Sarasinas, meton totz jorns lor entendiment en trobar et en chantar.   (Frank 1955:186)

One of the first and most basic problems encountered in an attempt to reimagine the cultural texture of this period is that many of the terms we must and do use can often be quite misleading. Foremost among these is the term "Islam" when it is used to denote the cultural entity that flourished principally in Spain and Sicily but that was also a significant force far beyond the geographical and temporal limits of its political boundaries. The term Islam has most commonly been used to denote that entity because it is the name of the religion under whose impetus military expansion initially brought it from the Middle East to Europe. It is also used in opposition to the term "Christian," which in Robertsonian and neo- or pre-Robertsonian views of the Middle Ages is assumed to be *the* cultural and intellectual force that strictly dictated and delineated the parameters and texture of both intellectual and artistic activities. As such, both terms are part of the general terminological apparatus that denotes an insurmountable separation between the two entities and that relegates to the category of non-European most of what is Islamic.

Such a perspective can be seriously misleading, however, because among other things it implies an identity between the religion and the cultural entity that, in terms of the way al-Andalus interacted with the Latin-Romance culture of the rest of Europe, was very often not perceived or was not the primary identification made. Its analogy would be of failing to distinguish, when dealing with the Middle Ages, between what is Latin (or Romance) and what is Christian, with the resulting misapprehension of the non-Christian cultural and intellectual strains and texts that are written in Latin (or in a Romance language).

But the problem is neither merely terminological nor due exclusively to the relative lack of sophisticated knowledge we tend to have about Islam and the Arabs in medieval Europe. It is also the case that there is much debate among scholars who are specialists (as well as among Arabs and Muslims who may not be scholars) on the question of the relationship between what is Arabic and what is Islamic. In any area of research where the distinction is potentially relevant, conflicting opinions on the nature of the relationship between these two terms almost invariably surface. All that one can say without much fear of contradiction is that Islam and Arabic culture are not *necessarily* identical and that at different times and in different places, the nature of the relationship has varied. At least this much can and should be said about their relationship in the Middle Ages in Europe: On the one hand, many different racial and ethnic groups were and became Spanish Muslims; on the other, the Arabic language became the prestige language for many who were not.

It would be risky to underrate either the importance of Islam in the context of its expansion into Europe (which without it would never have taken place at all) or the critical and highly complex role it played in the very formation and the bringing to such a high level of achievement of many of the aspects of culture relevant to the medieval world. It is also virtually undeniable that the fundamental cause of the importance of things Arabic in the first place is firmly rooted in the importance and success of Islam in this period, that the *primum mobile* in the prominence of the Arabic language as a vehicle of *haute culture,* even among those who were neither Arabs nor Muslims, was the dominance of Islam and its home language. In sum, there would be no question of the relative positions of Arabic and Islam if it were not for Islam in the first place, and the forces that brought Arabic to Europe were overwhelmingly in Islam. One can even accept, although it seems to me less self-evident, that many, if not most, European contemporaries would have been aware of that basic fact, no matter how dim or how inaccurate was their understanding of Islam itself.

However, just as risky as ignoring the role played by Islam would be to assume that, particularly from the eleventh through the fourteenth centuries, it was Islam itself with which other Europeans were principally acquainted, influenced, or preoccupied, or that Arabic was assumed to be the language exclusively, or even predominantly, of matters Islamic. Intensive knowledge of Islam was extremely limited and almost invariably distorted. It was ultimately as irrelevant, in its niceties as well as in its essential features (such as its monotheism), as the elements of Christianity were for most Muslims. Moreover, from the perspective of the power of a prestige language and the composite intellectual heritage adapted and created in that language, it might be seen that the Arabization of Spain and Italy was at least as successful as its Islamization. Witness the relatively simple fact that Maimonides, the greatest Jewish philosopher of his time (some would say of any time), wrote in Arabic without prejudice, and also that Arabic was the language of learning as well as the native tongue of Frederick II some two hundred years after the Arabs had lost all political power in Sicily and at a time when Frederick was actually carrying out certain repressive measures against Muslims there.

There is also a more complex, and more debatable, phenomenon: the existence of a particularly fertile and productive polymorphic culture in al-Andalus itself. Despite arguments to the contrary by some Arabists, there are many indications that to deal with al-Andalus as just one more Islamic country, one of the provinces and outposts of the larger Islamic world, is not appropriate. It was undoubtedly tied, through both Arabic and Islam, to the rest of the Islamic world. But that fact should not prevent us from seeing its peculiarly Andalusian character and the development of many cultural features that drew on non-Islamic sources as well as Islamic ones: features that in many cases—the *kharjas* certainly being a prime example—are directly attributable to the fact that total cultural hegemony was *not* achieved.

In any discussion of our perceptions of al-Andalus and Sicily within the rest of medieval Europe, as the two areas are likely to have been viewed at that time, it is critical to establish that religion often played a relatively minor role. Although the ultimate importance and impact of Islam may be critical, from the vantage point of a Christian living in the twelfth century the more important and influential phenomenon is better conceived of as Arabic in expression and Andalusian and Sicilian in immediate point of origin. The salient features of the world with which William of Aquitaine or the readers of the *Disciplina clericalis* of Petrus Alfonsi came into contact, and which we can legitimately claim they might have known in any degree, were secular. Thus, the ultimate sources of many of the cultural phenomena that became a part of the European mainstream because of the impact and prestige of Andalusian culture may be irrelevant, by and large. In other areas of inquiry, it is undoubtedly important to establish neatly and precisely the many different sources for the *Thousand and One Nights* or the *Disciplina clericalis*. But it is difficult to understand how one might imagine that such questions were raised by Petrus Alfonsi's readers or that answers to them by a modern-day scholar would alter the fact that Petrus Alfonsi was a Spaniard who told his readers he was going to relate to them some Arabic stories. The Andalusians' well-documented transmission of many material and technological advantages to other Europeans took place without much concern on the part of most of the beneficiaries about the religious beliefs, as they imagined them, of the bearers of these gifts. The Andalusians' knowledge of philosophy, medicine, astronomy, mathematics, and so forth rattled many fundamentalists, but the dissemination of such knowledge took place nonetheless and with little doubt in anyone's mind that the original language of the texts bearing that knowledge was Arabic. And, one might safely wager, the Andalusian songs heard throughout Spain and probably elsewhere in Europe too and the stories of Petrus and countless others who first heard them in Spain were appreciated (or not) without much consideration of whether they had existed in pre-Islamic poetry or had come to Spain from Persia.[2]

Remember, al-Andalus was also a cultural and intellectual entity that included many components that were not only not Islamic in nature but that in certain cases were antithetical to Islam, and in some cases this fine point was abundantly clear. Thus, for example, until well into the thirteenth century, and in some cases beyond that, Aristotle's work was perceived as being part of the Arabic cultural orbit. It had been assimilated into Arabic culture, and the Aristotle whom Latin-Romance Europe came to know was an Arabic Aristotle whose latest and most renowned commentator was Averroes. It is Averroes' versions and understandings of Aristotle (as well as selected aspects of Plato's work) that threw the Latin European community into a spin in the twelfth century, and it was Averroism, now more commonly referred to as "radical Aristotelianism," that presented the severe challenge to the primacy of Faith over Reason that so preoccupied and divided the intellectual communities of Europe as late as the fourteenth century.

On the other hand, it was also common knowledge among those who read Averroes—and they were legion—that Aristotle was part of the non-Islamic Arabic tradition. The variety of philosophic and scientific works and traditions that were accessible through Arabic texts was considerable, and they were read and accepted or rejected quite outside the context of Islam itself. In terms of its linguistic tradition and interpretation this was an Arabic Aristotle, and the perception of Aristotle in the rest of medieval Europe was inevitably tied to and associated with the Andalusian intellectual community, and this was an intellectual community that was not, in many cases, kindly regarded or dealt with by Islamic authorities. The Fundamentalist Muslims' persecution and eventual expulsion from Spain of Averroes for his strong and eloquent championing of radical Aristotelianism, his insistence that faith must be grounded in reason and philosophy rather than the other way around, was not unknown in the circles that read his work. It seems hardly audacious to assume that this would have engendered some sympathy on the part of Europeans whose own fundamentalist authorities, Christians in their case, looked equally askance at their own radical Aristotelianism or Averroism, and for very similar reasons. Under the rubrics Arabic and Andalusian, just as under the rubric of any other highly productive culture, we find a great diversity of ideologies, literary genres, and philosophical postures. In the tripartite culture of al-Andalus, the Christians' and Jews' contributions and adaptations of cultural and intellectual material were often expressed in the prestige language, Arabic, and many of the traditions of pre-Islamic as well as pre-Christian Iberian antiquity were important parts of the intellectual and artistic tradition. We must furthermore assume this to be even more true in the case of medieval Europe than in cases in history where cultures have been more homogeneous.

These examples, a small number of the many available, should serve to point out the essential fallacy in assuming that what is Arabic in medieval Europe is necessarily Islamic or that what was originally something else (Greek or Persian, say) was not received as Andalusian, as part of the great outpouring of material of al-Andalus that was so much a feature of the period. It is thus untenable to reject instances of possible Arabic-Andalusian influence on Christian Europe on the basis that the texts in question were not really—that is, originally—Arabic or Andalusian. Nor can we continue to maintain that many kinds of knowledge or interaction were inhibited by a fear and loathing of Islam.

The premise that Islam was essentially unknown and despised by Christians and that consequently it was not an influential force in the making of medieval Europe is accurate in great measure. But in most cases this is not true for what was Arabic and Andalusian. In this sphere in particular, one in which a close tie between religion and culture has so often been assumed by scholars, we should recognize that there is a critical difference between ideological, religious, and political domination on the one hand and cultural domination on the other. Material, cultural, and intellectual interaction and influence can certainly exist without ideological, religious, or political domination. At times, in fact, it may proceed even in the face of extreme hostility in the political and ideological spheres. Thus, if we posit that a certain important feature of medieval Europe had its origins in al-Andalus, we cannot maintain this by arguing that Islam dominated Christianity, which would be patently absurd. But such an assertion can certainly be made on the historically verifiable assumption that such a feature was part of a heterogeneous Arabic milieu that did, in a number of cases, dominate and shape Latin-Romance cultural features.

PETER, CIRCA 1142

In 1142, within a generation after William's death and at a time when the poetic vogue he had been instrumental in establishing was reaching its peak, Peter the Venerable, the enormously respected and influential abbot of Cluny, set forth on a trip to Spain during which he wished to gather the necessary material to make what was to be the first translation of the Koran into another language.[3] Peter's perspective on that world was quite different from William's. The monarch had been notorious for his apparent contempt for the dictates and mores of the Church and for his attraction to the unorthodox and innovative, the exotic and opulent. And the purpose of the great Cluniac could not have been more different from that of the troubadours, the successors of William whose own stays in Spain coincided with that of Peter.

In one of the documents Peter wrote, he explained the nature and purpose of his project for translating the sacred texts of Islam (actually he also translated some pieces of fiction that were assumed by others, and probably by Peter, to be part of the Islamic scriptures). In this explanatory text he reveals himself to be a worthy successor of Alvarus of Córdoba, since he notes that the problem among Christians is that they do not know or understand what a danger Islam is nor, consequently, do they put up any resistance to it: "I was indignant that the Latins did not know the cause of such perdition and, by that ignorance, could not be moved to put up any resistance" (translation, Kritzeck 1964:30). This revelation about the Latins' lack of resistance voices a complaint that Peter's fellow ecclesiastic, Alvarus, could well have understood and that was a source of considerable concern to the churchmen of Europe in the twelfth century, although the far more menacing spectre of Averroism was still a generation away. Both this passage and that of Alvarus, who had prefigured in Spain the reaction that arose farther north in Europe in later periods, reflect situations in which the Christian laity remained unaware of the sort of danger in their associations with "Islam" that was perceived by those more directly tied to the Church. Peter's statement (as well as his subsequent behavior) does tell us, as others have noted, that most Christians were ignorant of the doctrines of Islam. But his statement even more clearly tells us that those same Christians were not oblivious to many other aspects of Andalusian civilization and clearly had little hesitation in dealing with it, in showing no resistance to it, as he says. What is described with a sense of exultation by Raimon Vidal is a source of acute worry for Peter, and what is written between Peter's lines is as revealing as what he says. After all, if Christians were not coming into contact with those already seduced by that dangerous Islamic faith, then what danger could have existed? And it is worth remembering that the expression of fear comes not from the embattled Córdoban of the ninth century, but from the leader of Cluny, the heart and cynosure of Christian-Latin Europe, in the twelfth.

Indeed, from the perspective of the Church and its concern with protecting its dominant status (from Peter's perspective, in other words) there were good reasons to be worried, far too many reasons to explore here in any detail. Contemporary commerce was colonial in nature, with Christian Europe in the role of colony and the Europe of Islam and Arab wealth in the role of benefactor, and many of the advances and riches of al-Andalus would come to make it an important benefactor even of the Arab world to the east. Such luxuries had given many other Europeans a taste of what the good life could be, and it was a very good one, comparatively speaking. The many nouns whose Arabic names survive in our Romance languages give a skeletal picture of the innovations, the cultural nuances, and the revolutionizing technical and mechanical items, that were then becoming integral parts of Western life beyond the Andalusian borders—everything from oranges to pillows, glass, paper, the compass and astrolabe, sherbet, checks and other financial instruments, spices, chess, certain musical instruments, and on and on.

But no mere list or inventory, even if it could be exhaustive, could convey the overall nature of the impact that resulted from the virtual invasion of material wealth and luxury that the Arabs of al-Andalus and the rest of the Mediterranean then made available to a Europe long deprived of much of that kind of wealth. Because the Arabs were skilled traders and liberal acquirers of the benefits of all the societies with which they came into contact—and after the great expansion of Islam those contacts had been enormous—they enabled Europe to reap the benefits of many such acquisitions, as well as of the innovations of al-Andalus itself.

The situation may well be described as analogous to the impact of modern colonialism on many parts of the world and its spread of vigorous trade and material culture. Many Europeans who had not seen the Arab world firsthand understandably had the distinct impression that not only did the Arabs have control over the rest of the world, as it was in their imaginations, but also that the Arabs' lives were incomparably richer, easier, more luxurious, and superior, and thus to the Church more decadent. Such impressions were confirmed by returning crusaders who had themselves been dazzled by Islamic civilization. For the society against which they had fought on battlefields in Spain and Palestine was the source not only of immediate and tangible material improvements but also of the technical wherewithal to develop further amelioration in their daily lives. The Arab world was, in sum, a civilization apparently superior to their own in most if not all aspects of daily living, one whose trade goods were coveted and depended on, whose luxury was astounding, and whose *savoir-vivre* was often admired, however grudgingly.

By Christian standards, the Arabs were heretics, and what they had done to merit such a marvelous destiny was a mystery and a source of some concern. And, as would be the case when the situation was reversed in the modern period, the orthodox establishment was appalled. It viewed such an incursion, such commercial and technological imperialism and colonialism even beyond the boundaries of military and political control, as anathema, as a corruption of the sacred traditional values, and as something God-fearing men should avoid. Instead, much to the establishment's chagrin, a great deal of it was welcomed with open arms and paid for willingly. The foreign devil, with his material temptations and promises of a better life in this world (which subverted the foundations of a faith rooted in the primacy of the afterlife), has had many faces. It is one of the ironies of history that in Europe in the Middle Ages the foreign devil was an Arab.

No less significant was the increasing recognition that those who knew Arabic possessed the keys to the pagan and secular knowledge of the Greeks and of Aristotelians among the Muslims themselves, a whole body of science and philosophy that tantalized many. This was already emerging as no less a menace to the primacy of unadulterated Christian faith than the more tangible fruits of Islamic civilization, and Peter the Venerable, one of the most eminent and reasonable defenders of the faith, clearly did not intend to let the threat pass unchallenged.

His mission must have seemed of some urgency because of the alarmingly degenerating situation in the fifty years or so before he went on his mission to Spain. That half century had recorded events and vogues that indicated a multiplication of contacts with dangerous Muslim temptations: the fall of Toledo in 1085, the beginning of the First Crusade in 1095, and the introduction into the Christian courts of southern France of songs that were in many ways rather like those of the Arabs and that in any case were strikingly and distressingly unorthodox and secular in character. Dangerous contact with the seductive culture of the Arab world, that of the Holy Land as well as of al-Andalus, was on the increase. The crusades had in any case also expanded the areas of contact, often intimate contact, with that world, and little of its mystery and appeal was lost through such meetings, which revealed at closer range some of the many advantages the Muslim possessed. In many cases, as has happened before and since in history, the ravages of war were also accompanied by a measurable increase in the estimation in which the enemy and his society were held by many Christians.

At much the same time, the conquest of Toledo opened doors for Europeans that had previously been restricted to Andalusians. The great increase in the flow of translations from that city, whose name would come to be synonymous with the art and science of translations of Arabic texts, posed a different kind of threat and represented a different kind of evil. It instilled the fears and worries that secular philosophical knowledge and the sciences have always invoked in religious establishments, whatever the creed.

Peter, like many others before and after him, feared that the combined material, cultural, and intellectual seduction of Arabic culture, plainly visible in a number of different spheres, would ultimately be destructive of the Christian values it was his duty, and in his interest, to preserve. The situation and the reactions it produced are far from unfamiliar in other periods of history, including our own. It requires no great imagination to hear the sound of the keepers of the old faith preaching against the dangers of change and its ultimate destructiveness to traditional religion and values. Worst of all, in many cases, is the insidious acculturation provoked by the material advantages and cultural chic of the foreign influence. Most common is the fundamentalist association of new styles in clothing and music and literature, or new technologies, or new philosophies and forms of knowledge with the destruction of important values. Particularly if they seem to be coming from some foreign source, such pernicious influences are closely tied to assorted ideological, religious, and political dangers.

It was from this vantage point that Peter viewed his challenge. He saw an ideological danger clothed in cultural chic and material desirability, an enemy that was thriving both in Europe and on the battlefields of Palestine and that had already infiltrated or seduced many ignorant Christians. It was to combat all of this that Peter undertook his task of translating Islamic scripture, in the hope that the revelation of its true evil would somehow awaken fellow Christians to the dangers lurking in that culture. It is to his credit, and is part of his relatively liberal intellectual credentials, that unlike his hard-line Dominican brethren, he believed an appeal to reason through a knowledge of the enemy's religious failings would be most effective.

Both the texts that Peter translated and his own two texts, which became part of the group of translations known as the Toledan Collection, are of great interest. Although Peter is widely acknowledged to have been the first person who was interested in providing a reasonably accurate picture of Islamic doctrine for Christians, it should not be overlooked that of the five texts he translated, only one—the Koran—is not an imaginative or literary text. Moreover, in both his *Summa,* which is his summary of the doctrines of Islam as he understood them from the texts he had translated, and in his refutation of the doctrines of Islam as he construed them (the *Liber contra sectam sive haeresim Saracenorum*), Peter actually helped to perpetuate a very imaginative vision of Islam.

This is worth noting because many scholars have worried about the inaccuracy of the views of Islam held by Christian Europeans in the Middle Ages, and Peter's translations, his *Summa,* and his refutation have rightly been at the center of such discussions. But it is just as important to remember that to a great extent Peter's appeal to reason, however noble, was essentially misguided. Most Christians had little or no accurate knowledge of or interest in Islam, since the appeals and seductions of al-Andalus and everything else the Arabic-speaking world offered were hardly theological or religious, and most Christians were no more interested in the niceties of doctrine in the Middle Ages than they are today (despite some of our romantic notions to the contrary).

The central importance of the venerable Cluniac's texts is quite different. The significance of a set of seemingly authoritative texts such as those disseminated by Peter the Venerable is in the literary forms and imaginary visions associated with Islam and the Arab world that such texts created and perpetuated. As such, the texts served two functions, which embodied two of the reactions to Arabic thought and letters that would emerge in subsequent centuries.

First, part of what captures the imagination of both intellectuals and artists are forms and images, and in this respect Peter's texts provide examples of several critical forms and images. Two of the translations are of semiliterary forms that were already becoming important rhetorical vehicles in medieval letters: the dialogue and the fictive and rhetorical exchange of letters. It was the beginning of the era of *sic et non* among the Latins and the height of it among the Arabs. As a matter of fact, varieties of both had just been written by one of the most controversial intellectuals of that generation of Christians, Peter Abélard. His works banned by the council of Sens in 1140, Abélard nonetheless found refuge at Cluny with Peter the Venerable, who not only comforted the less orthodox Peter in his last two years but wrote the letter of condolence to Héloïse when he died in 1142. And before setting off that same year on his trip to Spain to study and translate the doctrines of the Muslims—a journey long planned, researched, and studied for—Peter made sure that Abélard's oddly named son was taken care of. But perhaps the name Astrolabe did not seem so strange to the ears of Peter the Venerable.

That Peter's translations of what was presented, and to at least some degree accepted, as the holy scriptures of the Islamic faith was written in such familiar forms would have at least helped to perpetuate the already prevalent impression that, as far as rhetorical, philosophical, and semiliterary forms were concerned, the styles and approaches of medieval Europeans—be they Muslim or Christian, Latin or Arabic—were very closely related. In fact, and this is the most important point, such texts document the extent to which it is difficult to point to a radical difference between the two traditions from the perspective of the twelfth and thirteenth centuries. Even before working with Averroes became *de rigueur* among intellectuals of Paris and London and before Aquinas responded because the Dominicans could no longer pretend that the new Aristotle was not there to stay, it is perilous to imagine that the other world would have seemed so unfamiliar to a reader of the Toledan Collection.

The second function served by Peter's texts is also tied to the fact that, despite their spurious nature (except the Koran, of course), they were presented and accepted as authentic scripture, and in both his *Summa* and his refutation Peter presented important parts of what he believed to be the Islamic vision of the afterlife, of heaven and hell. Peter's summary of what he considered to be the most important features of the texts was an important contribution to the Christian's fantasies about the Arab and his world, because the apocryphal material presented by Peter as part of Islamic scripture depicted a vision of heaven that itself was emblematic and illustrative of the terrible seductiveness and danger of Islam and the Arab world: the Islamic paradise is an appealingly (and for a devout Christian appallingly) sensuous and materially rich one, one in which the lascivious and materialistic desires of such people were gratified. This thinly veiled transformation of the real attractions of that world into a degenerate notion of the afterlife of bliss became, during several centuries, an important source of information on the subject of the Muslim concept of paradise for interested Christians.

As in all intercultural contacts, what proves to be significant and influential, and consequently what scholars of later generations may focus on, are the impressions created between such cultures, the notions they have of each other, whether accurate or not. The validity or accuracy of one impression does not determine that of others, and the ultimate or absolute validity of the impression is not the yardstick by which we can or should measure the degree of its impact. After all, it is the image itself, regardless of its accuracy, that causes both the reactions and imitations that are thereafter called "influences."[4]

It is thus important to shun the notion that influence by one culture on another is in any way dependent on accurate, or even particularly well detailed, information. Perforce, the vision one culture acquires of another is quite different from the one that culture has of itself, and it will rarely be accepted as accurate. Moreover, the selection process involved in the formation of the image may well not provide either a coherent or an orthodox view of the other culture by the standards of the culture being imagined and characterized. Such "errors," however, are a part of the truth of the image that becomes a formative element, and later scholarship dealing with the question of interactions between the two cultures must deal not only with the "truth" of what one culture was but also with the even more telling and influential truth of what it seemed to be to the other. Quite often an erroneous, oversimplified, or distorted image is the framework for much influence, whether adaptive or reactive.

Indeed, in the interaction between Arabic culture and Latin/Romance culture in Europe in the Middle Ages, historical evidence would indicate that the perception of what was Arabic was something quite different from what we would normally (or accurately) imagine as being Arabic or Islamic. The view Europeans held of the religion itself was one that not only did not reflect the fundamentals of Islam, such as its strong and basic monotheism, but that assumed it to be either a pagan religion or a Christian heresy. Of even greater importance when we try to reconstruct the framework within which Arabic texts, stories, or songs would have been received is the fact that Europeans imagined that cultural/religious entity to be characterized by moral licentiousness, permissiveness, self-gratification, and cultural decadence (that is, by an intense cultivation of secular dance, music, and so forth).[5] Within that context, the other more specific components of the image of what was Arabic, those that were the framework for any further influence, make a great deal of sense.

Islamic civilization appeared to be a materially much more comfortable and civilized world, since the religion did not cultivate any sense of restraint or puritanism but rather the opposite. It was the vehicle (because of its supposed lack of orthodoxy and guiding theological or moral principles of the kind that governed the Latin orbit) of an unrestrained intellectual tradition that fostered and furthered studies unknown or interdicted in the Christian tradition, studies as varied as astrology, medicine, and Aristotelianism. It is important to remember that such impressions were very much aided and abetted by those who were presumed to be authorities on the subject—Peter the Venerable for one. As we try to reconstruct the cultural and intellectual forces that shaped medieval Europe, it is necessary to keep in mind that these were the impressions that, by and large, Latin/Romance speakers had of the Arabic cultural milieu, impressions that were, in different measures, both fact and fiction.

A further question: To what extent did hostility on some fronts limit the possibility of interaction and influence on others? Here we can rely on observations of comparable situations and on what we do know about such matters in the medieval period. Aspects of a foreign culture that have to do with material well-being and cultural and artistic innovations, for example, are quite often readily accepted, both for the improvement in life-style afforded by the former and the stimulation and innovation provided by the latter. The acceptance of such material benefits or art forms may well proceed in the face of even quite hostile political or ideological differences. The subconscious cultural ideology can be quite separate from, and seemingly contradictory to, a well-articulated conscious ideology in a culture. One group within a culture may be more open to foreign influences than other, more conservative groups.[6] The literary or cultural historian of a later period should not fall into the trap of concluding either that the society as a whole was monolithic—that all groups had shared values or that those of a ruling group, whose tastes and prejudices survive more amply through official or canonized documents and texts, necessarily dominated or dictated those of others.

Here one must deal with the undeniable and often-cited fact of ideological (that is, theological) and military conflict, both of which were fought out not only in Europe but also in the Middle East when the crusades became a feature of Christian political policies. There are also several important modifications that we must make in our imagining of what such conflict meant—and did not mean. There is much disagree-ment among scholars about the nature and motivations of the crusades and their fundamental impact on medieval society in Europe. Within this framework of disagreement there is a particularly thorny debate over the idea that the very notion of a crusade, a holy war, is a cultural borrowing, a direct response to the Islamic *jihād* or holy war, a feature of Arabic cul-ture of which Europeans were aware. Whether or not one accepts so spe-cific a dependence on Islam and its power, it is sufficient for the purposes of this argument to accept the fact that the crusades, both within and outside of Europe, were an important fact of life, whatever may have been their motivation, whether political or religious, patristic or bor-rowed from Islam. But the question is what role the state of conflict represented by the crusades and the continuing anti-Islamic Christian rhetoric throughout Europe played in the overall picture of cultural and intellectual relations.

What is most frequently maintained, or assumed, is that the essential opposition and concomitant conflict between the two religious/political entities effectively blocked or prevented any significant degree of interac-tion at other levels. The most common view is that what was being com-batted on the battlefield or from the pulpit was not something that could or would be admired or emulated at the court or at the university, that the enemy, in sum, is the enemy, something one combats not just militarily but through disdain and rejection, culturally and intellectually. But is this really a tenable view of how cultures interact in general? And how does one account for evidence from the medieval period that suggests, in any case, that such a view is not specifically applicable to that period?

At a theoretical level, and given what we are readily able to observe about other major cultures in conflict, both historically and in our own time, it would be naive to posit that ideological, political, or military conflict necessarily precludes important interaction at other levels. Just as being a convinced Marxist or living in a militantly Marxist society com-mitted to the elimination of capitalism in no way guarantees, however much the political and ideological leadership would want it to, that one does not listen to rock and roll, living in the Christian society of medieval Europe did not predicate that one would find silk or sherbet distasteful or Arabic songs not worth listening to. Frederick II's position as one of the leading campaigners in the crusades did not deter his unabashed adoption of Arabic culture, from clothes to harem to intellectual traditions and other cultural patterns. His example is flamboyant and spectacular, but in many essential features it is representative. One of the things that must have driven the church authorities mad was the well-documented fact that so many crusaders, both in Europe itself and in Palestine, were culturally converted.

Warfare, actual or figurative, does not exist equally at all levels of culture, and political or ideological warfare is in many cases accompanied by a very different, more adaptive relationship in intellectual and other cultural arenas. It is quite often the case, and it would appear that this was so in the European Middle Ages, that certain important segments of the general population (artists, intellectuals, the avant-garde in cultural matters) are very often at odds with the elders and keepers of the flame of a community and a culture, and these are precisely the individuals most likely to ignore or reject the exhortations of fundamentalists to shun or avoid the temptations of an encroaching or threatening enemy. If we were ecclesiastical historians, it would be wholly appropriate to stress the importance of the enduring and omnipresent conflict between Christianity and Islam in medieval Europe. As literary historians, however, we must bear in mind that we are by and large dealing with individuals and cultural phenomena whose own standards and inclinations were in many cases dramatically different from and oblivious to the official pronouncements of Christian political and religious authorities.

Many of the writings of those very authorities reflect this phenomenon. From the lament of Alvarus of Córdoba to Peter the Venerable's explanation of the need for the translation of Islamic scriptures and to the ban on Averroist philosophy in Paris, we should be readily able to perceive the seductive power of the Arabic cultural milieu for the European intellectual and artistic community—despite the importance of the territorial threat that Islam posed for Europe. The real threat, indeed, was a cultural one, and this threat had little to do with either Islam or territorial conquest. What encroached on and in many ways eventually conquered Europe in the eleventh, twelfth, and thirteenth centuries were intellectual, artistic, technological, and philosophical phenomena, things that ideology cannot control effectively and that warfare cannot combat or preclude.

All of this would seem to indicate that despite the many kinds of hostilities that did exist between the two cultures, there were ample opportunities and stimuli for influence in the intellectual and artistic realms of literature. We are justified in considering the different kinds of literary influence and interaction that are possible under such circumstances. If we have established that the historical circumstances did not preclude such contacts, we must be equally careful in exploring the implications of the fact that those same circumstances would make many of those contacts less than straightforward and that would enmesh them in different kinds of linguistic or ideological difficulties.

ELEANOR, CIRCA 1146

Shortly after 1146, Eleanor of Aquitaine, granddaughter of William, followed in her well-known grandfather's footsteps by insisting on accompanying the first of her two husbands on a crusade to the Holy Land.[7] But, also like her grandfather before her and partially because of the less-than-pure quality of the Aquitainian courts in which she grew up, the courts of the well-traveled troubadours she encountered there and would herself cultivate, this was hardly the first knowledge Eleanor would have had of the non-Christian, non-Romance-speaking worlds. And because she reigned over courts in northern France and then Norman England that were the beneficiaries of the translations that so shaped intellectual life in the twelfth century, she would continue during her long life to have many other reasons and opportunities to be familiar with the culture of Arabized Europe, and that would include the intellectual culture of Spain as well as that of Palestine.

Some of the translators engaged by Peter the Venerable to work on those Arabic texts, apparently at a very pretty price, were already associated with the school of translators at Toledo, whose prestige and dissemination of translations continually increased and widened in Europe throughout the twelfth century, roughly the century spanned by Eleanor's life. Among those who worked on the translations of the Koran and other texts for the Cluniac abbot was Robert of Ketton, one of a half dozen Englishmen who came to be instrumental in the diffusion of translations of Arabic texts in northern Europe. He would not be the last, but neither was he the first, prominent intellectual to enlighten the Norman courts on both sides of the Channel about the learning and literary texts of al-Andalus.

Ketton's most eminent predecessor was certainly Petrus Alfonsi, the Spanish émigré whose other name was Moshé Sephardi, a converted Jew who had brought his vast learning of Arabic and Hebrew science and letters to London earlier in the century. It is true that as royal physician to Henry I, Eleanor's second father in law, and as savant in residence he played a prestigious role at that court. But his influence as a scientist, an astronomer, a veritable repository of knowledge of the Arabic and Hebrew worlds, great as it was in his lifetime, was no greater than the popularity he was to have as a litterateur. As the author of the widely read *Disciplina clericalis,* a collection of *novelle* derived from his storehouse of knowledge of the literature of al-Andalus, Petrus Alfonsi and his text would continue to figure prominently in courtly intellectual and artistic circles, the same circles in other ways dominated by Eleanor of Aquitaine.

Indeed, it would be fair to say that Eleanor's prestige and influential role in the making of civilized life in the twelfth century was shared with the Petrus Alfonsis of her time. The expansion of Norman political power in the late eleventh century and its consolidation in the twelfth and thirteenth centuries played an important role in the dissemination of learned Arabic texts in translation. The blood ties, as well as the political and cultural interactions among courts scattered from Sicily to England, with France in-between, meant that there was a considerable amount of free exchange of intellectual and artistic activity, much of which, in any case, tended to be carried out by peripatetic scholars and artists.

Further, the close ties with both Sicily and Spain meant that Eleanor and her entourage, much like her grandfather and his crowd, were familiar visitors to their relatives in courts where, since knowledge of Arabic was often *de rigueur,* translations from the Arabic were not as important as they were in London. One of the daughters of Eleanor and Henry II married the Norman king of Sicily, a Sicily just recently taken from the Arabs but so heavily Arabized culturally and intellectually that it was to become one of the most important seats of Arabic learning anywhere. A second daughter had married into the royal family of Castile, and as the wife of Alfonso VIII of Castile and an eminent figure in Toledo, this other Eleanor (she had been named for her mother) welcomed visitors from throughout Europe who came to Toledo to drink from its fountains of knowledge—and to take much of that knowledge back to England, France, and Germany. Both Joanna, queen of Sicily, and the younger Eleanor would be as familiar with that hybrid world as their great-grandmother Philipa of Aragon had been, and Blanche of Castile, brought up in Toledo and Burgos, descendant of William of Aquitaine, Philipa, and Eleanor on one side and of the Alfonsos of Castile on the other, would be Louis Capet's queen of France.

Contacts with the seats of learning and translation in southern Europe were anything but rare, indeed they were virtually incestuous at times. In Sicily in 1154 Idrisi was to call his magnificent geographical work *The Book of Roger* in honor of his Norman patron, Roger of Sicily, the first of the two "baptized sultans" of that island. But on that island, where Arabic was unapologetically the language of learning, a significant number of learned and scientific works and translations were dedicated to Henry II, Eleanor's second husband and Roger's relation several times over.

Eleanor herself, as her progeny would also do, played a key role in the cultural and intellectual revival of those courts of Europe considered by many literary historians of France to be the origin and home of the French literary renaissance of the twelfth century. A key role, however, was also played by the learning and attitudes, transmitted both directly and through example and translation, of the courts where the secular learning and cultural admixtures often voiced in Arabic were formative and key features. Eleanor was undoubtedly in the intellectual and artistic avant-garde of European court life, but she invented neither the attitudes nor the learning that transformed that world. Petrus Alfonsi, after all, was not an outsider at the Norman court. He was the king's doctor and his scholar in residence.

And he, and others like him—Adelard of Bath, Robert of Ketton, even Michael Scot at the end of the century—were important and prestigious, and not just because of the technical knowledge of Arabic culture they imparted through translations. Indeed, they were men of learning and book knowledge, but no less important, as the popularity of the *Disciplina clericalis* well indicates, was their intimate knowledge of a world that fascinated people on many levels. Their unrecorded accounts and retellings of the world they knew so well, the anecdotes and insights of such world travelers, would have held notable attractions. The *Disciplina* was written down, and written in Latin, and was thus preserved for posterity. But we can hardly suppose that at such times and in such courts they would have been the only stories from the Arabic world to fascinate and intrigue the members of the courts of northern Europe.

One of the best-told stories, in fact, came from Eleanor's own trip to the Middle East, for Eleanor not only accompanied her French husband, Louis, on the Second Crusade, which began in 1146, but reputedly created quite a scandal while she was there. Among other things, it was rumored that she had taken more than one Arab, including the great Saladin, as her lover. There can be no accuracy to the story, at least as far as Saladin was concerned. The man who was to proclaim the Holy War of 1186 and take Jerusalem the following year, thus rocking all of Europe, was but a boy when Eleanor and her entourage were enjoying the pleasures of Palestine, as other crusaders before them had done.

But the ultimate truth of such a rumor about Eleanor is not nearly as important as the fact that such a legend not only arose but apparently remained quite popular throughout her lifetime and during the rest of the

Middle Ages. The association of Eleanor with Saladin—who was to become a symbolic character in his own right, the personification of Arab honor and magnanimity in the northern European imagination and in later medieval literature—and with other Arab princes at a sexually intimate level is a more interesting reflection (from a literary point of view) of other, less titillating kinds of intimacy. It remains a good story, an indication, in part, of the degree to which the Arab world—the dominant Other, whether in al-Andalus or the Holy Land—was an entity associated with great appeal and seduction.

In myth or legend, the seduction or rape of a woman as the image for the succumbing of one culture or political entity to another is certainly common, and in archetypical terms the attraction of the Other at one level is often commensurate with his repulsiveness at another. Eleanor's sexual attraction to the enemy of the crusade fits such patterns all too neatly, and in this case it is perhaps even more telling that it was never thought that Eleanor had had anything but an active and willing role in her intimate associations with the Arab prince or princes with whom she consorted. This too is part of the story, since in fairly short order the Europeans who had participated in the First Crusade had embraced the cultural and material amenities of their supposed enemies.

It is a story, finally, whose meaning is obscured if we evaluate it as a straightforward recounting of historical facts. The "facts" may be no more or less accurate than those told of Charlemagne at Roncevaux in the Roland epic. In both cases the truth is less straightforward, it is to be sought less directly, it is ultimately more important than the facts.

One of the most likely kinds of influence of Andalusian culture on medieval Romance literature that one would accept as possible or likely under the difficult circumstances of antagonism is that of reaction. It is precisely because of the many instances in which adoption and adaptation in other spheres took place that instances of opposition in the cultural and intellectual orbit were likely to occur. The phenomenon of cultural interaction that leads to some kind of assimilation is bound to lead, in the same instance, to a demarcation, an identification, and an elaboration of the ways in which the cultures do differ and of the instances in which assimilation does not take place. What this means, however, is that in providing a vivid sense of a different culture, the Arabic cultural presence in Europe in many instances played the critical formative role of an identity against which many other Europeans might define themselves. Thus, when we study a writer such as Dante, for example, it is incumbent upon us not to ignore the role of Arabic culture, because it was influential not in the sense that he embraced it but in the sense that his work may have been a considered reaction against its encroaching presence in his intellectual milieu.

One of the important kinds of influences often present in medieval Romance literature (as in much other literature, including modern literature) is the definition of the self as being, in critical and distinctive ways, different from the other. In medieval literature the other is often, explicitly or implicitly, embodied by the Arab world in some guise. As such, it must be taken into account as an important defining and shaping element in much of that medieval literature. Part of this influence is the explicit imagery of the exotic other world that pervades medieval narrative, imagery that literary critics often account for merely in its detail and specific occurrences rather than in the context of a general cultural framework as an integral part of the imaginative world of medieval literature. Again, the accuracy of such notions and images is all but completely irrelevant. What is important in a text such as the *Song of Roland*, for example, is not that the Arabs are portrayed as pagans, which is inaccurate, and thus that the medieval French vision of Islam and the Arabs is one to be discarded or ignored. Nor, to take another example, is it sufficient to say that Boccaccio's setting of a number of specific *novelle* in oriental settings is incidental or has no value in terms of the rest of the elements of that story. Rather, our criticism of the text should focus on the paradigms of oppositions developed in the text and dependent for their comprehension on the views and understandings the audience was likely to have of the world thus alluded to. The image of the Saracen is constructed on the basis of a literary definition of what the Christian is, which, in this text, is what the Saracen is not. And the image of the world of Saladin—the image of a quasi-Greek, quasi-oriental world in which learned men hold forth—certainly embodies in part a concept of a world where learning is an openly conducted feature of everyday life. Such definitions are as dependent on the audience's knowledge and opinion of the other to which Christianity (or Florentine society) is opposed and contrasted as it is on its knowledge and opinion of the nature of Christianity (and Florentine society). In these terms, it becomes impossible to ascribe to the images of the pseudo-Muslim armies or to the pseudo-Arabic setting in the text a merely incidental role, though this is often done. In many cases, it might well be something more closely resembling the opposite, a feature critical in a text's very existence and elaboration as part of a definition of self, a crucially important counterpoint.

What presupposes this position is the observation that in imaginative writing, just as in other activities of the human conscious and subconscious, definitions are comprised more of implicit oppositions than of expository explanation. (If this were not the case, the texts in question would be less literature and more rhetorical or expository writing.) Despite the assertions that still abound, in different guises, that medieval man was artistically and psychologically more primitive than his modern descendant, it has become increasingly difficult to maintain such a position. Most medievalists have put aside the self-serving modern notion that medieval literature is not as complex artistically or its writers as perplexed psychologically as we are.

Fortunately for the sake of medieval texts, the era is passing away in which one could speak of a medieval writer as if he were an earlier version of the human being and his text a cartoon. Indeed, one of the reasons that it is necessary to review and redefine the different kinds of possible Arabic influence is that even though many medievalists have developed more sophisticated notions of literary confluences and currents, and thus borrowings, these refinements are almost invariably bounded by the limits of an older view of what constituted medieval Europe, one that excluded the presence of the Arabs.

In a more complex view of this literary universe, or a view of a much more complex universe, there exists an often-silent but far from unimportant other. As the entity that in many different ways supplied the locus and texture for a sense of other in medieval Romance literature, the Arab world must thus be reckoned a potent influence. If it had not been there in Europe, challenging in so many ways the sense of the European's identity and place in the larger scheme of things, medieval texts would be very different indeed.

There are several other things we should consider regarding influence. First, it might be perceived that there are many kinds of imitative or behavioral influence, even in the literary sphere, that do not require translation in order to be possible and that are particularly likely to take place under the circumstances of combined jealousy and fear seen in medieval Europe. If there is evidence (and such evidence is ample in our knowledge of medieval Europe) that one culture was aware of the existence of another, that it acquired certain views and specific or general images of the nature of that culture, and that it was stimulated in some way—perhaps by something as simple as viewing it as chic or challenging—to want some of the same or similar things, then influence in the sense of emulation or adaptation is not necessarily dependent on anything further. The image that William of Aquitaine, or his granddaughter Eleanor, had every reason to have of Arabized monarchs presiding over courts where the patronage of poetry and advanced intellectual pursuits was part of the very definition of a monarch's role can certainly be identified as a certain kind of influence if it was this image that precipitated or encouraged either one or both to take on such a role in their own courts.

Second, one is compelled to imagine that under the historical and cultural circumstances posited, there must have been a considerable amount of hidden or "anxious" influence. Although Bloom himself, in coining the term "anxiety of influence" and making the notion a commonplace in literary criticism, dismissed the medieval period as part of "the giant age before the flood, before the anxiety of influence became central to poetic consciousness," this view is part and parcel of a general vision of the primitive Middle Ages that is anachronistic. Scholars familiar with the ways in which Petrarch, to cite a well-known example, denied and repressed his knowledge of Dante and the impact it had on his own poetry are able to dismiss the generalization about writers in the medieval period out of hand. Also to be considered as a logical possibility is the proposition that because of the complex nature of the relationship between the Arabic and the Latin segments of medieval Europe, the impact of one on the other may in many instances be hidden rather than overt. It was, after all, a relationship of the sort that is most likely to produce anxiety, both antagonistic and dependent, loathed at one level but inescapably influential at many others, the culture of a world damned by one's faith yet seeming to be rewarded by God with affluence and often with stunning military victories.

It is not just ideological or theological orthodoxy that would govern or dictate a choice to leave unacknowledged something inspired by the enemy, although that too is a consideration that cannot be altogether disregarded. It must also be assumed that in many cases the anxiety was all too real. An anxiety that Peter the Venerable voiced audibly would have reverberated differently in a literary text and in the creative mind, whose "desperate insistence on priority" would have been all the more desperate if the source was as unspeakable as the Arabic one might understandably have been.

PARIS, CIRCA 1210

If one were a novice student of philosophy in Paris—or in London, for that matter—shortly after the turn of the thirteenth century, al-Andalus would have been very close at hand.[8] Several prominent Andalusians played a pivotal role in the intellectual and philosophical revolution then germinating, and the shared interests and methods of philosophers from both the European communities made the differences between the traditional Latin Europe and the avant-garde Arabic Europe progressively fewer than their similarities.

The intellectual revolution sparked and fanned by the knowledge of a series of critically important philosophical texts then emerging from al-Andalus was accompanied by an institutional revolution that would transform the modes and places of learning in northern Europe. The two worlds had more in common than mere fascination with Averroes, the most influential philosopher of his time. From many perspectives, the history of philosophy and education in the twelfth and thirteenth centuries is the history of one movement rather than two, and it is a history much involved with the predominance of the forms of thought and the expressions of thought that had originated in the south, in Spain.

Education was in a state of upheaval, and it is curious that so many of the revolutionary additions to and transformations of old modes of thought and expression were shared with thinkers whose Arabic writings, once translated, had permeated Europe. The acceptance of the *sic et non* method, which would become the hallmark of scholasticism, and the addition of the new logic, the new mathematics, and the new astronomy to the older Latin trivium and quadrivium are but several of the many features of the world of learning that now tied the two intellectual worlds together.

The transformations in these modes of passing on knowledge and of perceiving the role of knowledge itself, begun in the previous century, were the product of prickly innovators, difficult iconoclasts, such as Peter Abélard and Hugh of St. Victor, about whose orthodoxy suspicions and doubts had abounded. There was no doubt that access to the works of many of those who wrote in Arabic was more than abundant, because it was provided, not only surreptitiously but also through the most respectable of Christian channels, by the translations of the venerable abbot of Cluny himself, for example. The modes of thinking, writing, and teaching of the Muslims were no longer unknown, and they certainly were not alien. Peter the Venerable had suspected that the threat this knowledge represented to the Christian establishment could no longer be dismissed and that it was strong enough to require active resistance. He was probably more right than even he could have suspected.

In England in about 1200 a number of prominent philosophers who had been connected in one way or another with Spain or Sicily began to write on the "new Aristotle." Lectures on Aristotle's *libri naturales* were begun in the first decade of the thirteenth century by a scholar named John Blund. In Paris in 1210 and 1215 there appeared the first of the famous ecclesiastical bans against the study and reading, in private or in public, of the *libri naturales* and, significantly, of Aristotle's commentators and abbreviators. There is little doubt that the bans were promoted by the theology faculty in an effort to block a serious danger spreading rapidly in their midst. They were frightened by what were for them dangerous philosophical proclivities in the Faculty of Arts. But neither London, Paris, nor Bologna, all in the midst of a similar upheaval, were for long able to resist the invasion and the revolution it brought. Repeated bans would ultimately prove ineffective. In fact, the most successful enemy of the new knowledge was one who followed a variation of the dictum that "if you can't beat 'em, join 'em" and that it is most effective to fight the enemy with his own weapons. Thomas Aquinas would win the battle by approaching it differently than had the watchdogs of earlier generations, by assimilating the teachings and the teaching techniques of the revolutionaries into his own attack on them and his defense of the old order and the faith.

Many philosophical revolutionaries became enmeshed in the controversy that would so engross and transform European thinkers, but at its very center stood one man, a Spaniard. His name was Ibn Rushd, but he came to be known as Averroes among those who knew his Arabic works only in translation, and they were legion. For several centuries to come, his name would be universally known and would invoke loathing or inestimable respect, would be either sacred or anathema. It is he, in many ways and for some time, who was the new Aristotle of Europe.

Averroes was born in 1126 in Córdoba a scant ten years before the birth there of Maimonides, who, as a prominent philosopher and doctor in his own right, was for many as much a transforming writer as was Ibn Rushd. Both devoted their lives to the unencumbered pursuit of knowledge and the belief, which some of their enemies would come to share, that such freedom of thought did not go against the teachings of the faith: the Jewish faith for Maimonides, the Muslim for Averroes, and the Christian for Aquinas.

Averroes was above all devoted to the study of and commentary of both Plato and Aristotle, two of the leading lights of the Arabic philosophical tradition in which he was educated. The series of commentaries he wrote on these philosophers and their work, the major thrust of which was a defense of the philosophical study of religion as opposed to that of the theologians, was disseminated throughout Europe with astonishing rapidity. Not surprisingly, the commentaries earned him few friends among the Muslim and Christian theological establishments. Before his and his followers' works were banned in Paris, he himself was condemned by the orthodox Muslim authorities of his own land. He died in exile because of his compelling arguments for this early version of secular humanism. But before his ignominious expulsion from Spain and Europe, he succeeded in reestablishing there the interest and the ability to deal with two of the ancient world's most gifted and renowned thinkers. The works of Plato and especially Aristotle had been the *sine qua non* of his own education, but they represented an astonishing and revealing new corpus for most of his contemporaries who could not read Arabic. The centuries-long neglect of these philosophers in the Latin world was at an end, and the agonized Christian struggle with Averroism and Aristotelianism was just beginning.

London, Paris, Bologna, and Sicily enjoyed extremely close relations with the centers and sources of both Averroist and Avicennist philosophy, and the revolutionary texts spread quickly and efficiently. The texts were those of Averroes, Avicenna, Maimonides, and countless others who wrote on mathematics, medicine, astronomy, philosophy, and all the other new sciences. No student at Paris, Bologna, or London would have ignored these works—they had been banned, after all—and since they were all Andalusian, or had come through al-Andalus, al-Andalus and its prolific intellectual outpourings were at the very center of the students' attention.

So too were many of the go-betweens, the men whose lives were devoted to making such knowledge and such texts known to other Europeans who, unlike themselves, were ignorant of Arabic. That role is perhaps best exemplified by a man who was one of the scandalous and controversial figures a student in the first half of the thirteenth century would have heard much about, one of the most tantalizing objects of personal and professional gossip: Michael Scot. Among the best known and most often reviled intellectuals of his time, he had to his many and diverse credits the role of court astrologer, resident translator, and intellectual luminary of the court of Frederick II of Sicily. His trips throughout Europe and Spain yielded rich results and abetted the increasingly heated debates in intellectual circles. His translation of Averroes' commentary on Aristotle reached Paris at about the same time as it did Frederick's court at Palermo, sometime between 1230 and 1240. It may have reached Bologna even earlier, since Scot is known to have stopped there on several occasions early in that decade on his way from Spain back to Frederick's court. It may well, in fact, have been one of the many Averroist texts that Guido Cavalcanti would study at Bologna.

In Paris, Scot's translations had numerous repercussions, and they precipitated decades of heated discussion leading to the unprecedented growth of Averroist-Aristotelian scholarship. A similar outbreak of controversy took place in England, where Roger Bacon went so far as to question the accuracy of Scot's translations, some say out of professional jealousy. In Bologna and Tuscany, Scot became a symbol of the new knowledge and a mysterious cult figure whose lasting fame after his death was assured by Dante's and Boccaccio's literary characterizations of him several generations later. But most of all he should be remembered and his importance understood in terms of the court he loved best and of the monarch he best served, Frederick II of Sicily, *stupor mundi, immutator mundi.*

Although we are primarily concerned with literary history, it is virtually indisputable that the vicissitudes and trends of intellectual history are crucial factors in the general milieu within which literary texts are both created and received, and as such they are an indispensable part of our considerations. Moreover, contemporary divisions between literature and other artistic and intellectual phenomena are not always congruent with those that prevailed in the Middle Ages, when the dividing lines might be quite different. Translations of many texts that we now consider to be part of such disciplines as science or philosophy were available and of interest to those who would write imaginative texts as well. It is not possible to continue to maintain that the Arabic influence, mediated through translations of critical texts, was limited to areas other than the literary, since such a position is dependent on an anachronistic view of what constituted literature and assumes an arbitrary division between different segments of the intellectual and artistic communities.

Nevertheless, when so many translations in clearly nonliterary areas have survived, the question of why so few clearly literary texts, such as poetry, have survived has been an intriguing one for many, although such an absence of preserved texts hardly constitutes evidence that the literary realm was resistant to such influences in ways that other areas were not. This is largely a red herring. There are many aspects of artistic or literary phenomena that do not require direct translations or representational accuracy in order to become part of a different culture. Moreover, given the

hierarchy of importance of the different kinds of material for the sub-
culture of translators (and their commissioners) and the relative lack of
prestige or respect they accorded to European imaginative literature in the
vernacular in Europe (and this includes both the Arabic- and Latin-
dominated worlds), it is logical enough to suppose that the perceived
value of such works was hardly considered commensurate with the time
and effort required to translate them. The demand for translations of
works deemed essential was such that the relative neglect of purely imaginative material, which served no other purpose but pleasure, is hardly
surprising. Then too, the translators were scholars, and they undoubtedly considered popular literature to be considerably outside (and below)
the realm of their professional work, no matter how much they might
themselves have enjoyed it in their spare time. The fact that such literature
is now part of the canon to which scholars may honorably devote their
time does not mean that such was always the case.

In addition, certain aspects of the literary corpus needed little or no
scholarly translation in order to be transmitted and were accordingly left
untranslated. Songs and music, which is what we really mean when we
say the medieval lyric, certainly belong to this category. Language barriers cannot reasonably be said to prevent the transmission and eventual
adaptation of songs and music from the culture of one language to that of
another, particularly when, as was the case here, the two are geographi-
cally proximate and exhibit some degree of interest in each other. But in
any case, it is also evident that translations of the sung, performed poetry
would have been utterly unnecessary in many of the cases in which we
have believed they were necessary to prove influence. Why should anyone
have translated Arabic songs at the Aragonese or Sicilian courts, when
most of the learned and refined men there would have understood and
enjoyed them in their original language?

Even in the area of narrative the supposition of insuperable language
barriers is misleading. If we suppose that narrative (or lyric) literature was
transmitted from one generation to another through written texts alone,
or even predominantly through written texts, then the absence of widespread knowledge of Arabic outside al-Andalus and Sicily, and the lack of
known translations, would constitute a serious barrier to the acceptance
of any significant intercourse. But the moment in literary historiography
when one could safely hold such a view is long over, and our understanding of the vitality, power, and effectiveness of oral transmission (and not
just that embodied in so-called formulaic literature) has greatly increased.
If in his more than one hundred *novelle* Boccaccio includes some stories

he had heard from someone else, why should some of these not have ultimately come from a storytelling tradition that in Europe was first voiced in Arabic or Hebrew? And do we need to prove that he had a good edition of the *Disciplina clericalis* or the *Thousand and One Nights* on his desk in order to postulate these works as sources?

As long as Arabic culture was a force in Europe, word of its *matière* reached other Europeans who certainly knew no Arabic and who did not get such information exclusively from official written translations that we can now hope to uncover in some dusty archive. The impact of the numerous, wide-ranging, and quite influential translations that were made transcended the impact they had on the readers of the translations themselves. Numerous other factors ensured that those Europeans who knew no Arabic, particularly those, such as artists, whose curiosity may not have respected official bounds, would have indirect access to those texts. All of al-Andalus and Spain and a large segment of the Sicilian population constituted a body of unofficial oral translators, bi-, and tri-, and even quadrilingual individuals who moved freely among the different languages and cultures of medieval Europe and prevented the possibility of the complete ignorance of one community on the part of another. Particularly in the heyday of translations, the translators themselves were peripatetic and could be found roving throughout the courts and intellectual centers of Europe. Men such as Michael Scot and Petrus Alfonsi served not only as translators of written texts but also as less formal translators of many aspects of the culture. Undoubtedly, a no less important role was played by the large numbers of émigrés, many of them learned, who fled northward from the ravages of the wars in Spain, and by the less learned but certainly not cultureless men and women who lived as servants and slaves in courts such as those of Aquitaine after the conquest of Barbastro.

It requires no more than one instance of oral translation—one singer's rendition in Provençal of the gist of a song in Arabic, one retelling in Italian or English of a story from the *Thousand and One Nights*—to effect the transmission of a bit of literature from one language and culture to another. It is an anachronism to assume that developments in literature were solely a scholarly enterprise. Particularly before the advent of widely available books and in an era in which the oral performance and transmission of literature was commonplace, such sources were not frequently verified for accuracy or dealt with only in definitive editions or translations. Most important, we must banish the notion in this sphere, as in others, that influence means or implies servile copying, that its effects result in a text indistinguishable from the one that has influenced it, or that complex intertextual refractions are solely the domain of the modern writer or one limited to "truly" European texts. Influence is clearly more diffuse in some cases than in others, sometimes explicit and marked, and other times not, sometimes manifest in absorption, adaptation, and rewriting, and other times in a denial, a countertext, or a void. Sometimes we use the term to mean and evoke the general cultural and literary milieu, sometimes something more specific, and sometimes a very general inspiration. All of these subtleties in perception and analysis are applicable when we are discussing the Andalusian influence, for it was obviously as conditioned by the complexities of textual and cultural relationship as any other.

FREDERICK, CIRCA 1240

The Norman court in Sicily, first under Roger II, who ruled from 1130 to 1154, and especially under his grandson, Frederick II, who ruled from 1215 to 1250, was a glittering jewel in Europe.[9] The courts of the baptized sultans were centers of Arabic learning and, especially under Frederick, the sources of the kind of culture and learning that could be characterized by the words *stupor* and *immutator*. The two characteristics—the cultivation of the Arabic and what constituted *stupor* and *immutator*—can hardly be separated from each other in that century.

Frederick had from his infancy grown up with Arabic, and it was not simply one of the languages of his court; it was one he mastered so well in its classical form that he was at times able to correct his own official translators. But it was more than academic or book knowledge of the Arabic world that shaped Frederick's court. Acculturation there was so complete that visitors might have taken it for something else. There were no language barriers, and Frederick's court became a magnet for literati and intellectuals from throughout the world. The king wore a crown of Byzantine design and robes embroidered with Arabic. Indeed, he most resembled a powerful emir or sultan, with a harem, a royal bodyguard of Muslims, and a palace teeming with Arabic and Greek servants and functionaries. Frederick himself conducted extensive correspondence with learned Muslims and Jews from both al-Andalus and the Middle East. But most important, and most frightening to the Church, Frederick was an assiduous cultivator of knowledge from any and all sources, a collector of manuscripts from all parts of the learned world, and, indeed, an author in his own right of learned treatises on a variety of subjects. His court was the intellectual capital of a world already in upheaval because of the translations from Spain that were spreading throughout the north, and Frederick jumped right into the middle of it and became as much a patron of the new knowledge as any one man could have been.

Even a sketchy inventory of the intellectual activity at his court gives one an idea of how deeply immersed Frederick was in the new learning of Europe—and how much of it was Andalusian and Arabic. He had both Aristotle and Averroes translated quite early in his reign and sent copies of both to Paris and Bologna. His own letter accompanying these translations, directed to both students and teachers, reveals how deeply he believed in the centrality of Averroes' work. And because Averroes was the thinker who interested him most, he did not rely much on the Greek scholars he had at hand, scholars who could have given him direct translations of Aristotle. Instead he relied on the many Hebrew and Arabic scholars he had brought from Spain. He was fascinated by Maimonides' *Guide for the Perplexed* and had translations of that Jewish Hispano-Arabic work disseminated. Frederick's correspondence with the learned men whose languages were Arabic and Hebrew was prodigious, and he was in the habit of addressing to them long lists of questions on any number of subjects. His most important protégé was certainly Michael Scot, whose translations include parts of the *Metaphysics* and its Arabic commentaries and the *De animalibus,* dedicated to Frederick. Fibonacci, a student of Arabic mathematics himself, was also presented and favored at his court. His second edition of the *Liber abaci,* which would finally establish the Andalusian number system as the basis of modern mathematics, would be dedicated to Frederick. It was also at this court—a court teeming with luminaries from al-Andalus, ringing to the sounds of Arabic singing from the harem and Arabic poetry from the many learned men, and resounding with the new learning of the day, the learning of Averroes, Maimonides, Fibonacci, and Scot—that the first school of lyric poetry in an Italian vernacular was born and thrived under Frederick's own seemingly indefatigable encouragement. Indeed, by the midpoint of his reign, Frederick's court not only rivaled Toledo as the seat of translations but also rivaled many other centers in Europe as a seat of great learning and culture.

Frederick was an author in his own right of learned treatises on a wide variety of subjects. When he wrote the one that was to be best remembered, on falconry, he used as reference works a number of Arabic treatises on the subject. But he must have been somewhat difficult to work with, since he carefully scrutinized the translations of those sources by Theodore of Antioch, one of his most highly prized Arabic translators. Finding them wanting, he apparently corrected the translations himself before setting about his own writing. Frederick was also both a poet and a generous patron. The *scuola siciliana,* the first poetry of the new Italy, owed its very existence to his beneficence. How much it owes to the culture, predominantly Arabic, that filled and distinguished the court at which it was first performed has never been explored.

Frederick's reputation during his own lifetime tells us much about the view many other Europeans held about the cultural and intellectual world from which the king himself, who was at least nominally a Christian, could scarcely be distinguished. He was unabashedly both a cultural convert and a proselytizing patron of Arabic culture. His court was one of the apogees of European culture, and Frederick himself was widely respected, admired, and envied in certain circles. But he was anathema to fundamentalists and was excommunicated on several occasions, just as William of Aquitaine had been. At the Council of Lyon, Pope Innocent III made it clear that his associations with heretics (to Frederick they were simply scholars and learned men) had caused Frederick's own heresy. It cannot have helped much that Frederick was never without his counselors, men such as his Arab tutor in logic, even on his crusade in 1228. Indeed, his cordial fraternization there with the crusaders' enemies—using the crusade as simply one more opportunity to learn what there was to learn from that world—was less than ingratiating to the ecclesiastical establishment.

Thus, the awe and respect with which Frederick was regarded were tempered with a certain suspicion that his great culture and learning had fundamentally tainted his Christianity. Whether he was a heretic or the most learned man of his time was purely a matter of ideological perspective. Like al-Andalus itself, he was viewed with astonishment, admiration, and envy combined with fear and suspicion. The astonishment and admiration were generated by the observations and reports of the advanced learning of the Arabic courts, those of al-Andalus and of Sicily alike, where to translate a Greek codex or to read Aristotle in long-established Arabic translations with their commentaries was an everyday event but one that was beyond the reach of those not associated with such circles. It would still seem a barely obtainable dream to an Italian of a full century later. Petrarch, for example, struggling with his uncultivated and offensive Greek tutor, not only loathed the Arabs who had had such benefits but saw them as quite inferior to himself in learning.

Such an attitude was already manifest in the previous century, and it derived from an envy of the conspicuous material wealth and comfort that, for other Europeans, must have at times appeared to go hand in hand with the ability to read Arabic. The fear and suspicion are traceable to multiple causes. Frederick not only sheltered but embraced and cultivated the likes of Michael Scot and the translations and translators he brought him from Spain. Frederick also fostered learning in areas such as medicine that Europeans viewed with deep-seated hostility and fear. Averroism itself was still a source of consternation and fear in many quarters in Europe, and both Frederick, who was his student and proselytizer, and the Andalusians, who had produced him, were regarded with considerable trepidation by the old guard. When they looked at Frederick's court, when they learned of the esteem with which it was regarded, and when they realized that Averroism was more than a passing fad, they must at times have seen themselves as a rear guard.

I believe that we can justify a very different reading of the narrative of medieval Europe from the eleventh through the thirteenth centuries. Our reading of that text would tell us a story rather different from the one we have grown up with of the role and fate of the Arabs who became Europeans at that time but who never lost their own language or cultural patrimony. Our reading would note that at one time or another during the Middle Ages the intellectual and artistic centers of unconquered Christian Europe literally teemed with the activity sparked and fueled by continued contacts with al-Andalus and its material, cultural, and intellectual offspring. The parts of Europe never conquered by Islam were nevertheless strongly affected through the more complex, and often more compelling, mechanisms of cultural and intellectual imperialism. Far from being peripheral or secondary to the principal concerns and activities of those who remained speakers of Latin and her vernacular progeny, the dominant world of the age in which Arabic was the classical language was rarely out of mind and never out of reach, and the effects of such contacts were widespread and central. They were often the intellectual lifeblood of northern European centers, and just as often they fed a dangerous and banned avant-garde.

And what of al-Andalus, Spain itself, and of Sicily, lost by the Arabs to the Normans in the eleventh century but thereafter an even more vibrant center of Arabic learning? Both were, this story would certainly tell us, not only parts of Europe itself but in many ways and at many moments centers one went to and looked to for any number of material and intellectual amenities. In both places, but especially in al-Andalus, a new, symbiotic European culture developed, a uniquely rich tripartite culture based on the relatively peaceful and often prosperous cohabitation, for a time, of the offspring of Abraham, the children of Ishmael and Isaac alike.[10] A milieu existed where new hybrid literary forms, such as the *muwashshaha* and the *zajal,* were able to develop and thrive. Al-Andalus created an atmosphere within which the inherited learning of the three separate cultures had come together and were actively and in many cases fruitfully exposed to each other. And the products of this exceptionally rich breeding ground dazzled both of the worlds to which they belonged. Averroes would shine in the West but be largely forgotten in the East, and the writings of Ibn Ḥazm were more studied in the East than in the West. But al-Andalus was a part of *both* worlds, not, as our old reading has often told us, a part of neither.

Thus, for the reader of medieval texts, it is of some use to conjure up this image of our medieval past and heritage. Such an image emphasizes that the presence of this new and different cultural entity *within* Europe was a significant force in intellectual and literary developments of the rest of Europe. Sometimes its power was negative, the power of reaction embodied in the works of Peter the Venerable and Aquinas, but this was the stimulus and provocation for many great texts of the period. Sometimes the effect was more positive; for every Peter or Aquinas there was a William and a Frederick. Overall, given the combination of the pressing and often immediate political and ideological conflicts between the Arab world and the rest of Europe on the one hand, and the often highly visible material superiority and intellectual and artistic achievements of al-Andalus on the other, it would be surprising if some significant dialectic had not occurred.

Al-Andalus thus was both a major center of learning from which a variety of intellectual traditions were introduced to the rest of Europe through numerous means of translation and a living and very present Other whose material and cultural features, those aspects of a civilization that need little or no translation to be appreciated, were regarded with significant admiration throughout Europe and in numerous cases were adopted and adapted. We also have many indications that, despite the political enmity and the theological *mépris* that other Europeans had for the Arab culture of both al-Andalus and Sicily, these official objections from the entrenched establishment never completely succeeded in mitigating the seductiveness of those cultures or their numerous attractions for many who emulated them and believed they had much to offer.

What I would like to evoke is a vision not of two separate worlds but of one, in which a powerful push-pull relationship characterized the relations between two members of a community. Such a perception also recognizes that the tantalizing possibilities presented by the Andalusian model to non-Andalusian Europeans was a significant presence and a shaping force. Whether it was accepted or rejected, in whole or in part, it was a powerful defining element in European history, a civilization that was not isolated from the rest of Europe. The case was quite the contrary, especially from the eleventh through the thirteenth centuries. Indeed, al-Andalus was very much at the heart of the renaissance of the twelfth. It was a center of Europe, the locus from which radiated so much of what was the new, the exciting, the dangerous, the controversial.

None of this, of course, proves anything about any particular literary text of the medieval period. It is not intended to. It is meant to show that if we select these facts from our inventory of facts about the Middle Ages, we write a history within which many texts must be seen differently from the ways in which we have seen them before. It is a version of the story that does not relegate Petrus Alfonsi to the status of outsider, does not view William of Aquitaine's knowledge of Arabic song as something remote or difficult to imagine, does not imagine that later troubadours ignored the world in which Christians, Jews, and Arabs sang, and does not forget that the poetry of the *scuola siciliana* was sung in a court where Arabic was heard just as often as the vernacular Romance in which it was written. How this might ultimately change the ways in which we read and understand such texts is something we cannot yet answer.

I will undoubtedly be accused by some of ignoring in this scheme all of the other cultural elements that have traditionally been assumed to be central to the medieval world of letters. I propose no such thing. I have not suggested, nor would I suggest, that the Church and Christianity were not an essential and critical feature or that Ovid was not an important text. But these seem to me to need no apology, and most scholars do not need to be persuaded that they were important. My task is certainly not to argue unnecessarily for the centrality of Latin and Christian elements in medieval European literary life, nor to argue for the canonization of Ovid, Augustine, or Virgil as an essential background for medieval Romance vernacular literature. Those have been the concerns of the bulk of the work done in this area since it has been an area of scholarship. They are positions not in further need of cogent argument or persuasion.

But I am also not arguing against them, as others who have discussed the plausibility of this or that Arabist influence have been accused of doing, nor am I suggesting that we discard or ignore what has been obvious for so many years: the Christian, Latin, Germanic, and Celtic substrata that are essential to medieval literary history. I am arguing that these are not the limits of the essential factors or focuses of the medieval world, the necessary borders of our studies, the only shaping forces, the only background. And I would argue without hesitation that by ignoring other forces that are just as obvious in their importance and centrality once we are rid of certain ideologically conditioned preconceptions, we have largely impoverished our views of medieval literature and its world.

Notes

1. For William, on his life and times, his crusades to both Palestine and al-Andalus, the admixture of cultures in Provence, and the traffic of troubadours at recently reconquered courts of northern Spain, see Bezzola 1940. Defourneaux 1949 is a useful reference work on the extensive contacts and interaction spanning the Pyrenees, including everyone from Cluniacs and pilgrims to troubadours, merchants, and others. Denomy 1953 is helpful for additional intellectual contacts and the accessibility of Andalusian thought to non-Arabic speakers. See Frank 1955a on the cultural admixture of the Catalonian courts and on the continuous presence of Provençal troubadours in northern and *fronterizo* Spain (for which see also Marshall 1972, introduction, and Alvar 1977); Lasater 1974, Marks 1975, and Payen 1979 offer more recent descriptions of the strongly Andalusian cultural admixture in the intellectual and artistic ambience of the first troubadour. The Arabic account of the Barbastro incident is translated in Dozy 1881 and is recounted in several of the sources cited above. Farmer 1926 and 1930, Ribera y Tarragó [1927] 1975, and Lemay 1966 offer further details on Andalusian music and musical instruments and their spread into the rest of Europe. On Gerbert, see the sources cited below for the scientific revolution; see also Southern 1953 and Wolff 1968. For the general literary and cultural history of al-Andalus, the clearest and most recent source is Monroe 1974, one of the earliest histories of that literature is Schack 1865. Pérès 1953 is a classic and insightful study. Vernet 1972 is a useful reference source. See also the recent Spanish translation of Pérès (1983).

2. This may be construed as an argument in favor of ignorance on my part, but it is actually an argument for perspective. I grant the importance of knowing what the various ultimate sources were for the narrative tradition embodied in a text such as the *Disciplina clericalis*, and I do not contend that the efforts of Arabists to uncover or establish the *muwashshaḥas'* possible ties with other, perhaps pre-Islamic Arabic poetry are not worthy enterprises. But the question is whether it can be reasonably argued that that knowledge or those studies are relevant to a study of the role those texts played in the shaping of medieval Romance literature. Part of the duty of literary scholarship and historiography is, of course, to establish the truth, and it is thus critical that we know the complex strata of the narratives recounted in the *Disciplina* and the ties of the *muwashshaḥas* with other Arabic poetry. But an equally important obligation of the scholar is to define an appropriate perspective and understanding of which truths are relevant and which merely obfuscate the issues.

3. For Peter the Venerable and the Toledan Collection, the essential source is Kritzeck 1964. See also the relevant sections of Cerulli 1949 and 1972. On the effects of Toledo as an "open city" from which massive amounts of new material emanated, see additionally G. Menéndez Pidal 1951, Procter 1951, R. Menéndez Pidal 1956, Lemay 1963a, and, par-

ticularly useful as summaries of a vast field, Metlitzki 1977 and D'Alverny 1982. See also the sources cited in note 7 below on the Norman courts and in note 8 on the philosophy and the intellectual revolution. See note 10 below for the impact of trade and material incursions. The effects of Andalusian-Arabic philosophy on rhetorical and educational institutions are specifically addressed in Makdisi 1974 and 1981. For a discussion of religious attitudes, the most comprehensive studies are Daniel 1960 and Southern 1962. Addison [1942] 1966 provides a brief but succinct description. Defourneaux 1949, Daniel 1979, and Richard 1966 discuss the relative importance (or lack of it) of religious barriers among the laity, and both explore possible reflections of this situation in popular literature.

4. Analogies are always imperfect and are sometimes dangerous, but they can also serve a useful function in helping us to conceptualize what is evident in one sphere but seems unimaginable in a parallel or comparable sphere. Thus we should remember in this regard how important the role of an imperfect image is in our own world. After all, if not all Americans wear blue jeans and listen only to rock and roll and jazz or believe in taking over and colonizing and exploiting the Third World, that does not render any less important or powerful the *impression* many have that such is the case. Nor, moreover, does the simplicity and inaccuracy of that image mean that it should not be labeled "American," for that is the role it plays elsewhere. Nor does it mean that we can afford to ignore the influence such an image may have, whether the influence it provokes is that of adoption or reaction.

5. One is struck by the irony that is involved here. This view of materialism and sensuousness would undoubtedly astound most Muslims, since they have had, and continue to have, the opposite view, that it is the West that is materialistic, sexually permissive, and so forth. The pointedness of the irony lies in the fact that to a great extent such attitudes fall back on the general fear that the foreign devil will corrupt the traditional society and its values. Little wonder, then, that the attitudes of Muslims in the period of Western cultural and intellectual imperialism are so similar to those of Christians when the roles were more like the reverse.

6. Again, analogies are simplifications, but they are potentially helpful: The overt and often strident ideological anti-Americanism that has been characteristic of important segments of the youth and intelligentsia of much of the world in recent decades has not prevented the adoption among those same groups of any number of the cultural and material trappings that are characteristically American. Those who denounce the pernicious effects of American influence are often the very people who wear Levis and smoke Marlboros and listen most to rock and roll and American jazz. In many cases they seem oblivious of what might strike others (and this often does strike Americans abroad) as a flagrant contradiction. As for the constraints of official ideology, it is difficult to sustain any belief in its power when confronted with the popularity of the same kinds of American influence even in countries officially dedicated to its eradication. The French have passed laws against Americanisms in the language that have had about as much effect as the medieval Parisian bans against Averroism; smuggled blue jeans command staggering prices in the Soviet Union; the music of the West is often sung by those who do not know the language of the lyrics they are singing and whose elders and officials, for the record, vigorously deny its influence.

7. On Eleanor and her involvement with cultural and intellectual matters, see Kelly 1950 and Lejeune 1954 and 1958, as well as the more recent collection of studies in Kibler 1976. For views on the interactive aspects and results of the crusades, see the summary and bibliography in Metlitzki 1977 and the lucid and succinct discussion in Kritzeck 1964, as well as, more recently, the multiperspective views in Finucane 1983. On the Norman courts and the importance there of such itinerant intellectual figures as Petrus Alfonsi, Haskins 1915 is still authoritative. Paris 1888 is still useful on literary interrelations among the Norman centers. Also, see the introductions to the following translations of the *Disciplina clericalis:* Hermes [1970] 1977, Keller 1978, and M. J. Lacarra 1980. For sources on the intellectual upheaval at these courts, see note 8 below.

8. On philosophy and the intellectual upheaval of the twelfth century and after, the classic work and starting point is still Haskins 1927. Kristeller 1961 offers an excellent supplement in his section on medieval philosophy and Aristotelianism. Indispensable on Aristotle, as interpreted and reworked by the Arabs and then read in northern Europe, is Peters 1968. Kelly 1979 provides a useful supplement on the *Poetics,* and Lemay 1963 embodies a detailed and authoritative exposition on northern European translators and their translations. Specifically concerned with the revolution in the sciences and medicine are Haskins 1924, Sarton 1951, and Dunlop 1958. Haskins 1924 is also particularly useful for the role of Michael Scot, as are Amari 1853 (which provides the text of Frederick's questions addressed to Scot) and, most recently, Corti 1981. See also the numerous sources on Frederick II in note 9 below.

9. On Sicily and the Arabic culture and learning there before the Norman conquest, see especially the classic studies of Amari 1933–39 and 1942, as well as the more accessible Gabrieli 1950, Ahmad 1975, and Rizzitano 1975 and 1977. For the reign of Roger, Norwich 1970 is useful. Sources of special interest are two contemporary Arabic writers: Idrīsī 1883 (on Roger's geographer) and Ibn Jubayr 1952 (on an Andalusian pilgrim stranded for a time in Sicily). On Frederick, his court, and the centrality of Arabic learning and culture in Norman Sicily, see Haskins 1924. Haskins focuses on scientific thought but provides much additional information. Heinisch 1968 includes citations of Arabs' opinions of Frederick's learning. Gabrieli 1952 offers a concise overview, and Rizzitano and Giunta 1967 provides a broad cultural perspective spanning the entire Norman period. Kantorowics 1957 and Van Cleve 1972 are the most comprehensive biographers of the life, times, and achievements of Frederick and are outstanding sources of information. Nolthenius 1968 offers a pointed description of Frederick and his culture in the context of the rest of Italy. For other studies focusing on the impact of Arabic learning and culture on other parts of Europe, see Parodi 1915 and Kristeller 1955 on Cavalcanti and Haskins 1924 on the education and migration of scholars such as Fibonacci and their interactions with Scot and others of Frederick's entourage. Cerulli 1949 and 1972 are essential for Andalusian material in northern Italy that arrived via Toledo and Paris, and Corti 1981 deals with Averroism in Bologna, its revolutionary effects on Tuscan and Bolognese intellectuals, and the probable Sicilian provenance of many influential works. For northern Italy, see also the outlandish Fiore 1964; Gabrieli 1977 on Petrarch; and Kristeller 1964 on Pico della Mirandola and the survival of Arabic and Hebrew studies in the Renaissance.

10. For al-Andalus, besides the literature-oriented histories cited in note 1, see the classic old histories of Dozy (1861 and 1881). Of special interest are histories written by Arab historians from the perspective of a lost homeland, principally al-Makkari (1856–60) and the widely read and admired Ibn Khaldūn ([1958] 1967). Ribera [1896] 1972 provides a fascinating view of Hispano-Islamic libraries. Baer [1961] 1971 focuses on Jewish history; see also Silver 1974. The most commonly used, relatively brief general historical overviews are González Palencia 1945, Lévi-Provençal 1948a, and Watt 1965, whereas Chejne 1974 is more extensive and also provides an ample bibliography. Glick 1979 explores usually neglected subjects, such as agriculture and demographics, and applies some of the methods of more recent historiography. On the issue of the hybrid character of al-Andalus and thus medieval Spain, see Menéndez Pidal 1947, Castro 1948, and 1954a and b, Asensio 1976, Sánchez Albornoz [1956] 1966 and 1973, Maravall 1954, and Cantarino 1968b and 1978. Some specialized studies that are not involved with the Castro-inspired dispute over cultural hybridity and polymorphism but which explore the special fertility of Andalusian culture are Jargy 1971, on music; and Lemay 1963a, on translations, and 1977, on mathematics and the number system. Vernet 1978 focuses on al-Andalus as a center of new learning and hybrid forms that spread both to the east and the rest of the Arabic world and to the north and the rest of Europe. On the spread and effect of Andalusian material prosperity and culture to the rest of Europe, some of the most succinct and accessible descriptions and analyses include De-

nomy 1953, Fuertes Montalban and Gimeno-Besses 1954, Gabrieli 1954b, Gibb 1955, Bausani 1957, Menéndez Pidal 1956, Sánchez-Albornoz 1965, Watt 1972 and 1974, Schacht and Bosworth 1974, Daniel 1975a and 1975b, and Makdisi 1976. See also the numerous individual studies from the Spoleto Conference in *L'Occidente e l'Islam nell'alto medioevo* and the more recent SUNY conference in *Islam and the Medieval West*.

CHAPTER THREE

The Oldest Issue: Courtly Love

This makes it clear without further ado why love as passion is our European specialty—it absolutely must be of aristocratic origin: it was, as is well known, invented by the poet-knights of Provence, those splendid, inventive men of the "gai saber" to whom Europe owes so much and, indeed, almost itself.
—Nietzsche, *Beyond Good and Evil*

Perhaps no area of medieval Romance literary studies so well illustrates the decisive effects of a preconceived image upon scholarship as does the problem of the origins and formal characteristics of the vernacular lyric. At the very center of this wide-ranging subfield is the lyric poetry written in southern France and variously referred to as "troubadour," "Provençal," "Occitan," or "courtly love" poetry. Its centrality for scholars derives directly from its assumed centrality in the history of vernacular European poetry itself. For most of its students it has been the oldest, the most exemplary, the most central flower in the history of lyric, and particularly of the love poetry of medieval and modern western Europe. From this, our histories of literature tell us, derived any number of the distinguishing characteristics of the lyric forms that are, or were until relatively recently, so vital and so lustrous a part of the literary heritage and makeup of western Europe's vernacular tradition.

The centrality of the Provençal lyric has also traditionally been determined by its pivotal position in literary history. It was always believed to be a pioneer in a number of critical ways, ranging from its language (the vernacular) to its forms (the song, *canso*, with a number of apparently new formal features, among other things), its prestigious role within its own society, and most of all its best-known theme, dubbed "courtly love" more than a century ago. But just as determining as its chronological primacy was the fact that in our western traditions, many or most of these essential features, modified or not, remained salient traits of the poetics of lyric poetry in general and of love poetry in particular. A more accurate statement of why troubadour poetry has been so central, then, is that it has been perceived as being the originator of a whole branch of European literature, one that left its imprint, either formally or thematically, on many other types of literature long after the school had itself ceased to exist. It is certainly emblematic that Ezra Pound, a critical figure in the creation and nurturing of modernism, was a devotee and translator of Provençal troubadour poetry.

Origins and originators were, after all, the stuff of Romance studies ("Romance philology," as it was often designated) when it coalesced as an academic discipline in the nineteenth century. The validity of genetic studies—as they would come to be referred to, somewhat disparagingly after they were displaced as a central pursuit—was rarely questioned in the long first stage of literary studies, when they were still married to studies in historical linguistics. Moreover, this was a linguistics that was fascinated and preoccupied with the written word and its earliest attestations, a field at first untouched, and later unconvinced, by the theories and practices of the Neogrammarians.

Little wonder then that within such a framework the earliest literature in Romance in attested written form was the beneficiary of such lavish attention. Not surprisingly, of all of the questions raised by studies of the poetry, none was more fascinating than one whose answer, assuming there was a coherent and convincing one to be found, would in some measure undermine at least one of the reasons for the poetry's preeminence: Where had it come from?

Perhaps in part because an answer would so rob us of a cherished and rather romantic notion of a neat and pretty beginning nestled in southern France (that quintessence of Europe creating itself, as Nietzsche described it), perhaps because an answer would so disrupt a hierarchy as well established as this one, and perhaps for many other reasons an answer agreed on by even a slender majority of scholars in the field has never been found. Given the amount of thought and hard labor that has been dedicated to finding the answer over so long a period of time, one cannot help but be impressed that the cloud on the Provençal horizon is still as dark and mysterious in many ways as it once was. Or perhaps, to see it in a more positive light, the efforts devoted to such a labor are only commensurate with its difficulty, with the elusiveness of seeing what lies behind the cloud, if anything. Even the origin of the name of the poets themselves, the verb designating their art, this symbol of poetry at the most basic level, has been most elusive, perhaps the longest debated and most extensively written about etymology in all of Romance linguistics.

But the history of Romance philology and of interest in Provençal poetry goes back considerably further than its more formal and codified academic beginnings in the last century. Dante's *De vulgari eloquentia,* written in 1303–1304, can be adduced as the first work of scholarship in our field, and it is characterized by those combinations of literary and linguistic thought, theoretical speculation and practical instruction, and historical and descriptive perspectives that would become the discipline's calling cards. As would be so many of his academic progeny, Dante was fascinated by the Provençal lyric and its relation to the other earliest vernacular poetry in which he was interested, primarily that of the different parts of Italy. Further, as the title of his work indicates, the problem of writing in the vernacular was what interested him most.

And a problem it was. For Dante, and for others after him (particularly in Italy, the most Latinizing of Europe's cultures), the legitimacy of writing in the vernacular was far from well established, a situation with which we might legitimately have some trouble sympathizing, since diglossia is a linguistic state few of us have experienced in its full form, and to write in the language that seems to us to be the one we speak (despite marked stylistic differences and a more rigorous codification in its written form) requires little justification.

But obviously, the situation was not always thus (and still is not in many other cultures and languages), and Dante's interest in the lyrics of the troubadours is in great measure due to his search for legitimate and legitimizing antecedents, those who had made writing in the vernacular—in Romance per se—a reasonably respectable enterprise. But the poets and the poetry of Provence did not solve all Dante's problems, although they were indispensable as antecedents. He was plagued by a further problem, which was, ironically, to be one of the banes of all writers born in the Italian peninsula for centuries to come and even well into the modern period, that of the specific form of Italian to be adopted and codified as the new Latin, the written lingua franca.

Nevertheless, the poets of Provence, the troubadours, were propitious models and it is as models that Dante treats them in the second half of his treatise, which resembles a manual on poetics more than anything else. The *De vulgari eloquentia* thus identifies, or ratifies (in a document precious also because of the status acquired by its author thanks to the *Com-*

media), many of the essential features that would come to characterize troubadour scholarship. First, the *De vulgari* leads the way in its perception or tacit depiction of its importance as the first, exemplary, and guiding model of literary writing (which meant predominantly poetry) in the vernacular. Dante himself, who in turn would be perceived and treated as the progenitor of Italian literature, regarded the Provençal poets as the begetters of the relatively new and in some ways struggling tradition of which he was a part. The question of lineage and ancestry, moreover, was not limited to the mere problem of the language of choice, although this was indeed a critical issue that clearly concerned Dante enormously. The consideration of lineage, in poetic-linguistic terms, in fact led him to an accurate historical linguistic observation of great importance, whose validity is all too often forgotten or ignored by the keepers of the flame of our cultures: that languages are mutable, always have been and always will be. He noted that all great writers, including those of antiquity, of whom he was also the offspring, had written in their own vernaculars. Thus, if the language he and his contemporaries used was structurally different, that was only because language is mutable and is continually changing. From a contextual and functional point of view, however, it was the same.

But, although Dante's observation was certainly accurate in the abstract and in terms of the more objective (descriptive) current understanding of language and its mutability, the break from the Latin written tradition appeared no less revolutionary contextually. Not only the subject of Dante's book but also its language (Latin) attest amply to the momentous break that was indeed taking place. And the choice of a new language was not the only break involved: hand in hand with the new vehicle for poetry went a new substance, a new purpose for which it was and would be used, and this was the poetry of love.

Although Dante's own love ideology would itself differ sharply from that of his Provençal and Sicilian ancestors, the essential orientation, the focus on that particular subject as a defining characteristic, of the vernacular lyric, remained unchanged. This too, from Dante's perspective—and it was a perspective we would come to adopt in fits and starts—was as revolutionary as the new language, and it played the same double role as a break with the past and a basis for the future. Even in the area of form, Dante sets the standard for later work: He unequivocally identifies the *canzone* as the exemplary form, and he defines it as a rhetorical composition set to music and as the action or passion itself of singing, making its link to both music and moving emotion its defining characteristic. He insists that the stanzaic or strophic structure is requisite and distinctive.

In most ways, then, Dante's appreciation of the earliest period of Romance lyrics and his identification of its critical features and its most lasting contributions to European poetry are strikingly akin to those that would prevail when, centuries later, research and thought in this area would become a fundamental part of our branch of the academic profession. But there is one major difference, one noticeable, and even stark omission: Dante seems not in the least concerned with the bases, inspirations, or roots of the Provençal poets themselves. His silence concerning these subjects is noteworthy, and it is conspicuous, because the *De vulgari* is palpably driven by the desire to establish antecedents, authorities, and standards in an area where they are totally lacking or few in number. Dante's work is a document saturated with a sense of the importance of literary history and precedence, imbued with a sense of the wisdom of resorting to the past, even while canonizing a revolution, in order to give credence and legitimacy to the future. In such a context, the lack of preoccupation with the problem of his revolutionary ancestors' own inspirations and provocations, their claims to legitimacy, is indeed startling. What would be anachronistic would be to postulate that Dante's inattention to this subject is due to any belief that it is not a question worth asking. The tenor and substance of his book, as well as Dante's preoccupation with and detailed cognizance of the history of poets and literature before him, would belie this. One is left to assume that the question remains unasked either because the answer is too obvious to him and his readers to be worth setting out explicitly or because the question raised issues, and possible answers, that Dante did not, for some reason, want to discuss.

But the sources and the setting of the poetry (two concepts closely intertwined) would come to dominate work in this area, an area so vast in terms of both volume and variety of approaches that one can hope to complete even a book-length study dedicated to the history of scholarship in the area only if the full bibliography is not commented on and if the subject is presented schematically and telegraphically.[1] Thus, generalizations about the directions and features of so prodigious a field are fraught with danger and are open invitations to contradiction and the citation of exceptions. And yet, as I have pointed out elsewhere in this book, there is a certain value in tracing broad patterns, in attempting to see the most general of frameworks from which may hang even the most widely variegated specific works. In this case, a synoptic overview would include two principal points, neither without its exceptions. But these general observations are not, I believe, invalidated as observations on the state of canonical studies and knowledge by the practice of pointing out the exceptional scholar or study nor explained by such a generalization.

The first point is that the background, the origin, of this first Romance lyric has never ceased to be dominant. Even when it has not been the explicit subject of study, assumptions made about it have significantly dictated the orientation of synchronic or structural studies. The second generalization is that the most general concept of that background is very much grounded in—even exemplary of—a quite strict construction of what constitutes the Western tradition. Or, to formulate it negatively, it is a general concept of the background that has denied or excluded the hypothesis that any significant part of that background could be Arabic-derived or inspired—Andalusian for the Provençal troubadours or Sicilian for the *scuola siciliana*.

Even after protracted examination of the relevant studies, these hardly appear to have been crippling or impoverishing constraints. Indeed, few specific areas of literary, particularly historical literary, study show such a range of theories, hypotheses, and speculations about the origins and, in part derivatively, the nature and meaning of a group of poetic texts. Moreover, the number of specific issues ancillary to the discussion of the historical background raised in the course of such explorations is considerable, and substantial disagreement on them still plagues the field (or blesses it, depending on one's notion of the goals of the profession).

Most fertile among these issues is certainly the central thematic question of what, if anything, was courtly love, the "religion of love," as it has been dubbed. Opinions on the subject run the whole gamut. At one end is the detailed set of rules that presumably were established, known, and followed in most or all poetic compositions. This is most commonly characterized in the following terms: the poem involves the adulterous or at least extramarital love of a woman who is superior in status to the male suitor. She is impossibly beautiful and clearly superior to all others. The suitor is rebuffed or the possibility of consummation is sabotaged by evil enemies, spies for the husband, or malicious gossips. In the rebuff or the lover's frustration and subsequent pain lies his redemption and the power and beauty of love . . . and so forth. At the other end of the spectrum is the rejection of the idea that such a phenomenon ever even existed, the assertion that no system so amoral or immoral could have been exalted in the medieval period any more than in any other and that courtly love is critical conceit, an invention and/or a fallacy.[2]

Even within any subcategory of opinion in this range there is more than ample room for divergence of opinion. Within the rulebook school, for example, which in great measure has Andreas Capellanus as its model, the questions of what the specific rules or conventions were, how strictly they had to be adhered to, who set them and who did and did not follow them, the extent of their formal ties with lyric poetry, whether and how they could be transposed to a literary genre such as the romance, are all asked, or assumptions about them are made, in studies that do not wish to question them. At the other end lie disputes about the nature of a society that might create or borrow and codify such rules of love, and the continuing effects on both literature and Western society of the glorification of such a perverse, antisocial, un-Christian, and self-punishing conception of love. Nietzsche's statement, although he clearly approves of the notion of passionate love, reveals how deeply ingrained the notion is that this is, for better or worse, a fundamental feature of Westernness.

Discussion of these issues has invariably raised others, some of which dovetail nicely with more general issues in literary studies. Why is woman idolized and respected, made the center of the poetry and the master over the male, and what (if anything) does this reflect about the society in which such a system arose? Is this condition a fairly direct reflection of social circumstances, the product of a situation in which many women were lord and master over feudal domains while their husbands were off on crusade? Or is it a case of the literature of a society reflecting what does not exist in it in reality, a wish projection or dream fulfillment? Or is this the case of a society in which women themselves were not revered but in which certain female images that derived from its religion were?

Thus courtly love poetry has provided fertile territory for the consideration of both general and specific questions about the relationships between society and literature. No less so has it provided the provocation for raising questions related to different kinds of literary and sociological perceptions of the relations and roles of men and women, as poets and protagonists of the poetry itself. What does one do in this context, for example, with the poetry of the *trobairitz*, the women troubadours, texts relatively neglected until fairly recently but which appear to be remarkably like those of their male counterparts and present similar features and problems?[3] Or, again, how do we handle somewhat bizarre features, small but appearing significant to some, such as the use of *midons*, a masculine form ("master" rather than "mistress"), as applied to objects of love who are women? Are there indeed, as some would have it, two sets of rules, two ideologies, one for women, the other for men, one embodied in a courtly love in which the female is idolized and the other manifest in songs that are more accurately perceived as women's lamentations, related to the courtly love ethic in some ways but quite separate from it in others?[4]

The relationship such courtly poetry may have had with more popular songs is a closely related issue that has engendered no fewer discussions. At least one of the major theories about the origins of the more formal poetry, in fact, is based on the assumption that it is closely related to more popular, less formally codified poetry, much of it belonging to the female brand of love songs. And there is the other side of this coin, namely, what relationship the poetry of the courts had, whether it was originally dependent on popular poetry or not, with other later forms of literature and song. Was it, for example, incorporated into, or did it influence, songs sung outside the setting of the courts? And what of its ties to music? How central and formative were the poems and how long did they last? What was the difference between the *trobador* and the *joglar?* between the singer of love songs and that of narrative poetry? or between the composer and the performing artist? Ultimately, was all this much too variable for us to codify with any hope of verisimilitude?

The troubadour lyric has also been fertile ground for those interested in the ways in which literature can manifest an ideology. Have we constructed this love ideology ourselves, or have we borrowed and adapted it from such prose texts as Andreas's *De amore* and then read these poems to fit it? Is it legitimate to apply Gaston Paris's description of Chrétien's *Lancelot* to earlier lyrical compositions? The question, then, is not only whether they really fit such a system, but in more general terms, can any group of poems really reflect or embody a coherent ideological system, or even a coherent set of ideas? This poses the further question of the relative objectivity or subjectivity of such poetry. Why and how, some have noted, usually in some discreet fashion, could a group of poems that all seem to be saying the same thing have become so popular and so highly regarded and have remained so for so long? And, in the transition from short lyric pieces, the *canso,* to longer narratives, how would such an ideology hold up? Or how would it be applied?

But these are merely hints and suggestions of the richness and variety of the critical issues deriving from the study of this body of poetry, and the range of solutions and opinions on them offered through the years. Such wealth and variety is commensurate with one aspect of this poetry on which there is at least a general consensus: that it was immediately influential in a number of other areas of Europe and that its form and themes were adopted in other Romance vernaculars.

The lyric poetry of *langue d'oil* in northern France was for a considerable time very much under the spell and dominance of the Provençal troubadours, and no less can be said of poetry on the Italian peninsula. Since a decline in the vigor of Provençal poetry coincided with political upheavals in southern France that forced or coaxed into exile a number of the troubadours of the last generation, some of their domination in foreign parts derived from their physical presence at foreign courts. But those courts were also hospitable to them personally, because the reputation and prestige of the singers of Provence had preceded them.

Moreover, even in cases when the poetry as such was not fully adopted, many aspects of it were influential in other genres. The influence of Provençal poetry was felt throughout Europe in one form or another, directly or indirectly, for hundreds of years, and in some cases even down to the present. More than one prominent and influential writer of the twentieth century has revered such poetry and sung its praises. In sum, exposure to the poetry itself or its progeny, the notion of "courtly love," or some other aspect related to the lyric poetry of Provence is virtually unavoidable.

The agreement, at least at the most general level, on the impact and formative effects this poetry had is in no way shared, however, in the related issue of how and why, in terms of its own past, it was so pivotal. The intricately intertwined questions of the ways in which it differed dramatically or substantively from some or most of its predecessors or, conversely, what it took from other forms of poetry have largely shaped the field of troubadour studies. Even many aspects of the formal description of the poetry are shaped by such considerations.

The focus on this question has remained compelling even in a period in which genetic or origins studies are not only not *de rigueur* but in many quarters are distinctly out of fashion.[5] This is in part precisely because of the influential and formative position the poetry holds vis-à-vis later European literature. Scholars perceive that this position may reflect a paradox: that in great measure the poetry achieved such eminence and popularity because it was perceived as new, revolutionary, and fresh in some ways. At the same time, it must have had at least some roots somewhere, as all revolutions and innovations do. Thus we have the long quest for its origins, the Holy Grail of Romance philology.

Although Dante did not pursue the search, it was undertaken formally quite early on. Perhaps the earliest case is that of Giammaria Barbieri, who wrote *Dell'origine della poesia rimata* in the middle of the sixteenth century. As the title indicates, Barbieri identified the governing use of rhyme as a distinctive new facet of that poetry, and he would not be alone in taking such a position. But his search for the origins of this feature of the poetry, as well as others that had contributed to its influential position in the development of European literature, led him to al-Andalus. Although the "Arabist" theory, as it is so often called, might thus claim the distinction of being chronologically first in Provençal studies, it was not destined to become the first in importance. Far from it.

The theory was reiterated in the eighteenth century following the publication of Barbieri's work in 1790, although it was apparently known and circulated extensively before its transformation from manuscript to book. Its second champion was the Spaniard Juan Andrés, a Jesuit exile in Italy whose *Dell'origine, progresso e stato attuale d'ogni letteratura* (1782–1822) was apparently at least partially motivated by shock and consternation that his Italian hosts, and other Europeans, were unaware of how deeply indebted they were to the Spanish Arabic tradition.[6] Andrés' sympathies were thus with the theory expressed in Barbieri's *Dell'origine*, and in his own, more ambitious work he supports the notion that in the refined and artistically innovative courts of Islamic Spain were to be found the roots and inspiration for what would become the most renowned poetry of Europe.

But a negative reaction to such notions was not long in coming. The first refutation of the Arabist theory was Stefano Arteaga's *Della influenza degli Arabi sulla poesia moderna* (1791). As in the case of the *Dell'origine della poesia rimata*, the title provides significant indications of the orientation of the writer: Arteaga rephrases the question of where one would find the origins of modern poetry, and in his view it certainly was not in the Arab world. Many scholars of later generations were to agree with his position.

But Arteaga's firm rejection of such a possibility did not immediately produce universal agreement. In fact, the Arabist theory reached the peak of its popularity, and the peak of its support among *literati* (Sismonde de Sismondi, Claude Fauriel, Stendhal, E. J. Delecluze, and Eugène Baret, for example), in the first half of the nineteenth century. It has been pointed out, and it is an observation that might surprise many, that by the middle of the nineteenth century the notion that the origins of troubadour poems and courtly love lay in al-Andalus was a conventional maxim of criticism.[7] But even so, at this same time virtually all the other theories that would eventually be spun out were first postulated, at least in rudimentary form.

Madame de Staël (*De la littérature consideré dans ses rapports avec les in-*

stitutions sociales, 1800) and Chateaubriand (*Génie du Christianisme,* 1802) both laid the foundations for seeing the basis of Provençal poetry as Christian and European, and both were in some measure reacting nega- tively to the suggestion that it is in some way Muslim, or at least not Christian. More telling, they insist that it was fundamentally a European phenomenon, and they exclude Islamic Spain from their definition of that community. The many other theories first developed at more or less the same time shared two distinctive features with those of de Staël and Cha- teaubriand. First, although they might be at odds with each other in terms of *which* European and Latin/Romance tradition they thought had been formative, they shared a view of the Middle Ages in which the dominant forces were those of Christianity and Latinity. Secondly, they fundamentally opposed the Arabist theory, either directly or through their depiction of a medieval Europe within which Islamic Spain was a hostile or foreign force, a culture with marginal connections or no con- nections at all with what was clearly becoming the "real Europe."

Thus Schlegel directly disputed the validity of the Arabist theory on the grounds that Arab society was too repressive toward women to have produced courtly love. His view is noteworthy in this regard as an early example of a trend to dimiss the Arabist theory on less than a firm and knowledgeable footing, and the concomitant tendency not to question too deeply the accuracy of such arbitrary assertions. Dante Gabriel Rossetti laid the groundwork for an intepretation of troubadour poetry and its origins as a vehicle of religious dissent, the embryo of a theory that would see in courtly love the literary propaganda of the Albigensian heresy. Later in the nineteenth century Paul Meyer and other philologists would see the troubadours' roots in the Latin tradition that had preceded them and with which Meyer and the others increasingly perceived there to be a continuum. Meyer singled out the writings of Ovid as particularly formative and influential. Yet another school of thought originated and blossomed during this period: Gaston Paris's folkloristic theory, which saw the missing link as being that of popular poetry, especially the poetry of the *fêtes de mai.*

It is evident that a number of critical perspectives on the poetry of the troubadours and on the Europe in which they lived had crystallized shortly after the midpoint of the nineteenth century. But this was also a period of crystallization and definition, both for the field of Romance studies and for the Europe within which that area of inquiry was formed. And it was a Europe, as I discussed at some length in the first chapter, that was at precisely that moment shaping its views of the Arabs as colonial subjects. Napoleon's first campaign in Egypt at the turn of the century (1798–1801) is a convenient benchmark for the beginning of this key period. By 1831 Disraeli would write of that world from Cairo: "My eyes and mind yet ache with a grandeur *so little in unison with our own likeness*" (emphasis mine), and just before the midpoint in the century Marx would write of those "others" that "They cannot represent themselves; they must be represented."[8] The fairly specific and well-articulated view of the Arab and the Muslim world, developed and refined through what was by then an extended and cumulative colonial experience, was one whose assumption of the irremediable inferiority of the Arabs (and that of other colonized nonwhites) might be untenable today, but it was completely acceptable then, and it was destined to remain so until close to the middle of the present century.

The vaguer, more romantic, and in some ways more positive views that had been common even fifty years before were replaced with far less tolerant ones. Within this broader context, Romance studies came of age and achieved a level of respectability and interest that had not been accorded them before, and medieval studies was not the least among them. Further, the establishment of the centrality of such studies—"modern philology," as it would be known for some time—was part and parcel of the general tendency to define and respect modern Europe. The study of that culture's literature, its contribution to the finest of the world's cultural monuments, was both a reflex and a handmaiden to such a general cultural self-definition. Finally, the need to distinguish more coherently what was European from what was not was triggered by an expanding colonial experience, or at least it took place in its shadow. It would be incongruous to imagine that the general views of the emerging European nations did not affect an area of scholarship so intimately tied to that emerging sense of Europeanness in other ways. And the defining ideologies of self and other that contributed positively to making the study of the Romance languages and literatures so central a discipline at this time cannot but have affected scholars in the field in other ways as well.

It is clear, in any case, that it was at this moment that the Arabist theory not only ceased to be one of those theories advocated, denied, or discussed; it became virtually taboo. While the other theories, none of which violated any fundamental principle of Europeanness as it was then emerging, were spun out and set against each other, the older Arabist one, which was clearly at odds with the larger views that were affecting not only members of the profession but all Europeans' views of the world and of themselves, slipped into oblivion and undiscussability.

The groundwork had been laid, *grosso modo,* for continuing and ever-popular discussions of the origins and importance of Provençal poetry, the ancestor of all European literatures. The preeminent issues for debate were whether the sources of inspiration for the troubadours were popular or learned, in the local vernaculars or in Latin or Late Latin; whether its relationship to Christianity was heretical or transformational, the rebellion of the Albigensians or the secular transformation of ecclesiastical hymns and the adoration of the Virgin; and whether its other seemingly original features were really original or were instead inspired by some aspect of their background. But the possibility that their background may have been the Arabic component of Europe in the Middle Ages was so effectively banished (despite the idea's popularity as little as a generation before) that one might never have known that the theory of Arab influence in Europe had ever even been proposed. By the time Nietzsche was writing, as one can deduce from the citation above, the possibility could scarcely have been voiced without being greeted with derision. By the time the great debate about the etymology of *trobar* formally commenced in 1878, two years after Victoria had become empress of India and four years before the British occupation of Egypt, it would no more have occurred to any of the participants to trace the word's etymon to Arabic than to propose an origin in classical Chinese.

This academic conceptual banishment of the Arab from medieval Europe was to have extraordinary power. While versions of the Arabist theory were to be brought up again and again, it would not be reinstituted as part of the mainstream of philological thought. The sporadic suggestions of Arabic influence on this or that aspect of medieval European literature or on salient features of its lexicon, such as *trobar,* were largely ignored, were dismissed as unworthy of serious consideration, or at best were subjected to unusually heated and vitriolic criticism.[9] The proponents of such ideas, predominantly Arabists, were dismissed as individuals who simply had an ax to grind rather than a conceivably legitimate contribution to make and who, in any case, were not knowledgeable in the field of European literature.

Stern's stunning discussion of the *kharjas,* published in 1948 under a rather unassuming title, was proclaimed by some to signal the beginning of a new era in medieval Romance scholarship.[10] The addition to the corpus of medieval literature of what would prove to be a significant number of lyric poems in a Romance vernacular, Mozarabic, would in and of itself have broadened the horizons of the field, because here was a Romance language not previously included in the inventory of those languages that had produced literature. But what seemed to assure that the field would be shaken and transformed was the fact that these Mozarabic poems not only preceded those of the troubadours, thus dislodging them from their chronologically primary position, but at first glance they also resembled the poetry of Provence in some fundamental structural features and thematic characteristics. Some scholars suggested that something akin to courtly love was being voiced in these Mozarabic refrains. It also seemed to some that the origins question would again be pushed to the forefront and the Arabist theory reestablished in a position of, if not preeminence, at least credibility and respectability. It would be hard to dismiss textual evidence of the existence of vernacular love poetry in Romance that was clearly tied to the Arabic tradition, since the Mozarabic refrains were part of Arabic and Hebrew *muwashshaḥāt,* and that existed before the rise of the Provençal lyric and shared at least some of its major characteristics. It was all plausible and logical enough.

In fact, despite the wishful thinking of a relative minority of scholars, who were intrigued by these texts and whose views on Romance literature even before their discovery were well disposed to the Arabist theory (Menéndez Pidal and Américo Castro, among others), it would be inaccurate to say that the views of medievalists in general were revolutionized or that the borders of medieval Europe were redrawn to include al-Andalus. Beginning with Stern himself, who denied in no uncertain terms the possibility that such verses in any way affected those of the troubadours (the latter being part of a very different world), scholars were able, with very little difficulty, to reconcile the discovery and the existence of such texts with established views that effectively shut out the Andalusian world.[11] In fact, for the majority of scholars working in the field, no such coming to terms was even required. The *kharjas,* to say nothing of the *muwashshaḥāt,* were simply ignored by the mainstream of scholars and students, as they had been for the previous eight centuries.[12]

There were and are exceptions, of course, but the fact that they are exceptions serves to demonstrate that the notion of what was European and what was not was certainly not shaken in a way that would cause it to be redefined. In fact, the very existence of something called "*kharja studies*" is a ratification of the gulf between Arabic and Romance literary studies. That such a subdiscipline exists at all clashes with the essential characteristics of poems that would otherwise seem to defy such segregation, because the poems are themselves so obviously a part of a mixed rather than a segregated culture.[13] Clearly, it would be premature to say that Stern's discovery has brought down any walls or barriers. But those are walls that could well be breached, and our current view of the Middle Ages, and specifically of the world in which the troubadours first wrote and thrived, could well be replaced with a more expansive concept, one that assumes that the Arabist theory is as plausible and compelling as any.

But what of the specific arguments that have been adduced to refute the various formulations of the Arabist theory? And what other arguments might justify a different view of the medieval lyric, seemingly already so meticulously explored, or a reopening of the question of its origins, when such approaches are now effectively eclipsed by other very different orientations? And from the simplest of perspectives, what would one have to gain?

I have attempted to answer the first question, at least implicitly, in the first two chapters of this book. A significant number of the arguments against specific parts of the Arabist theory have been assertions of the impossibility or implausibility of attributing textual similarities or congruities to direct interaction between the two cultures or knowledge on the part of members of the Latin-Romance orbit of the literature of the Arabic world, even those living in al-Andalus or Sicily. Thus it has been argued that William of Aquitaine could not have adapted any element of Hispano-Arabic songs to his own poetry because he could not have known enough Arabic to have understood them.[14] Following a similar line of reasoning, it has also been argued that it is more plausible to imagine that where there are similarities between the sung lyrics of these two different worlds, parallel development accounts better and more logically for the phenomenon than any theory of direct connection.[15]

But both a more realistic definition of influence (one that does not trivialize it by making it mean copying or rob it of other possible complexities) and the historical evidence tell us that such assertions about William and his complete ignorance of the songs of the Arabic world are unreasonable hypotheses. Similarly, it would be more reasonable to assume something other than parallel development when one observes the appearance of quite similar and distinctive features in two schools of lyric poetry, one arising in the wake of the other, in two regions near each other and with no lack of communication, indeed with all sorts of traffic, between them. Significant, too, is the cultural prestige one of the two regions possessed in the eyes of the other. In fact, most of the refutations of the influence of Hispano-Arabic poetry on that of the Provençal troubadours derive their validity from the basic assumption of the unreasonableness of such a proposition, an assumption that is itself strongly governed and shaped by ideology. Once such a proposition is discarded and the hypothesis adopted that such influence is plausible, the force of the refutation is deflected. What is at stake is hardly whether William sat down and copied out some Arabic poetry, any more than it would be when we talk about an Ovidian influence on William. Rather, the question is whether an Andalusian factor was a significant part of his cultural background.

Among the least legitimate and most easily overturned is the argument first made by Schlegel: that courtly love, or poetry in praise of women, could not come from a culture that so despised and repressed them. There are two weaknesses to such an argument, and they are even evident in refutations more sophisticated than this one. The first problem is that the statement is based on incomplete or inaccurate assumptions about Arabic poetry. Poetry in praise of women, for example, certainly was and has been written and sung in Arabic, and perhaps this and other general features of such poetry, particularly as it existed in al-Andalus, will soon become more widely known.

The second problem regarding such an argument is that it is based on a very strict construction of the relationship between a society's values and those of its literature. One could point out, of course, that the canon of Arabic poetry is replete with wine songs despite (or because of?) the strict Islamic prohibition of alcohol. One might also point out that the actual social position of women in European society in the medieval period was hardly the exalted one that might be suspected if one regularly read literary texts as if they were sociological treatises or interpreted images in poetry as if they were direct representations, faithful mirrors, of society. Nor can literature, any more than any other art, be expected to follow party lines, yet this assumption, too, has fueled many refutations to the effect that if ignorance did not prevent a Provençal poet's use of Arabic songs, repugnance certainly would. The problem, of course, is that such views, problematic as they may seem when one analyzes them from this critical perspective, have in many cases been enshrined in the scholarly literature. The refutation of the Arabist theory expressed by Jeanroy, for example, is somewhat sanctified by the fact of Jeanroy's other achievements in troubadour scholarship. But the validity of the rest of his work—or that of Curtius, Auerbach, Gaston Paris, or Leo Spitzer—does not mean that we must continue to accept their views on this particular matter.[16]

But there do exist refutations, or what might appear to be refutations, that are not based on the exclusionary ideology. They are considerably

more complex, and they are really more suggestions of some of the interesting problems that might be explored than they are barriers to such avenues of discourse. Curiously enough, the poetic complexities raised by
many of these arguments are very similar to those that in the past, in a
more restricted context, have made the study of Provençal poetry so fascinating for so many scholars.

Many of these seeming refutations of the Arabist theory revolve
around the notion that Hispano-Arabic poetry, particularly the *kharjas*
and *muwashshaḥāt,* is more complex than scholars may have thought and
that its forms and themes may not be so readily associable with those of
Provence as some earlier enthusiasts had believed. For example, in some
critics' views, the love lamentations so often found in the *kharjas* (and
with which the *kharjas* are invariably associated) are more akin to the
female poetic love ethic of popular poetry than to the male one that is so
characteristic of courtly love poetry—and of the main part of a *muwashshaḥa.* Complicating this issue even further is the suggestion, a quite reasonable one, that while the main body of the *muwashshaḥāt* is part of the
tradition of classical Arabic poetry, the *kharjas* were originally quite independent of them, being part of a body of Romance popular poetry with
congeners throughout Romania. In this view, such a priori compositions
were later embedded in the classical poems. The conclusion some might
draw from such observations is that it is not a question of Arabic poetry
influencing Romance but the reverse.

These discussions, these questions, even the suggestion that the obverse of the Arabist theory is possible, reveal all the more why an alteration in our perspective is so desirable and potentially profitable, for if the
Andalusian world is part of the medieval West, and indeed a critical and
often central part of it, then detailed discussions of the complexities
of Provençal poetry can only be enhanced by parallel and intertwined
discussions of significantly similar complexities and problems in the
Hispano-Arabic sphere. It is telling that these arguments over the very
nature of Hispano-Arabic poetry reveal that many if not most of the
problems involved are similar to those that have been discussed ad infini-
tum by Provençalists: the differences, similarities, and relationships between the masculine and feminine branches of love poetry of the period
and the nature of the relationship between courtly and popular poetries.
Was the poetry part of a long tradition that was merely given a new twist,
or was it really revolutionary? This latter question is as heated and problematic for Hispano-Arabic poetry as for Provençal, and many of the ar-

guments focus on the poetry's apparently revolutionary features: the way rhyme is used, the strophic form, the use of the vernacular instead of the classical language, and so forth.

At a minimum, the sharing of insights and the comparison of possible solutions to these questions, remembering how parallel they are, could not help but be fruitful. But if to such a rudimentary concept of the value of shared knowledge in similar fields we add the incentive provided by remembering that we are talking about bodies of poetry that may very well have interacted at some level—the popular one in the county of Barcelona and the more courtly one at Palermo, just to name two of the myriad possibilities—then the case could be made that it would be a dereliction of our duty not to explore conjointly such multiple parallels.

It all seems to boil down to the question of what we have to gain and what we have to lose. An important part of what we have to gain is the addition to the canon of our commonly read secondary texts an extensive body of literature, much of it quite cogent, whose authors have concluded that the role played by the prestige and the songs, the neo-Platonism and the music of al-Andalus, were significant inspirations for the creation of what would become Europe's first poetry. What we might lose, of course, is the somewhat romantic notion that the question of the bases for the revolution in Provence are *introuvable* or, in a more recent version of the argument, that they are insignificant.[17] We would also lose a good part of our long and closely held ideology that sets us apart, as Europeans, from all others.

But even if we eventually conclude, as we might, that the Andalusian influence was only one of many, and perhaps not the decisive one, we gain in expanding our canon of medieval courtly love poetry by including texts that in critical ways parallel the poetry of Provence and also share many of its difficulties and mysteries, much of its fascination, all of which are singificant common bonds in both their background and success. We should see that this can only enrich our perception of so momentous and pivotal a period in our literary history.

Notes

1. Boase 1976 is the major full-length study of the history of scholarship on Provençal troubadour poetry. Although he concludes that the Arabist theory is the soundest overall, Boase's general recounting of the history of the scholarship is both nonpartisan and thorough. See the 1978 review by Cummins. In Menocal 1981, also a review of this book, I provide further bibliography and an analysis of why Boase's evenhandedness vis-à-vis the Arabist theory is valuable and convincing. It is unfortunate that Boase does not, however,

come to grips with the problem of why the Arabist theory has continued to be rejected, especially in light of the fact that he has found it the most reasonable and convincing overall. Nevertheless, this is certainly the best study of both the earliest history of scholarship on the question, that which precedes the institutionalization of Romance studies, and the more recent intellectual history. It may be supplemented by Cremonesi 1955, which is also a detailed history and evaluation of origins work in the modern period (that is, after the middle of the nineteenth century). Cremonesi pays special attention to the question of how scholarship has dealt with the distinction between popular and courtly literature (5–35). She also notes that theories of Arabic origins "non incontrano il favore della critica"(25). These two sources have provided much valuable information for the discussion in this chapter.

2. Besides Boase 1976, the two best discussions of our understanding of "courtly love" are Frappier 1959 and, especially, Frappier 1968, which is an extensive, lucid and highly informative critique of the series of essays in Newman 1968. Since the Newman collection includes Robertson's well-known article, "The Concept of Courtly Love as an Impediment to the Understanding of Medieval Texts" (Donaldson 1970 is also dedicated to the same proposition), Frappier's response is particularly important and valuable. See also an earlier critique in Silverstein 1949.

3. Recent *trobairitz* studies include the sketchy Bogin 1976 and Paden et al. 1981. Although in both cases the authors focus on what distinguishes them from their male counterparts, the similarities and parallelisms that emerge from these studies are substantial. See further discussion of this issue in Chapter 4.

4. Dronke has explored this position in depth and has canonized the distinction between male and female love songs. See Dronke [1968] 1977.

5. Note especially Payen's 1979 attempt to dismiss the question: "Les romanistes ont perdu trop de temps à énoncer de vaines hypothèses sur les origines de la lyrique troubadouresque"(98). He goes on to conclude, however, as the title of the article indicates, that William created a "révolution idéologique" (106).

6. For information on Andrés himself, the expulsion of the Spanish Jesuits, and his text, see Mazzeo 1965.

7. This is Boase's conclusion, and he documents it thoroughly. See, for example, Fauriel [1860] 1966. Studies not devoted to this issue in particular but rather to the question of the "Orient" in eighteenth-century French literature and literary studies would lend support to his thesis. See, for example, Martino [1906] 1970.

8. Said 1978:xii and 102. He includes, particularly in the first two chapters, an extended discussion of the development of largely negative attitudes toward the Arab world in the period of colonialism.

9. The best and most succinct example is certainly that of Jeanroy 1934, whose brief negative appraisal of the Arabist theory is capped by the statement: "Puisque la poésie arabe est pour nous autres provençalistes un livre scellé, c'est à nos collègues arabisants à venir à nous." (1:75). In fact, judging from some recent evidence, even that does not necessarily work very well. A pointed example is the 1972 Saville study of dawn songs, which ignores the 1965 Stern and Wilson investigation of the same motif in Mozarabic poetry.

10. "Les vers finaux en espagnol dans les muwaššaḥas hispano-hebraiques" (Stern 1948); also in English in Stern 1974.

11. See Stern's "Literary Connections between the Islamic World and Western Europe in the Early Middle Ages: Did They Exist?" (1974) a question to which the resounding answer is No. The paper was originally delivered at the Spoleto conference and is thus published in Italian in the *L'Occidente e l'Islam nell'alto Medioevo*. See Stern 1974 for a complete bibliography of Stern's work. Note also Zumthor 1954, which identifies the *kharjas* as further proof of the separation of the two cultures.

12. As I have noted in Chapters 1 and 2 about Hispano-Arabic literature, the *muwashshaḥāt* are relatively rarely integral parts of courses, anthologies, or histories of medieval

literature. Knowledge of their intricacies is admirable in a Hispanist and exceptional in a French or Italian medievalist.

13. Yet segregation and partition are still, perhaps even increasingly, the dominant features of *kharja* scholarship. *Kharja* studies have become a specialized subdiscipline within Romance medievalism and are largely segregated from the mainstream. See my more detailed discussion in Chapter 4 of how the study of the *kharja* itself is often characterized by segregation: it is studied independently of the *muwashshaḥa* and is seen as part of one tradition or the other, but not both.

14. There is a series of articles that deal with the interconnected questions of whether William of Aquitaine knew any Arabic and whether there is textual evidence of Arabic words or expressions in some Provençal poems. These articles, several of them exchanges and responses to others, include: Roncaglia 1949 and 1952, the first on the use of *gazel* (< Andalusian *ghazal*) in a Provençal poem and the second on a poetic motif of possible Arabic origin in a Bernart de Ventadorn poem; Riquer 1953 is a response to the latter; Lévi-Provençal's 1948b suggestion (1:298–300; reprinted as Lévi-Provençal 1954) that "babariol-babarian" in a poem of William of Aquitaine's was decipherable as Arabic provoked the response of Frank 1952, which includes a succinct presentation of the arguments of why it is absurd to imagine that William could have known any Arabic. On this problem, see also Sutherland 1956. Later specialized studies of lexical or refrain echoes include Dutton 1964 and 1968 and Armistead 1973. Gorton 1976 is a review of some of these and of other such studies. Gorton himself is very negative on the question of the possibility of any direct knowledge of even spoken Arabic by any troubadours, principally because of the state of warfare and ignorance of each other that existed between Muslims and Christians.

15. Again, Dronke is the primary exponent of such parallelism.

16. Nor, of course, is the obverse true, that because we reject their views on this issue, we need discard their accomplishments wholesale. I will, in fact, argue in Chapter 5 that many studies that have ignored the Arabic-derived component dovetail remarkably with the view that emerges if one introduces into the global image the crucial participation of the Andalusian and Sicilian orbits of medieval culture. As I have indicated in this chapter, many of the questions posed about the origins question in troubadour and courtly love studies are prime candidates for the integration of Andalusian material into their proposed solutions.

17. Payen 1979 (see note 5) and Guiraud 1971 and 1978 (see Chapter 1) are two good examples of unsuccessful attempts to bypass the origins question.

CHAPTER FOUR

The Newest "Discovery": The Muwashshaḥāt

Mort estes pur l'amur de mei:
Par raisun vivre puis ne dei.

—Thomas, *Tristan*

The first and principal benefit of the reorientation of our scholarship should be to enable us to bring to fruition a new type of comparative textual analysis, an analysis not focused on the question of origins as this question has previously been profitably and legitimately carried out in the study of the medieval lyric. What is altered in reshaping our view of the medieval cultural ambience is that it becomes as potentially valuable and revealing (and as legitimate) to compare Hispano-Arabic poetry with Provençal or Sicilian poetry as it has always been to compare Sicilian and Provençal texts, for example. But even when the focus of such a study is not genetic, the question of origins is never completely irrelevant, as I have previously pointed out. Some assumptions about the poetry's origins inevitably affect purely comparative studies in two principal ways: assumptions regarding possible or likely origins and filiations govern the choice of texts compared, and the results of the study will explicitly or implicitly validate or invalidate the supposition that the compared texts are in some way related to each other.

Thus, to begin with the second of these two points, if we use such comparisons for the purpose of establishing possible genetic affiliations (who influenced whom, what innovation in one group of poems was inspired by what feature in another, and so forth) then it is incumbent on the scholar to distinguish clearly, in any given case, the complex and variable nature of the relationships between the different groups of texts. If one has assumed that Hispano-Arabic poetry was in some way part of the general poetic background of a poet writing in Provençal in the twelfth century, for example, then it is also necessary to sketch out a hypothesis concerning what kind of relationship was probably involved. But is this requirement really much different from that which is (or should be) in force in justifying the texts chosen for any comparison in the first place?

If we are to maintain, in studying the poetry of that same troubadour, for example, that a given image or form is drawn from contemporary Church hymns, say, or from Ovid, is it not legitimate to require that a hypothesis about the kind of relationship involved there be set out? Unless we assume that all possible artistic and intellectual sources are read by a given artist, and are thus used indiscriminately and equally, then we are in all cases obliged to clarify which sources were oral rather than written, which may have been interpreted reverently rather than in a hostile fashion, and which were of high prestige rather than being perhaps not fashionable. Such a procedure, even if in some cases quite brief, is applicable not just in the more prickly case of dealing with Arabic texts and songs in a European context. The troubadour's knowledge of and attitude toward Ovid, or the Church and its hymns, is no more self-evident or exempt from speculative or hypothetical clarification than is his attitude toward songs sung in Arabic by servants or by visiting scholars at some of the courts at which his own songs were being sung.

Thus, although it is possible to do comparative literary work when no genetic question is explicitly at stake or when this is not the major focus of a particular study, such comparative work in medieval studies has generally been limited, by common consent, to comparisons of texts that have been considered comparable in terms of the broadest genetic framework and relationships. It has not been sufficient, and perhaps it should not be, to note that two texts have shared features and then to compare those features that invite such comparative work. The implicit or explicit rule has been in force that there must be a plausible historical relationship between the texts, at least in terms of their being part of the same general literary universe.

As a result, the exclusion of the Andalusian and Sicilian Arabic literary world from the general medieval European frame of reference has affected more than just the question of origins. It has also prevented much potentially valuable comparative study from being carried forward, for although comparative work is not ultimately separable from genetic questions in this realm, studies whose focus is synchronic can produce insights that other studies may overlook, because of the difference in focus.[1] The insights, in turn, may better inform and elucidate discussions of the origins question, diachrony, and genetics when one returns to the old question of where it all came from. The Arabist question has thus doubly suffered from neglect: Not only has it been dealt with from the distorting perspectives I have already discussed, but it has also been impoverished in ways that other theories have not been, by being dealt with from a purely diachronic point of view.

Moreover, given the ever-shifting notions, relative prestige, and perceived value of various modes of literary criticism, it is important to establish that our revisionist view of medieval European cultural and literary affairs can be of value for something more than establishing which came first or where any debt is owed. This is a view that can also be used as the basis for different readings of the texts themselves. In other words, acceptance of the basic premises of the Arabist theory can produce something more than further insights into the origins question itself. It may also be used as the basis for a more enlightening reading (at least by the standards of those who advocate the primacy of synchronic over diachronic studies) of a series of texts and the identification of possible structural and thematic connections among a series of medieval texts. The comparative exploration of selected medieval lyric poems that follows derives its legitimacy from the revisionist historical analysis already discussed and from the concomitant conceptual and procedural norms that have been suggested.

> Tears that are shed and a breast that is burned
> > Water and fire!
> Things never joined save for matters of moment!
> > By my life, it is harsh, what the censor has said,
> > For life is but short while love's toils are long.
> > O, for the sighs that betray one who loves!
> > And O, for the tears that flow like a stream!
> Sleep is taboo, visitation is far;
> > No peace and quiet!
> I would fly, yet I find no place to take flight!
> > O Ka' ba to which all hearts journey forth
> > Torn by passion that calls and answering love,
> > You called on a sinner returning to you;
> > Here I am! I heed not the words of the spy!
> Allow me to travel and worship therein;
> > Make no excuse!
> My heart is the gift and my tears are the stones.
> > Welcome is he, though he expose me to death;

One supple of waist and languid of eye.
O hardness of heart which love sees as soft,
    You have caused me to learn that thoughts can think ill!
Since he made off from those nights which were short
    My tears gush forth
As though my lids were sharp-pointed swords!
    I've chosen a lord who unjustly condemns;
    To him I allude not revealing his name;
    My justice is wondrous in view of his wrong!
    Him you may ask for the tryst and refusal.
He tore from a passion well proven my share
    Of obedience,
Though shunned. Joy after him may choose whom it wills.
    I cannot resist him on any condition;
    A lord who accuses, treats harshly, delays;
    Who left me in pledge to despair and disease,
    Then sang with an air between boldness and love:
"Meu l-habib enfermo de meu amar.
    Que no ha d'estar?
Non ves a mibe que s'ha de no llegar?"

("My beloved is sick for love of me. How can he not be so?
Do you not see that he is not allowed near me?")

(Al Aʿma aṭ-Ṭutılı, number 23 in *Hispano-Arabic Poetry,*
translated by James Monroe.)

Who will be my ally against a gazelle who hunts lions in the jungle and who reneges on a debt when I threaten suit?

With her I lie between hope and desire. I do not show signs of despair even when she prolongs her injustice towards me. Indeed, I said: "Oh my heart, shelter her close to you and keep her from your evil thoughts. And you, my soul, melt away." You who delay fulfillment for so long, execute your judgment since I will accept it whatever it might be.

You who so unjustly reject me although I have no patience, cannot wait infinitely. I would not even mind it if I were to waste away to nothing, as long as you did not desert me. You have left me barely alive when, somnolent, you shoot from your dark eyes arrows that do not miss their mark, arrows that hit the heart.

What do you do with my heart that it never ceases to be troubled? It complains to you of its passion in vain. Have pity, since its life and its death lie in the palms of your hands. Oh you, my sickness and my healer, in but a word from you lies the cure of my illness. And yet, because of you, I have melted away to nothing. Do what you will, then, since you have already decided.

Why should I try to slow down those looks that bring only death for me? Even when she passes by me with her head turned aside, she is still the essence of beauty. If I wanted to fully describe her charms, it would be quite impossible. The eyes of a troubled man leave his face and wander into a garden, but those gardens remain inviolate, protected by other, sharp and vigilant eyes.

God, what a cautious and wary gazelle, frightened by separation, a girl of thirteen. Tearful and sobbing, intoxicated, yearningly, she says to her mother: "*Ya mamma, meu l-habibe baiš e no mas tornarade. Gar ke fareyo, ya mamma: No un bezyello lešarade?*" ("Mamma, my lover is gone and he won't come back—what will I do? He won't leave me even one little kiss.")

(Anonymous, number 21a in García Gómez,
translated by Adel Allouche and María Rosa Menocal)

When the new Andalusian poetic form called the *muwashshaḥa* came to be known in other parts of the Arabic-speaking world, it was promptly rejected. It was not perceived as a legitimate poetic form, because, among other things, it violated the first law of Arabic poetry, that it be written in the standard classical language. While the principal strophes or stanzas did adhere to this principle, the final strophe, the *kharja,* did not; it was composed in the Romance vernacular of al-Andalus, Mozarabic. This incursion of the vernacular made the entire poetic form illegitimate. But the Arab literati who made such pronouncements would be much amused, no doubt, to find that in our own times some literary critics have discovered a different solution to this perceived problem. Since the *kharjas* were first deciphered in 1948, many scholars have performed conceptual and working excisions on the poems to enable them to deal with the *kharja* separately or to allow them to view the entire poem as part of the standard canon of classical Arabic poetry.[2]

This practice has produced two results. First, we often deal with the vernacular part of the poem as a separate and separable poetic entity from the part of the poem written in classical Arabic. Second, we do not deal with the poem as a whole as part of the larger tradition of Romance courtly poetry to which it is, even at first glance, related thematically and structurally. If it had occurred to those earlier purveyors of good poetic taste, the Arab critics who refused to accept the *muwashshaḥa* into the standard canon, to resort to such a device, the *muwashshaḥa*'s main strophes, at least, would not have been denied a place in the canon of classical Arabic poetry. They could merely have done what we now do on a regular basis: deal with them as different poems, as if there had been no dent in the classicism of Andalusian literature at all.

Of course, no such thing was done at that time, for the simple reason that the two parts of the poem were—and are—inseparable, and the Romance or Romance-influenced part marks it clearly as not classical. The *muwashshaḥa* is a poem, a poetic form. It has, like many other poetic forms, distinguishable components within the poem. However, to posit those separate components as separable poems defies conventional good sense in literary analysis. From some perspectives the operative division of *kharjas* from *muwashshaḥa,* one so deeply engrained that it is reflected in our nomenclature (which establishes a dichotomy between the two and conveys the impression that the *muwashshaḥa* somehow stands in opposition to a *kharja*) makes as much sense as it would to perform a similar operation on the quatrain and tercet parts of a sonnet or, in our normal way of referring to such poems, to talk about sonnets on the one hand and tercets on the other.

In order to explain the subdivision of what was originally composed and presented as a single poem, it has been argued that because of the linguistic and stylistic rupture that exists between *muwashshaḥa* and *kharja*—that is, between the main part of the poem and the final strophe—and because the *kharja* resembles other examples of early Romance popular poetry, we must assume that the *kharja* comes from a rather different poetic tradition than the rest of the poem. It is further argued that the specific *kharjas* lifted from that popular tradition almost undeniably antedate, in composition and performance, the strophic sections that were part of the courtly tradition. This argument, and its numerous variants, has much interest and validity, and *kharja* scholarship, viewed from this perspective, has undeniably accomplished many of its stated aims and has greatly enhanced our knowledge of early Romance popular poetry.

Such an approach has been especially important in terms of the origins question, since it has successfully established that the *kharjas* (or at least the proto-*kharjas,* the poems that provided the inspiration for the final strophes of the *muwashshaḥa,* and in some cases exact verses or whole refrains) are an important part of the common Romance corpus of popular lyric of medieval Europe. As such, in fact, the successes of this scholarship provide significant evidence for the sort of revisionist medieval image we are proposing here. They clearly indicate, through the relationships that have been established between the reflexes of popular poetry adopted by courtly Arabic poetry and the examples of other Romance popular forms, that what we are dealing with is a community of popular poetry that was as much a part of the Arabic cultural orbit as of that of the Romance/Latin world. There can be no question that the work of the scholars who have demonstrated the morphological and genetic affinities between the popular poetries of the different parts of Romania, including those where Arabic was the prestige language, has been crucial in the attempt to establish precisely the kind of different view of the medieval world on which further comparative studies must rely.[3]

The unfortunate result of the lopsided emphasis of this kind of work, however, is that in great measure it has resulted in the dismemberment and the rather incomplete reading of the *muwashshaḥāt* themselves. Even more unfortunately, the scholars who have called most frequently for a restoration of the unity of the texts do so largely from the perspective that the entire poem can only be understood in terms of the classical Arabic tradition. Thus, to follow their line is to substitute one kind of dismemberment for another, to divorce the poem from its special Andalusian setting as well as to divorce the Romance *kharja* from the rest of the poem.

The dangers inherent in conveying the impression of the ultimate divisibility of these poems—either internally or, as a whole poem, from the Andalusian framework—is all the greater because of the relatively high degree of naiveté in regard to these texts that exists in the community of medievalists. The confusion created by presentations of the *kharjas* that do not make explicit their essential ties to the *muwashshaḥa* is greater than would be the case if a similar impression was conveyed about a sonnet. Few fellow scholars would go on to talk about its meaning and function without referring back to the original composition. And the confusion generated by claiming that the *kharjas* do not entail a clear break from the classical canon, and are thus part of the domain of Arabists exclusively, is one not likely to be remedied by those most able to do so. Students of the *scuola siciliana* or Provençal poetry who might perceive connections and thus deny the assertion that it is not comparable to Romance lyrics are also those predisposed to dismiss such poetry as part of the Arabists' domain in the first place.

The argument is occasionally made that we are justified in this division of our attention and reading by respectable precedents, the earliest critics of this poetic form. In fact, however, of the three premodern critics who discuss the *muwashshaḥa,* two make it perfectly clear that the *muwashshaḥa* with its *kharja* constitutes a single poetic form. In doing so, moreover, they indicate no less clearly that it is a peculiarly Spanish, Andalusian, form and that it is something quite apart from the classical canon. The observations of these early critics are cited because they sum up, quite simply and forcefully, what reasonable analysis and more detailed observation would eventually conclude. Moreover, they provide ample documentation of a certain historical perspective, the perception of the status of such poems among contemporaries or near contemporaries, a perspective that is sometimes obscured in more recent studies.[4]

Ibn Bassam attributes the invention of this new form to a specific author, an observation unlikely to be made by someone who perceived of the *kharja* as being something distinct and separable from the rest of the poem, let alone an autonomous poem. He then goes on to note the linguistic difference between the *markaz,* as he calls the *kharja,* and the rest of the poem, indicating clearly that this type of composition is not the normal poetic form. But he indicates no less clearly the integrity of this new genre, noting in the same breath that there are also formal differences between other components of the poem, between the *ghusn* and the *simt,* for example, two parts of the strophes that no one has as yet suggested we study separately for their individual meanings.[5]

The best-known premodern *muwashshaḥa* critic, Ibn Khaldūn, makes the case even more strongly, and it is worth quoting directly from the *Muqaddimah:*

> Poetry was greatly cultivated in Spain. Its various ways and types were refined. Poems came to be most artistic. As a result recent Spaniards created the kind of poetry called muwashshah. Like the qasidah, the muwashshah is used for erotic and laudatory poetry, and its authors vied to the utmost with each other in this kind of poetry. Everybody, the elite and the common people, liked and knew these poems because they were easy to grasp and understand.   (Rosenthal [1958] 1967:458)

Virtually every sentence in this passage reaffirms the basic assumption that the *muwashshaḥāt* were single poems, not double ones. Ibn Khaldūn likewise leaves little doubt that this is a new kind of poetry created by the Spaniards. The notion of creation refers to the new and novel mixture of popular and classical elements, and it was understood and enjoyed by all, presumably, at least in part, because there was some element in it from the different traditions that both elite and commoner were familiar with. One searches in vain for an indication that the separate parts were enjoyed by separate audiences or that this was not commonly regarded as a novel form created by the Andalusians. In fact, Ibn Khaldūn goes on to state the following:

> It should be known that taste as to what constitutes eloquence in connection with such poetry is possessed only by those who have contact with the dialect in which a particular poem is composed and those who have had much practice in using it among the people who speak it. . . . A Spaniard has no understanding of the eloquence of Maghribi poetry. Maghribis have none for the eloquence of the poetry of Easterners or Spaniards, and Easterners have none for the eloquence of Spaniards and Maghribis.   (Rosenthal [1958] 1967:458–59)

Ibn Sanāʾ al-Mulk is the third of these early critics, and he was, in some measure, one of those Easterners who might have had some difficulty in dealing with this peculiarly Spanish form. His testimony is at the outset the most suspect, because he was an Egyptian who dealt with a form of *muwashshaḥa* that had been modified for non-Andalusian tastes—and for those who could not understand even the language, Mozarabic, of the original compositions. In fact, it turns out that even Ibn Sanā' himself could not read it. Nevertheless, and even given his perspective and the fact that his motive for writing the *Dār al-Ṭirāz,* was to make the form acceptable and canonizable in classical Arabic terms, his testimony is often revealing. He is unable, for example, to explain how to scan the Andalusian *muwashshaḥāt* in accordance with classical Arabic meter, the only system he knew.[6]

A careful reading of what the earliest critics had to say about this new poetic form should thus reinforce the dual assumptions that the *muwashshaḥa* and its *kharja* constitute a single poem and that the genre is clearly distinguishable from other Arabic forms and differs from them in various ways. One of these is that the final strophe is composed in the vernacular, and thus in a different language. But the *muwashshaḥa* also appears to break with traditional Arabic poetry in its meters and in the use of rhyme, and these are features that appear to relate to its linguistic background. But the most striking thing that emerges about this form is that its novelty lies precisely in the unity of its disparate components. It is this feature that distinguishes this genre from others in the Arabic canon, and the *kharja* is necessarily an integral feature of it rather than a mere appendage.

What happens, then, if we assume that the *muwashshaḥa* with its *kharja* is a single poetic unit, a distinctively Andalusian creation? The first thing the casual reader is likely to note is that the final strophe, the *kharja,* is indeed strikingly different from the rest of the poem.[7] In fact, it contrasts with it in several complementary ways. The purely linguistic distinction between the strophes is classical Arabic and the *kharja* in the Mozarabic vernacular is coterminous with a difference in the poetic voice or speaker involved. While the sections written in the formal poetic language, the formal code, embody the equally formal courtly laments of a male speaker, the Mozarabic refrain, set off by its use of a much more casual code, is often spoken by a woman who does not use traditional formal expressions to convey her sentiments. The different parts of the poem are thus composed in different languages, not only from the strictly linguistic point of view but also in the sense that the parts are spoken by quite different poetic voices, with different tones and styles.[8] One notices further that the poet uses the linguistic difference to accentuate the characteristic voice and stylistic difference. Thus the strophic sections in the formal classical language express the courtly sentiments of frustrated love that have led to deep dissatisfaction and unhappiness. The final strophe, the *kharja,* on the other hand, which is also considerably shorter, has a style that is often as informal as the vernacular in which it is delivered. The female voice's lament is short, direct, to the point, often startlingly so, and decidedly uncourtly.

One way of approaching the problem of the relationship between the two parts (other than forgetting their unity in the poem and pointing out that they originate in different traditions) is to begin with a metapoetic reading of such alterities within a single poem. In fact, these texts lend themselves particularly well to a reading in which we understand that the poem is talking about itself and about literature and language at least as much as it is about its external subject. It is not difficult to perceive that in their structure the poems set up a series of overlapping oppositions, creating a dialectic between the two kinds of poetry involved. Not only are the two linguistic codes (one formal and classical, the other informal and vernacular) set in opposition to each other, but so are the male/female poetic dichotomy, the courtly/popular opposition, the traditional and canonized (or canonizable) in conflict and contrast with the renegade, uncanonizable form. At the metapoetic level, in the very structure of essential oppositions within the poem itself, the *muwashshaḥa* presents, in microcosmic form, the poetic alternatives that the poets probably had to deal with. From this perspective alone it is necessary to note how quintessentially Andalusian that makes such poems. They are embodiments of the different poetic traditions that had come together in al-Andalus, poems written, at least in part, to demonstrate the close juxtaposition of the two traditions.

Another achievement of the form is that while preserving a sense of opposition, contradiction, even seeming irreconcilability, between the two traditions, they are nevertheless ultimately unified as part of a dialectic within a single poem, a dialectic that establishes their fundamental congruence. Thus, whether the subject of the poem is what we would call courtly love or something else, the very structure of the poem is one that embodies, quite neatly in fact, the metaliterary problem of conflicting poetic voices and styles that we can safely assume from other external evidence must indeed have been a matter of considerable interest to the poets of al-Andalus. This is the poetry of a society full of dialectically opposed cultural alternatives.

But such poetry is an embodiment of the perception that such hybrids are productive, that diglossia and bilingualism are far from infertile. Al-Andalus was thus a dynamic crossbreed, for the two voices are tied to each other not because they happen to be part of the same poem but in other structurally essential ways: through the music, the metrics, and the rhyme scheme, which are the same throughout. The setting off of the two voices is thus neatly counterbalanced by the recurring and unifying metrical scheme and rhyme, as well as by the way in which musically they were part of the same song.[9] Although much or most of the evidence, both textual and historical, indicates that the unifying patterns of rhyme and meter were Romance in origin, this still-debated question is best left for others better informed than I to discuss.[10] The problem is, however, largely irrelevant to the present comparative, synchronic study, for this is fundamentally a question of diachronic importance and perspective. A synchronic reading of the poem or "hearing" of the song would not require detailed historical information to understand that structurally the dialectic is marked by a fundamental unity. When the linguistic breach occurs, signaling another voice, another alternative, an opposition, the continuing rhythm and rhyme signals just as clearly that this is still the same song, the same poem.

One might well describe such poems, at least from these perspectives, as constituting a dialectic of alternative poetics, and as with all good dialectics, it is one that thrives on both discontinuity (the oppositions implied by the different voices and languages, the different kinds of poetries that find a place in the poem) and continuity (the link provided by the unchanging and unifying elements of rhyme and rhythmic patterns.)

But what about at the thematic level and the actual subject matter of the poetry? If the poems examined are limited to those that can readily be labeled love poems, how do the expressions of unrequited love presented in these poems work within the peculiar dialectic nature of their structure?[11] Were it not for the fact that it is easy to be misled by the regnant assumption that these are two essentially separate segments, one might easily conclude that the poems present a form of dialogue: two voices, which have reasons for speaking different languages, are speaking—or at any rate, are trying to speak—to each other. But something else has prevented us from coming to this conclusion in the past: the fact that it seems to us impossible, because of *what* they are saying, that this could be a dialogue. What seems incongruous is the fact that both voices are expressing a lover's lament and that each one is saying, in his and her own language and style, essentially the same thing. Rephrased in contemporary colloquial English, they are *both* saying something to the effect of: "I'm in love with this person, and I'm terribly unhappy because she (or he) doesn't love me back" (or is cruel or indifferent, or some such thing).

It might seem at first blush illogical to assume that this is a dialogue, that the laments are directed at each other and that these are two would-be lovers, each of whom is rendered unhappy by the other. If this were a dialogue, it might be argued that there is then really no problem. If they are saying they love and/or want each other, then why aren't they loving each other and why aren't they happy? Although the metapoetic dialectic just discussed makes eminent sense, given our experience of dialectics, the subjective dialogue implied by this analysis does not correspond to our notions of common sense or the human experience. Hence the final and most convincing reason for the assumption that these are two separate poems joined together for the sake of some sort of novelty, or because it was the trendy thing to do to add popular poems to one's own courtly compositions, or because the court poets are folklorists *avant la lettre,* as García Gómez has claimed, or for whatever other reason one can think of.

But such a line of reasoning, however logical in terms of personal expectations and experiences, may be irrelevant in the case of a poem, unless, of course, we are expecting poetry, or at least these poems, to be like life. There is implicit in the reflexive avoidance of such a reading the assumption that the goal of the lovers' declarations of love and unhappiness is eventual union and happiness, as it is in the archetypical romance, and that a reading in which both lovers express something tantamount to "I love you. Why don't you love me?" *to each other* would be incongruous.

But what is involved here is a specific poetic system that, like many others, is not dependent on its logical consistency with rules of known human behavior for its meaning or value. In fact, within this poetic system it would seem that union and happiness in the external frame of reference are clearly not the goals. As a love song, the lament has no goal except for its own expression (in this case composition and/or singing). *Within* the poem the racking unhappiness, the treachery or coldness or abandonment of the loved one, the unrequitedness, are all things that are sung about. While in the world outside they may be obstacles to be resolved or overcome, our analysis of this as poetry must recognize that they are obstacles that are created and must be maintained if there is to be a song at all. The unity that validates the poem is internal. Satisfaction or happiness in an externally judged context is antithetical to the genre; it would in fact, negate such poetry altogether. Such a reading or understanding of the *muwashshaḥāt* would indicate that what is involved here, in terms of poetics and the governing love ideology, is necessary and desired unhappiness and mutual unrequitedness.

But all of this begins to sound familiar. In fact, if we pose here the question of what happens if we assume not only that the poem is Andalusian but also that as such it is comparable to other Romance courtly poetry, poetry to which it is related within a complex cultural network[12] and that is part of the same cultural universe, such a reading might not seem so odd. In fact, this particular view of a love system that is, by most people's personal standards, perversely bent on perpetual unhappiness, is far from novel in the literature we are more accustomed to dealing with. The existence of such a system underlying the courtly poetry of Provençal courtly love lyrics was widely publicized by the publication of Denis de Rougemont's *L'Amour et l'Occident*. De Rougemont's notions have waned in popularity in recent years, but such a decline is attributable in great measure to other factors: De Rougemont waxed normative at times, being preoccupied with what he assumed was the poor effect that such an ideology had had sociologically in the development of Western culture, its idealizing of unfulfillable love and deprecating of the virtues of fulfilling, married love. But his general concept is one shared, *grosso modo*, with scholars such as Gaston Paris, who preceded him and who coined the term "courtly love," and others whose research has followed.[13]

It is not easy to dismiss the general and fundamental analysis of the ideological system that governed the expressions of love found in most Provençal *cansos* as elaborated by such scholars, despite their very different perspectives on the source of such a concept of love. The passionate love expressed, and by extension defined, in these poems was both unhappy and what many call "adulterous" by its very nature—"interdicted" is perhaps a better term, since it is essentially disassociated from any specific sociological state. The love that one sang about, the true love of poetry, was a priori unrequited and unrequitable: requitedness leads to happiness and happiness leads to a very different kind of poem, or to no poem at all. One is tempted to paraphrase Tolstoy in characterizing the ground rules of much love poetry of this period: "All happy lovers are alike, unhappy lovers are unhappy in different ways."

If by adulterous we mean not the technical state of love outside the marriage contract but more loosely, as most poems indicate, the lack of a permanent and fulfilling union with the desired one, then it becomes quite difficult to quarrel with such a reconstruction of the poetics or "rules" of love that dominate the body of Provençal love poetry.[14] To counter this position by saying that not all *cansos* (or all *muwashshaḥāt*, for that matter) adhere to this scheme is not a convincing refutation of the conclusion that such a system does govern a sizable portion of the poems of these schools.

And if this view seems reasonable, the next logical step in our comparison is to ask what the *domna* of a Provençal poem would say if she too were given a poetic voice. If the similarities that can be noted at this rather elementary level are valid, perhaps they are manifested in other ways, and it would be a logical proposition that if the construct is valid for both poetic schools, she, like the female poetic voice in Hispano-Arabic poetry, would second or duplicate the lament of the troubadour rather than refute it or respond to it in a commonsense way. Conveniently enough, not much speculation along these lines is necessary, since there are several different sources for partially answering the question of whether the *domna* will show that, from her point of view too, love is unrequited.

Even though there are no poems that are directly parallel in form to the *muwashshaḥa*—one of the hallmarks of the classical Provençal *canso* is its single subjective "I" or voice—we do have poems written by the *trobairitz,* the women troubadours. Curiously enough, except for the technical changes imposed by sex and gender (that is, he for she, feminine rather than masculine adjectival endings, and so forth), many of the poems are or could be identical to those written by the composer's male counterparts.[15] The female poetic voice sings of the same kind of unrequited and unfulfilled love, and the concomitant unhappiness, as does her male counterpart, using formulas and images very similar to those that are characteristic of the poetry whose voice is a male "I." These are not, contrary to the sort of logical expectations that have been applied to the *muwashshaḥāt,* poems that express her disdain for her poetic suitor, her *mépris,* her lofty and cold role as a *domna.* It is clear, then, that as far as one can take the analogy with different single poems, the pattern holds. To argue that this is merely because the poet, male or female, is following a strict poetic convention serves only to reinforce the argument: the sex of the suitor may, one must conclude, be reversed within this system, but not his or her sentiments regarding the varieties of unhappiness produced by love.

There is another important source of information and comparison, and this is in the Provençal poems that are, or appear to be, parodies. A parody of such a system would be one that entailed a clear subversion and mockery of the system's established rules. One of the most problematic of the troubadours in this regard has been, curiously enough, William of Aquitaine, both the first troubadour chronologically and long considered to be the founding father of these vernacular love songs, the "creator" of courtly love poetry. One of the features that has generated a certain degree of curiosity and puzzlement among readers of his songs is the complete mastery he exhibits of both the forms and the themes that would make the Provençal school so distinctive. For some, such a virtuoso command of a less-than-simple poetic system in its very first poet has seemed hard to credit in a true pioneer, trying his hand at it *ex nihilo*.[16] Not surprisingly, the apparent lack of development in the earliest Provençal corpus, constituted by the poetry of William, is one of the factors that triggered the search for other sources, for a groundwork or inspiration or predecessors that enabled William to create the songs he wrote.

One of the most surprising features of his repertoire of eleven songs is that while several of them are classic expressions of the sentiments of courtly love, there are several that seem to be readable most readily as parodies of that same kind of love and its characteristic attitudes.[17] This is a delicate matter, since it is difficult to posit how there can be a parody of something that is still in the very process of coming into existence. To some scholars, such poems in William's repertoire have suggested that he was sufficiently cognizant of an already well-developed system that he was able not only to emulate it but also to mock it.[18]

In any case, it is not difficult to read, for example, his "Farai un vers, pos mi somelh," as a parody. If the poetics, the rules, of the mocked love system are that both parties are willing and active participants in the scheme of things, that both of them desire unrequitedness and unhappiness because they are essential to poetry itself, then we would expect to find quite the opposite in parodic poems. And indeed we do. This particular poem is about a trio of insatiables. In fact, as it turns out, the male is more easily sated than the females. This is a standard medieval misogynist theme, but it is also a clear mockery (whether intended or not) of the cold and removed *domna,* whose virtue is characterized by her inaccessibility and her desirability, in great measure created by her stoniness. Moreover, union is the object of all of these poetic characters, and union is indeed achieved. These women, antitheses and mockeries in their behavior of the one who is idolized in other poems, are yet described as "Domnas . . . de mal conselh . . . cellas c'amor de cavalier tornon a mals" ("Ill-advised women who turn to evil the love of a knight").

An equally intriguing example is that of one of the best-known poems of the *scuola siciliana,* the first school of courtly poetry in an Italian vernacular, a school whose dependence on the Provençal corpus is a part of the standard canon of criticism but whose interaction with the Arabic poetry of the same court, that of Frederick II, has been considerably less explored. The poem is "Fresca rosa aulentissima," written by one of Frederick's notaries, Cielo d'Alcamo. It is a lengthy poem in dialogue form. It is also known and often referred to as the "Contrasto," a title suggesting its essential structural feature, a dialogue of disagreement. As with William's poem, the parodied aspects of the courtly love poetics are several. Of special interest in this discussion is the role of the female voice. Along with the male voice to which it responds in the dialogue, the female protagonist is as interested in union as the suitor whom she pretends, at least for a while, to reject.

To describe the poem as a long poetic tease would not be inaccurate. Both parties are actively seducing each other, in different ways, and at the end we realize that the seduction has worked and that union and at least temporary happiness are the result. But long before that the reader has perceived that it is all a game: the pseudo- or mock-*domna's* double-entendres and not-so-veiled counterseduction leave little doubt as to her intentions. The point-by-point reversal of the rules of an underlying system where neither party hears the other's seductive advances because he or she is singing and is only listening to his or her own song of lament, is apparent. Here each one is attempting to outwit the other in achieving the most respectable possible cover for union, and the point is to outwit the system. Here they listen to each other quite carefully.[19]

Other examples that ratify the basic model abound. One of particular interest is a *tensó* of Rambaut de Vaqueiras, which begins "Domna, tant vos ai pregada" ("Lady, so often have I asked you . . ."). In this poem, which is also a dialogue between a male and a female voice, the male voice speaks in the classical *koiné* of literary Provençal and uses the standard lamenting formulas of courtly poetry. The lady, however, when she responds, speaks in a different vernacular, and the crudity and overt sexuality of her words and tone leave little doubt that she is, in fact, no lady, no *domna* at all, at least not in the way that the male voice's praise would have led one to believe. The parody is indicated both by the fact that the dialogue is productive—that is, both parties listen and respond to each other, in contravention of the most basic rule that the plea must be unheard, the love unrequited—and by the fact that both do wish to achieve union—which would be interdicted by courtly poetics, in which the virtues of this kind of love emerge only and precisely because union is unattainable.

As in William's "Farai un vers" and in the Sicilian "Contrasto," the most overt indication of the reversal of rules and mores is the hardly disguised lack of modesty and traditional virtue on the part of the females. In the Sicilian dialogue the lady at least pretends, but she gives herself away nonetheless through the crassness of her language, a dialect that is not the literary one but a garden-variety vernacular.

If from such a variety of poetic sources we deduce that one of the notable features of courtly love poetry is that it relishes dissatisfaction, being the poetry of love unsatisfied, then even the single highly subjective *canso* should reflect this. It is true that such *cansos* can only portray the feelings of the loved one indirectly through the prism of the dissatisfaction of the suitor, but all the same, and despite the tendency of some critics to externalize and sociologize the causes of the poet's sung unhappiness, many studies of the *canso* have concluded that it is, in so many words, sought unhappiness. This was the feature, after all, that de Rougemont singled out and found so censurable in his reading of Provençal poetry, the feature that Gaston Paris concluded was turned into adultery in prose narrative, the feature that Denomy found to be so fundamentally un-Christian, and the feature that seems so absurd to scholars such as Robertson, who view it as a description of real life rather than as a poetic system.

The principal value of reading the more subjective *canso* from this perspective is that it allows the reader to see that the obstacles in the way of the fulfillment of love, of the establishment of a satisfying union, are more internal and poetic than they are external and social. The cliché that courtly love is technically adulterous, that the *domna* is married to someone else and that this is a significant obstacle, is, indeed, illusory. Few *cansos* make explicit any commonsense, lifelike reasons for the nature of the disappointment they express. When they do, or appear to, as in the famous case of Jaufré Rudel and his *amour lointain,* numerous studies debate its meaning.[20] It is the disappointment itself, too often without logical reason, that is the subject of this poetry. The obstacles, when and if they are specified, are rarely if ever as significant as the simple fact of unfulfillment, which is clearly at the center of the poetry's concerns.

It only confirms the solipsistic nature of such poetry to note that it is very often explicitly concerned with itself, overtly cognizant of its own value. It is often its self-stated and self-centered divorce from external values and references that makes it more, rather than less, interesting and amusing. Such an attitude is succinctly characterized in William's "Farai un vers de dreyt rien" ("I will make a poem of exactly nothing"), but it also receives voice in numerous other ways in other poems of the Provençal and Sicilian schools. It is hard to escape the tentative conclusion that this is poetry very much for itself and conscious of itself as its own principal pleasure and subject, and that the recurring theme of unsatisfactory love is a thematic vehicle particularly well suited to this sort of poetic narcissism, so characteristic of modern poetry. Perhaps it is a recognition of this that has made such poetry a favorite with many modern poets and that justifies the praise of a poet–critic such as Pound, whose views on the superiority of "purely" self-referential poetry are as clear in his critical writings as they are in his own poetry.[21]

It is equally difficult to escape the conclusion that there are strong affinities between the original, and in some ways revolutionary, poetry of William and his progeny and the hardly less revolutionary Andalusian poetry of the *muwashshaḥa*, or that a study of these two groups of poems side by side can give us a more complete and convincing picture of the nature of the innovations that were taking place in lyric poetry throughout Europe in the eleventh and twelfth centuries. An examination of the poems of both schools aimed at seeking out the distinguishing features of courtly love from such a perspective would lead us to conclude that the "rules" of courtly poetry written in Romance are quite similar to those that must be assumed in order to read the *muwashshaḥāt* with their *kharjas* as integral and meaningful poems in their own right.

In the different schools of poetry there is an often hidden, but necessarily implied, dialogue in which the two would-be lovers do not respond productively (in external terms) to each other. This is not a literary love system in which the obstacles to fulfillment lie outside the poet-lover-protagonist himself (or herself), as in a *roman d'aventure*, for example. Rather, such obstacles are intrinsic to both the love and the poem and are not antithetical to what drives the poet-lover. As we can see in the muteness of the Provençal *domna* and, in a startling fashion, in the brief and extremely pointed reply of the female voice in the *muwashshaḥa*, the love qua love is in and of itself a dead end. It is a dialogue between two people who are deaf to each other, intent not on yielding to love but on singing of its unhappiness, the Francesca who does not name Paolo. Only in having an object, unrequitable love, that is unproductive can this poetry be so fertile, so continually able to sing of despair and of the kinds and causes of despair.

This thematic comparison is not the only factor that would lead one to conclude that there are affinities between the two schools of poetry that make them quite comparable. The radical introduction of the vernacular into courtly poetry, the use of rhyme in ways that were innovative in terms of classical poetic antecedents, the development of complex strophic forms that would set new standards—these are but the most immediately apparent features. A more refined, extensive, and detailed analysis of parallelisms, shared features, and contextual innovations is of considerable potential value. Such a study might well conclude that formal and thematic features characteristic of both the schools are tied to each other in essential ways. And such a study would have value whether or not it went on to conclude that there were also productive filiations, genetic and inspirational links, in the intricate developments of cultural and literary features present in both traditions.

What has been perceived as being of very questionable value, however, is the ideology of love that emerges from our reading of some of this poetry. One of the questions that has frequently presented itself to many is whether this can reasonably be described as poetry that is in praise of love, in any conventional sense. It might more plausibly be suggested that in being poetry in praise of itself and of poetry primarily, the poems actually subvert the apparent praise of love that the poet seems to be conveying to us. Is this really, as de Rougemont and others maintained, a glorification of such an attitude toward love? Perhaps in considering the Hispano-Arabic texts as part of the European body of courtly love poems, a different view might emerge. It would appear that the Arabic texts allow us to see, more clearly than could the Provençal poetry alone, that the poems embodying this love ideology could be read as excellent examples of a condemnation of the love whose praises they at first seem to be singing.

The structure of many of the courtly love poems, and this is equally but differently true in the Provençal and Sicilian texts, emerges as a closed and unhearing, uncommunicative dialogue. This constitutes a clear subversion of any direct verbal praise of the love or lover found within the texts. Many critics have long been aware that such self-subversion is far from rare in poetic texts, medieval as well as modern, and it is not difficult to note it in these poems. Unless we resort to mutilating the *muwashshaḥāt,* it is clearly a feature of the Andalusian texts, in which the overt praise of lover and love is almost viciously contradicted (and thus subverted) by the response of the loved one. Also, Provençal and other courtly love poems that are not explicitly dialogic often involve the same kind of denial of the validity of such love. This poetry is filled with variegated but analogous devices, such as structurally pairing emotions that cancel each other out and create voids and that in other ways indicate in a fashion quite similar to that of the *muwashshaḥāt* the essential unproductiveness of such love.

Thomas, the "courtly" *Tristan* poet, succinctly summarizes such characteristics in the verses quoted at the beginning of this chapter and elsewhere throughout the extant fragments of his Anglo-Norman poem. This is love that is equal to death; it is love, as he says elsewhere, without issue or product. So, too, do the poets of both the Provençal and the

Hispano-Arabic lyrics indicate in any number of ways that the love they sing of has no end but itself—itself as the poetry, that is—and for them this is apparently not only sufficient but delicious. All other issue is blocked, interdicted, by the nature of the love itself, which consequently has no other value, no existence except in the generation of the poetry, for it can generate nothing else. It is no doubt a glorification not of love but of literature.

It is equally apparent that this ultimately solipsistic and secular depiction of love, equally un-Christian and un-Islamic, was clear, and was ultimately unacceptable, to close observers, some of the closest, in fact. That it was judged negatively and often condemned by religious authorities, who had both a vested interest in protecting respect for traditional values and a far weaker interest in protecting poetry itself, is amply documented and neither surprising nor particularly intriguing. But dissent among the ranks of fellow poets, those more keenly interested in the uses of poetry than in ecclesiastical authority, is considerably more to the point.

Andreas Capellanus, whose *De amore*—so often cited as an encyclopaedia, guidebook, or rule book of courtly love—is unequivocal in his condemnation of it, although the existence and contents of the third book, the palinode, are less frequently adduced than the first two, which embody an inventory of the features of courtly love. His detailed knowledge of the system, revealed and set out in such detail in the first part of his work, is perhaps in some measure a rhetorical device. It establishes its author as one who knows full well of what he speaks—and of what he disapproves, a fact that cannot be understood if we disregard the third book, which rejects the teachings of the love apparently praised in such poetry. Andreas's overriding consideration, the praise of the more productive and legitimate love of God, is hardly incidental.

No less condemning of this love of self and one's own suffering and poetry, nor less knowledgeable of what he is rejecting, is Andreas's Andalusian counterpart, Ibn Ḥazm of Córdoba. His *Ṭauq al-Ḥamāma* (*The Dove's Neck-Ring*) is also, at first glance, a compendium of, and guidebook to, such poetry and to the love embodied in it. The *Ṭauq* includes numerous examples of the poetry itself, much of it Ibn Ḥazm's own.[22] His palinode, although briefer than Andreas's, is no less clear. But it is just as often ignored or dismissed—not surprisingly, perhaps, given how inconvenient it appears in the context of what is described as a poet's guidebook. And Ibn Ḥazm is indeed a poet, clearly a master of the very rules he ultimately condemns and proscribes as un-Islamic. Interestingly, and ironically, in both cases the palinodes have often been dealt with in a fashion parallel to that adopted with respect to the contradictory elements within the *muwashshaha*. They have been assumed, in one way or another, not to inform the rest of the text.

But perhaps the most masterful, perceptive, and creative of those who saw, understood, and were appalled by courtly love was a poet who was able to transform it rather than to detail and then reject it. It took an exceptional master to be able to take so many of the features of a poetry that was, indeed, virtuous and beautiful but not productive or useful by ethical religious standards and transform it and many of its essential features into the essential poetry of love of another and of God rather than of self. He would use it, indeed, as he put it, to "dicer di lei quello che mai non fue detto d'alcuna" ("to say about her what no one had ever said about a woman before"). And he did, in fact, more systematically and completely transform the system of frustration and unfulfillment, which before him had served no worthier cause than the regeneration of poetry, into emotions that would serve a much higher cause: the knowledge and love of God. From the point of view of his own moral system, he saw the weaknesses of his poetic predecessors, but he did not despise their poetry. He saw a way of developing it and using it so that his own poetry would have all of its merits but none of its defects. And when Dante wrote the *Vita nuova*, a prologue to his *Commedia*, he was referring both to a new life for the soul of the young protagonist and a new life for love poetry itself.

Notes

1. What we see here once again is that the diachronic and synchronic aspects of the question may be advantageously separated, as long as one does not forget that this is a question of focus rather than of any absolute independence. See my discussion in Chapter 1.

2. The length of the following digression on the question of the essential unity of the Andalusian *muwashshahāt* is justified by the extent to which the problems detailed here have almost overwhelmingly molded scholarship in the field. In great measure, scholars have been acting out the problem illustrated in the texts: that of the merging of two originally separate poetic traditions. Most critics, however, have not gotten beyond the separation to the question of how both are affected and transformed by the poetic union. In the discussion that follows, the segregationist views of Arabists, who believe that the *muwashshahāt* are understandable in terms of the classical canon of Arabic poetry, are best represented by Jones. See especially Jones 1983 and my discussion of his views in Chapter 1, note 5. There is some irony in his maintaining that the reunification of these texts can be achieved only in terms of a divorce from Romance. The degree to which *kharjas* have been studied without reference to what they mean *as part of* the *muwashshahāt* is reflected in the two basic handbooks. García Gómez 1965 was the first edition of the *kharjas* "en su marco" to appear after the 1948 Stern discovery. Almost all the studies detailed in Hitchcock 1977, both before and after the availability of an edition that would give the reader some idea of what the full poem was like, are concerned primarily or exclusively with the *kharjas* as entities that are clearly

considered separable from the main text in terms of their meaning. See also Armistead 1980 for an updating of Hitchcock's bibliography. Part of the explanation, of course, is that these texts have been and are extraordinarily difficult to decipher, and many studies have been philological in nature, concerned with establishing decent texts. But the larger question of whether they are Arabic or Romance supervenes and is often the focus of the discussion that follows the establishment of such texts.

3. The best examples of such studies are certainly Frenk-Alatorre 1975 and Cummins 1977. I must reiterate that there is nothing wrong with such studies, far from it. Clearly, the *kharjas* have meaning in terms of the body of popular Romance refrains and other poetry of which they are, from one perspective, a part. However, such studies do not tell us what the refrains meant in terms of the *muwashshaḥāt* into which they were woven by the poets. Poetic meaning (like all other meaning) is, after all, contextual, and while these studies have provided valuable insights into one kind of context (the popular one from which the *kharjas* derived) there are no parallel studies that approach the question of what they meant in the context of the courtly *muwashshaḥāt*.

4. As I discussed in Chapter 2, the question of appropriate perspective is not a negligible one. Thus, in terms of a discussion of the larger role played by the *muwashshaḥāt* in the development of courtly poetry in the adjacent courts of Provence (a question not addressed here, incidentally, but which might logically follow from my own comparative work), the fact that there *may* be some pre-Islamic antecedents for such poetry is irrelevant—and obfuscating.

5. For Ibn Bassam and a summary of the other earliest critics, see Monroe 1974: 28–30.

6. For Ibn Sanāʾ al-Mulk, see also Fish Compton 1976, especially Chapter 1.

7. The basic sources for full texts, as well as for general explanations of the poetry, are García Gómez [1965] 1975 and Monroe 1965 and 1974. See also García Gómez 1956 and Cantarino 1969. It is worth reiterating, since the objection will undoubtedly be raised to the brief analysis of the poetry that follows, that these are generalizations and are far from universally applicable to the entire body of *muwashshaḥas*.

8. It is as well established as anything in this thorny field can be that the Mozarabic *kharjas* are predominantly feminine voices. It is not insignificant that Monroe and Swiatlo (see Monroe 1979) have found that the Arabic *kharjas,* those more classicized, are predominantly masculine. Monroe's sociohistorical explanation of this phenomenon agrees with my own. Monroe notes that Romance was associated with the world of women both because of the poetic tradition and the fact that al-Andalus was, particularly at the outset, divided between male conquerors (Arabic speakers) and female natives (Romance speakers). Such an explanation adds, in fact, a further opposition that is present in such poetry, the social and historical one related to the effects of the conquest on the social structure.

9. The musical question is no less thorny in this case than it is in any other area of medieval music. But, once more, what draws one's attention is the fact that many of the problems faced by scholars working on troubadour musical composition are remarkably like the issues raised in the Hispano-Arabic sphere. See, as a general reference, Seay 1975 and Reese 1940:221. Reese discusses the problem of the disjuncture/unity of the refrain in the *canso* and describes a situation that could fit, verbatim, that of the *muwashshaḥa/kharja*. This issue is explored in greater detail in Haxen 1982. On the poetic fertility of diglossia, see Bakhtin 1981:76–78.

10. See especially Cantarino 1974 and Monroe 1976a, as well as the Jones-Armistead/ Monroe polemic cited and discussed in Chapter 1, note 5.

11. I will limit myself here largely to the erotic *muwashshaḥāt,* although I fully realize that that was not the exclusive subject of the genre. The legitimacy of a procedure of selecting one subgroup of poems unified by their common theme to be studied separately from others is indisputable.

12. There is a vastly complex network of possible ties and levels of connection among the many different poetries involved. Many of the influences may be two-way or even multiple interrelations: the Romance substratum of popular poetry in Iberia (shared with Provence) was instrumental in shaping the *muwashshaḥāt,* which in turn had an influence on the developments in the earliest troubadour poetry, which, again, had a certain foundation in some classical Latin poetry, but aspects of the latter, which were in fact part of the Greek heritage, influenced Andalusian neo-Platonism, and so forth. See Monroe 1975, 1976b, and 1979 for a discussion of some of these levels of interconnection.

13. C. S. Lewis 1936 was an early exploration of the subject. De Rougemont 1956 sought the origins of this distorted kind of love in the Cathar heresy. But Denomy (1944, 1945, and 1947) sees its origins in a variety of philosophical currents prominent in al-Andalus. See also Giffen 1971 for a skeletal presentation of most of the Arabic treatises on profane love, many of which are discussed by Denomy. Zumthor 1943 is useful on Andreas. See, more recently, the review of the various theories in Press 1970 and Frappier 1972.

14. As Frappier 1972 and other studies point out, the question of whether it is literally adulterous is a red herring. Gaston Paris's analysis was based on a narrative text, the *Chevalier de la charrette,* which may have transformed the prohibition of satisfaction—which is more amorphous in the poetry—into something that could be narrated.

15. See texts and commentary in Bogin 1976 and Paden 1981. In the latter study Paden states: "The value of Castelloza's poetry lies in part in its contrastive effect, since it shows us what a troubadour such as Bernart de Ventadorn did *not* sing, although he could. . . . [she is] . . . daring to suffer without relief" (170).

16. Here the concept of what is first, of what has primacy, is more elaborate than it would be later in literary history, extending to include the language itself as well as poetic forms and a very particular thematic system.

17. For William's texts and those of other Provençal troubadours, see Goldin 1973 and Hill et al. 1973.

18. It is useful at this juncture to reiterate that influence does not mean copying. Menéndez Pidal makes two points in comparing Andalusian and other European poetry: that there are too many affinities to be ignored, but also that there are too many differences for one to be an imitation of the other (1955:66–68). But this statement reflects, more than anything else, the kind of shackles with which those exploring the Arabist theory have had to work for so long, the need to prove extremely specific imitations or copyings. One of the major benefits in the revised operating image I have proposed is that it would see influence in this sphere in the same complex and invariably adaptive ways that we normally see in the results of literary confluence and interaction.

19. For editions of this and other Sicilian and Italian poems see Contini 1960. Note also that the geography evoked by Cielo d'Alcamo in the "Contrasto" includes such places (where he has searched for a "donna cortese") as Constantinopoli, Soria, Babilonia, and Barberia.

20. Some of the studies devoted to the question of just what that "love from afar" expression means are Frank 1942, Spitzer 1944, Cluzel 1957, and Walpole 1960. In his study Spitzer felicitously adapts the expression "to have and have not" as a description of the kind of love involved. Perhaps "to have not" would serve just as well. See Zumthor 1970 for a full and convincing analysis of the "circularity" of the *canso,* a description that would apply equally well to the *muwashshaḥāt* as I read them.

21. See Eliot 1972 and Kenner 1953.

22. There are several translations of Ibn Ḥazm: Nykl 1931 (English), García Gómez 1952 (Spanish), and Arberry 1953 (English).

CHAPTER FIVE

Italy, Dante, and the Anxieties of Influence

Lo buon maestro disse: "Omai, figliuolo,
s'appressa la città c'ha nome Dite
coi gravi cittadin, col grande stuolo."

E io: "Maestro, già le sue meschite
la entro certe ne la valle cerno,
vermiglie come se di foco uscite

fossero. Ed ei mi disse: "Il foco etterno
ch'entro l'affoca le dimostra rosse,
come tu vedi in questo basso inferno"

The good master said, "Now, my son, the city that is
named Dis draws near, with its grave citizens, with its great
garrison."

And I, "Master, already I discern its mosques there within
the valley, red as if they had come out of the fire."

And he to me, "The eternal fire that blazes there within
makes them show red, as you see, in this nether hell."
—Dante, *Commedia*

There can be little question that Dante Alighieri and his diverse works, both fiction and nonfiction, stood at a significant crossroads in the development of European artistic and intellectual life. Over the succeeding centuries, the vast power of his magnum opus alone has earned him a virtually unrivaled place in the hearts and minds of Europeans. Rumor has it that, after the Bible, no text is more studied in our tradition than the *Divine Comedy,* and its centrality to literature in a number of languages, English among them, is difficult to ignore. Fortunately, the seemingly endless richness of that text alone warrants the lavish critical attention it has received and undoubtedly will continue to receive. It is a well from which it appears impossible to dip too often.

But not all aspects of Dante's world and works have received equal, or equally tempered, exploration. The question of what role and what effect material, artistic, and intellectual incursions of Arabic-European provenance had on his world and on his worldview has been left largely unexplored by those who have devoted themselves to the study of Dante. This is in some measure because of the constraints of our own view of that world, one that has not considered those features central to the medieval period, and no less because Dante himself is so fundamentally a Christian and in terms of literary ancestry, so often explicitly Latinizing. It is hardly surprising that the general medieval image of the Graeco-Latin-Christian tradition should have had an especially tight grip when we have turned to study what can accurately be described (to cite just one of many accurate descriptions of so polysemous a work) as the greatest Christian apologia ever written.

Yet it was precisely in an atmosphere in which the primacy of the Christian system and the Christian ethos that Dante so deeply revered and cherished was under severe challenge that his *Commedia* and his many other works were written. It is time to explore the possibility that Dante was neither ignorant of the cause of many of the transformations that had affected (he might have said afflicted) Europe in the previous two centuries, nor that he was exempt from their influence, in that a reaction to them was an important conditioning factor in his own attitudes and writings. It could be seen that the fork at which Dante found himself led, along one path, precisely to the new choices, the new options, that had been created by the Arabic-inspired cultural phenomena to which many of his peers had been drawn. That he chose the other path makes it all the more important that we attempt to understand the road not taken.[1]

It was a path well traveled in thirteenth-century Italy, although most of our literary studies and textbooks hardly even suggest it. Both the early part of the century and the beginnings of Italian literature are dominated by the stature and the power, particularly on the cultural front, of Frederick II. Under his patronage was born and thrived (for as long as Frederick did) the first lyric poetry in an Italian vernacular. The sources and impetus for this poetry, the *scuola siciliana,* have always been identified as being in Provençal courtly poetry, but there is little doubt that other poetry was also present, other songs heard, in the hallways and *salotti* of Frederick's courts at Palermo and elsewhere. Part of one such song might well have been this:

Mi hanno ucciso sguardi di donne simili
a statue, fra un candore di denti e
labra di scura porpora;
Dopo aver detto che la mia giovanile
follia si era ormai conclusa, eccola
rendermi nuovamente pazzo di amore e di
passione;
Nel suo volto ho visto la luna,
sorridente nel suo viso radioso:
apparsami, ho interrogato il mio occhio:
l'aveva vista da sveglio oppure in
sogno?
Quello sguardo è un vero enigma! rende
infermo il corpo ma lo risana anche!

(I have been killed by the looks of
women like statues, between the
whiteness of teeth and lips of dark
purple;
After having said that my youthful folly
was now over, here it is once again
making me insane with love and passion;
In her face I have see the moon,
smiling with her radiant look. Did she
appear to me, I ask my eyes, while I was
awake or in a dream?
That look is a true mystery! It makes my
body sick, but it also cures it.)

(Italian translation from the Arabic is from Rizzitano 1958:376;
English translation from the Italian is author's)

This poem, and a reputed twenty thousand verses written by a hundred and seventy poets, remain almost completely unknown. Students of the *scuola siciliana* are deprived of access to that earlier *scuola sicilana:* the Arabic poetry written in Sicily, from the tenth through the thirteenth centuries, of which this fragment is but a minute part. This lapse in our knowledge of the period, of the flavor of court life, of this other world that existed within the same walls as the one we think we know so well, is a serious one.

For one thing, any student of Italian literature can see this lyric fragment's myriad connections not only with the Italian *scuola siciliana* but also with other trends in mainstream *duecento* (thirteenth-century) Italian poetry. The Arabic-Sicilian poem certainly contains its fair share of traditional courtly love motifs, which are also characteristic of the earliest examples of Italian vernacular courtly poetry, motifs it likewise shares with the Provençal courtly love tradition: the physical beauty of the white-faced Lady, her statuesque coldness and aloofness, the piercing and devastating effects of a single look from her eyes, the literally sickening effects of love and passion on the body of the lover, and so on. It also contains hints of thematic developments that would characterise the *dolce stil nuovo* and later Italian lyrics, including those of Petrarch: the ascription, to both the lady and the love itself, of an angelic, even beatifying, nature and effect, the confusion between dream and reality, between the earthly and the heavenly, even a suggestion of the topos of the "giovanile follia," or youthful error, which will become so fundamental a part of the poetics of love both in Dante, (especially in the *Vita nuova*) and in Petrarch, whose *Canzoniere* opens with exactly that image.

But the possibilities of exploring further the connections, parallels, and interactions between the Sicilian poetry—written in Arabic under both Arab and Norman rule—and that written in Romance during the last reign of a great Norman monarch are slim indeed. Our cognizance of the Arabic poetry of Sicily is conspicuously poor, for a variety of reasons, although the documentary evidence of its abundance before and after the Norman conquest indicates that this is hardly because it was inconspicuous in Sicily during those years.[2]

There are but two extant collections of the poetry of Sicilian poets who wrote in Arabic, those of Ibn Ḥamdīs and al-Ballanūbī, and neither is accessible to the Romanist. Such a situation clearly reflects a deeply ingrained belief in the utter separability of the Arabic and Romance traditions—even in Sicily, where they not only succeeded each other directly but overlapped for so long and in so many ways. But the greatest of the Sicilian *diwans* (anthologies of poetry), that which is known to have contained a vast and varied collection of poets (reputedly 170) and verses (reputedly some twenty thousand) did not survive to be neglected in the twentieth century. This was the anthology of the eleventh-century Sicilian philologist Ibn al-Qaṭṭāʿ. While knowledge and notice of it was widespread enough to inform us of its existence and of some of its general features, the original is lost, and today fragments are all that survive. These are mostly the bits and pieces in a mutilated form that were deemed worthy of posterior recollection and that were thus incorporated into later Arabic anthologies. Two fragmentary compilations of what was originally in the Ibn al-Qaṭṭāʿ collection, preserved in much later anthologies, have been published with some translations into Italian, although neither of these publications is easily accessible to an Italianist.[3]

There have been two principal causes for the poverty of surviving and accessible texts of the Arabic poetry of Sicily, poetry that, I reemphasize, flourished as much under the Normans, especially Roger and Frederick, as under the Arabic rule that preceded them. From the comments and insinuations of some of the later Arab compilers, as well as from the evidence provided by what they chose to include in, or omit from, their own *diwans,* it is apparent that much of the Sicilian poetic tradition, which deviated from the mainstream in certain ways, apparently seemed unintelligible, uninteresting, or scandalous to later compilers and philologists. It is a fate that should hardly surprise us, given the analogous fate of at least one part of the corpus of Hispano-Arabic poetry, the *muwashshaha.* What was preserved, clearly, was what was sufficiently classicizing to merit preservation. Some of the items excised on ideological or aesthetic grounds from the later pastiche of *diwans* are explicitly mentioned as unworthy of recollection, items such as odes to the Norman monarchs, including, apparently, a fair body of such elegiac poetry dedicated to Roger, Frederick's grandfather. We are left to speculate about what other kinds of poems may have been cut, what criteria, besides political and religious unsuitability, may have been applied to the process of selection for posterity.

Rizzitano believes, with much justification, that the only poems that were preserved were those that were sufficiently mainstream Arabic and not characteristically Sicilian in any way. Within such a general category, bilingual, bicultural poems, perhaps much like the *kharjas,* may have existed but were not preserved. If such compositions did exist, it is fairly certain that they would not have been included in later, highly pan-Arabizing and classicizing collections such as those that survive. That they existed (or at a minimum were known about) in Sicily is hardly less plausible. Sicily was very much under the cultural influence of al-Andalus, particularly during the latter's golden period and height of cultural preeminence while both areas were still under Arab domination. Numerous Sicilian poets made the pilgrimage to al-Andalus, among them Ibn Ḥamdīs, who went to Seville. The indigenous mixture of Arabic and Romance elements that allowed the *kharjas* to exist in the first place was no less strong in Sicily than in al-Andalus and, indeed, reached a special status under the Normans. If the *muwashshahāt* were never cultivated locally, they would nonetheless have been comprehensible to, and would have been appreciated by, the Sicilian poets, who clearly cherished and admired Andalusian literature.[4]

But the irony is that while in one sentence Rizzitano makes the point that the surviving Arabic poetry is hardly representative of what was written, sung, and appreciated in Sicily, he states in the next that such poetry has nothing at all to do with the Italian poetry written there, because the Sicilian Arabic poetry is too strictly classical to have anything to do with the new Sicilian Romance poetry. Thus, Rizzitano contributes in great measure to an additional impoverishment of our knowledge of the Arabic poetry of Sicily. This is in part because he makes the sweeping statement that none of it had anything to do with Italian vernacular poetry, including that which was *not* preserved by non-Sicilian Arabic anthologists because it was too Sicilian, too indigenous.[5] It is also because, as a result of this view, both he and other Arabists who share his beliefs have made precious little of what *has* survived available to their Romanist colleagues.

Although we are obliged to speculate on the probable nature of non-classical Siculo-Arabic poetry, little speculation is needed concerning the general status of the Arabic language and Arabic intellectual culture during the years of Norman domination, particularly under Frederick.[6] There can be little doubt, though one would never know it from our anthologies and histories of early Italian literature, that such poetry would have been far from ignored or marginal at the same court where the poems of the *scuola siciliana* were being written. This is true for both the poetry preserved—but for the moment unavailable—and for that which may be irreparably lost through the indefatigable editing of earlier generations.[7]

We do, however, have access to much poetry that undoubtedly was known by men of culture in Sicily from the tenth until the thirteenth centuries, a poetry they admired, studied, and sought out, the poetry of al-Andalus, the culture that was the fruitful and generous elder sister of Sicily's own under both Arabs and Normans. In imagining the cultural ambience at Frederick's court, we need to evoke the Arabic poetry of the Sicilians that had a long and prosperous tradition there, the odes to Roger and lost *muwashshahāt* and the classicizing poetry that is not.[8] But we might also remember that especially under Frederick, at the time of the rise of the *scuola siciliana,* the culture of al-Andalus was far from being a stranger at the Norman courts.

Yet every anthology and history of the literature presents a rather different picture of the ambience of that court. Seemingly, the only possible literary currents worthy of mention are the Provençal courtly lyric and the Latin tradition motivated by the revival of learning taking place in Palermo. But our image of this court and its culture needs substantial revision; it needs to be amplified to include a more accurate depiction of the other world that existed there and that Frederick cultivated so assiduously, and for which he was notorious throughout Europe in his own lifetime and beyond. Frederick's court was, indeed, a haven for those following that other path, and its poets wrote in an ambience literally saturated with every aspect of Arabic culture. As one of the most accomplished Arabists of his day, Frederick made his court an outstanding center of knowledge of all sorts, and traversing the hallways of his homes in Sicily were Arabic and Andalusian (Christian, Muslim, and Jewish) philosophers and other savants and translators, of whom the most prominent was Michael Scot. These were learned and cultured men, and, Andalusian or not, they knew and undoubtedly enjoyed the poetry that had put Andalusian literature on the map, the *muwashshaḥa* that had flourished in the previous century, the *zajals* of Ibn Quzmān, perhaps the poetry of Ibn al-ʿArabi, who was then still alive. And it was not just the "cultured" element of Frederick's court who cultivated and translated things Andalusian. Even the domestic aspects of the court were heavily Arabized, from harem to bodyguard to clothes—and who can doubt that music was as well?

To imagine that other members of his court, the poets whose names are so familiar to us—Cielo d'Alcamo, Pier della Vigna, Stefano Protonotaro—had no contact with this world is to be less than realistic. Frederick's palaces would have had to be neatly and tightly cloistered, his harem and its entertainers muted in their presence, the learned men for whom Arabic and Andalusian culture were the sources of all manner of enlightenment (from Michael Scot to Fibonacci) strictly segregated, the Arabic-speaking notaries a world apart from Cielo d'Alcamo, the Italian notary. A more convincing picture is certainly one in which such men rubbed shoulders, and the contemporary illustration at the front of this book depicts them just so. When they sat together to be entertained, the songs would have been in Arabic, or partially so, as well as in the nascent Italian literary dialect. Perhaps future studies of the *scuola siciliana* will begin to take such circumstances into account.

We can certainly be sure that such ties with the world of Arabic learning and culture were not ignored by the next generation of prominent Italian intellectuals. It seems likely that some of them, those who studied at Bologna, would have worked directly with the translations of Averroes that Frederick had sent to the university in 1227. However negatively some of them in the thirteenth-century may have felt about Michael Scot's and Frederick's adventures and proclivities, they certainly did not ignore them. That they and many of the other intellectual luminaries of the time were Arabized and Arabizing was no great secret, and that in the next generation Bologna had inherited the mantle as an intellectual hotbed, particularly of Averroism, would have been even more intimately known by Dante.[9]

No doubt such knowledge would have been a cause of some distress. Dante's tastes and ideology are well known, and such fraternizing with a world he clearly held in some contempt would have seemed reprehensible to him, but it certainly was known to him, at least from that perspective. One question this fact raises is why he remains so silent on the issue of the background and contributions of other kinds of poetry to that of the Sicilian poets whose poems he analyzes in the *De vulgari eloquentia*. Perhaps this question is answered in terms of his overall relationship with the Arabic-influenced Europe of his time and of the previous several centuries, the Toledo that Brunetto Latini had visited, the Sicily Frederick had made to rival Toledo itself, the Bologna that rivaled Paris and London in its study of Averroes.

The earliest prominent discussion of Dante's relationship with the Arabic culture of Europe in the Middle Ages did not get off to a propitious start. In 1926 an eminent Spanish Arabist named Miguel Asín Palacios published a book entitled *Islam and the Divine Comedy*,[10] which was the object of controversy, considerable derision, and ultimate banishment among Italianists. Asín argued that Dante had gotten his basic idea for the plot and some of the particulars of the *Divine Comedy* from the important Islamic tradition known as *mi'rāj*, the Prophet's descent to hell and ascent to heaven. Part of the rejection of Asín's thesis by Dante scholars stemmed from the seemingly outrageous nature of such a suggestion. If our view of the solidity and impenetrability of the Graeco-Latin-Christian heritage of the Middle Ages has been so deep-seated as to prevent, in many cases, reasonable consideration of the possible interaction of troubadours and their Arabic-singing confrères, its intractability with respect to *the* Christian author of the Middle Ages, Dante, can be well imagined. It is all well and good to suggest that poets of suspect dedication to the faith might have found something appealing and imitable in the world of Muslims. But Dante?

While this sort of reaction conditioned the rejection of the plausibility of such a borrowing, much of what Asín actually proposed did not help matters either. In fact, Asín was probably wrong in one important regard, and this would have been sensed and noted by even the most detached and evenhanded of critics. He assumed, or to most readers seemed to imply, that Dante had indulged in wholesale and quite detailed copying of a rather impressive body of texts. Most Dantisti justifiably reject any hypotheses of seemingly simplistic copying on the part of Dante. But Asín's instinct may have been quite correct.[11] Research on directly and indirectly related matters in the years since his book was first published, as well as the adoption of a different concept of the cultural gestalt of the Middle Ages and how we conceive of influence operating within it, all converge to indicate that Dante may indeed have been strongly affected, not only by knowledge of some variations of these specific texts, but also by the whole Arabic cultural and ideological entity, of which such texts may well have seemed emblematic.

There are several avenues through which Dante is most likely to have come to know something about the existence and nature of the texts that contain or summarize the legend of Muhammad's trip to the other world, a journey that begins in Mecca and ends at God's throne. But Dante would not have known them or about them in their classical Arabic versions, as Asín had speculated, but in several vulgarized versions of the legend that existed in both Latin and the vernaculars during his lifetime.

For a variety of reasons, in fact, knowledge of the *mi'rāj* tradition was quite widespread throughout Europe by the end of the thirteenth century, and surviving manuscripts of vulgarized versions of it in the Romance vernaculars are only one of the indications we have of its wide dissemination. In 1264, Alfonso the Wise, through the Toledan school of translators, which was the international European center par excellence for the dissemination of texts coming from the Arabic tradition, had ordered translated into French and Latin a previously existing Castilian version of the Arabic *mi'rāj* text that has come to be generally known as *The Book of the Ladder.* The translator Alfonso chose to carry out this particular task (at a center where many translators from many countries were available)[12] was a Sienese notary named Bonaventura da Siena.

It is quite a coincidence that another notary, the Florentine Brunetto Latini, who had been sent to plead the Guelf cause to Alfonso, happened to visit Toledo while this translation was being executed. But, although his sojourn was relatively brief (only a few months), the intellectual activities of the court that made Alfonso so well known can hardly have escaped Brunetto's notice. It is hardly surprising that his two major works, the *Tresors* and the *Tesoretto,* particularly the former, bear remarkable similarities to the kind of general encyclopedic-didactic work being translated and compiled in Castilian in Toledo at the time, although it is more common to find references to the influence of the *Roman de la Rose* on the *Tesoretto* than to the translations and new texts of the encyclopedic histories that characterize much of the work being done at Toledo.

It seems highly unlikely that Brunetto would not have known about the translation his fellow Tuscan, Bonaventura, was engaged in or that he would have kept this knowledge to himself during the twenty years after his return to Florence, when he played a particularly prestigious role as one of its leading intellectuals. But if he did choose to ignore the world he had personally witnessed, if he remained silent on the subject of the road he had traveled, others in Dante's extended intellectual circles certainly did not.[13]

Bologna in Dante's lifetime was permeated with the revolutions of thought and learning produced by the preceding two centuries of contacts, translations, and absorptions of texts from al-Andalus and other sources of knowledge of Arabic texts, such as Sicily. It would appear that Dante was an embattled exile in more ways than one. At least as significant as the physical isolation produced by his banishment from Florence was the increasing philosophical and religious isolation produced by the rapid and vigorous spread of radical Aristotelianism—that is, Averroism—in Bologna, the intellectual capital of Italy. The rationalist challenge to unreasoning faith and the correlative cultivation of the sciences (including modal linguistic philosophy) or such pseudosciences as medicine and astrology, which were based on a flourishing and sustained commerce with Frederick II's Sicily and also with Toledo, Paris, and London—all of which were sources of significant bodies of translations—was very much the movement of the day.

In the first half of the century such material had come from Frederick's court in ways as direct as from Michael Scot himself—the impresario, as Corti so well dubs him—of translations of Aristotle, Averroes, and Avicenna, among others. Discussions of the medical treatises of Avicenna and the Avicennists were widespread and influential both at Salerno and Bologna. Knowledge of the modistae and their universalist linguistic philosophy crept in during the latter half of the century. Its ties to Averroism and other Arabic thought on the one hand and to the linguistic philosophy of Italian writers of the *trecento* on the other are suggestive and have just barely begun to be explored.[14] The compelling attraction of the new philosophy and its handmaidens was hardly diminished as the year 1300 approached. The evidence of this is as varied as Taddeo Alderotto's vernacular translation of Aristotle's *Etica Nicomachea,* which had previously been translated into Latin from an Arabic edition, and the work of another Florentine doctor, Dino del Garbo.[15] In fact, the climax of interest in and discussion of all these different but related currents of thought came in the first decades of the fourteenth century in Bologna and Tuscany.

No matter how extensive, any itemization of such intellectual intercourse in the world of which Dante was a part would, in and of itself, fail to convey the general impact of such currents on people like Dante. But several general features of the late thirteenth- and early fourteenth-century intellectual currents in northern Italy, which were very much a part of Dante's background, do merit attention. The intellectual avant-garde of the period had turned to, and was excited by, philosophical texts and ideas of both Arabic and Greek provenance (Averroes and Avicenna on the one hand, Aristotle on the other) that were revolutionizing attitudes toward many issues, from medicine to linguistic philosophy.

Although postmedieval scholarship has largely ignored the fact, contemporaries were more than aware of the sources for such fascinating new theories, the provenance of coveted texts, and the translators of newly discovered tracts. They were Arabic, either in origin, translation, impetus, or orientation. For the Bolognese or Tuscan intellectual at the turn of the thirteenth century, the roots and often the texts of the intellectual revolution of which he might or might not be a part, were indubitably in the European Arabic tradition. They were available through commerce with Toledo or with the other capitals that had already taken advantage of the translations disseminated by that city: Paris, London, and Palermo (whose translators, thanks to Frederick II, had been able to do much of their work *in situ*). Finally, and perhaps most significant from the perspective of how Dante might have viewed such matters, much or all of this—as with most if not all revolutions or apparent revolutions—had for some time been anathema to many, and it still was.

What would have seemed to a conservative such as Dante to be the seduction by Averroism or its like of the best minds of his generation (or indeed, of his *primo amico* Guido Cavalcanti) must have been a horrifying and discouraging scene for Dante, since for him, as for Peter the Venerable, this intellectual seduction would ultimately result in spiritual perdition and eternal damnation. It is through Peter, ironically, that we can be relatively secure in our knowledge that Dante was at least aware of the supposed Muslim notions of heaven and hell and of the existence of a text that described the Prophet's voyage *oltretomba,* accompanied and guided by the Archangel Gabriel through mysteries both physical and theological.

In the middle of the twelfth century Peter the Venerable had sought to provide Christians with ample proof of the true dangers of Islam—dangers, Peter indicates, to which all too many Christians exposed themselves, though by and large unwittingly. His proofs and arguments for the pernicious nature of the religion of the Arabs is the Toledan Collection, a series of texts that includes the first translation of the Koran from Arabic into any language. But except for his translation of the Koran itself, Peter's translations were spurious and apocryphal, not part of Islamic scripture at all, although they served quite adequately his purposes of discrediting Islam. As I pointed out earlier, there is little or no reason to doubt that the material presented by Peter and described in his *Summa* and decried in the *Liber contra sectam sive haeresim Saracenorum* (all of which were integral parts of the collection) were widely accepted and believed to be part of the sacred books of Islam. And Peter's texts include allusions to and descriptions of both general Muslim concepts of heaven and hell (particularly in the *Summa*) and more specific references to Muhammad's trip to the other world (this primarily in the document called *Fabulae Saracenorum*).

Most astonishing of all is the discovery of Cerulli, who has extensively studied the fortune of these texts in Europe, that to the Toledan Collection were added versions in Latin or in the vernacular of, of all things, the *Kitāb al miˁrāj*, the *Book of the Ladder*. It is clear from textual evidence, in fact, that in at least one case it was the version of the *Libro della scala* that was translated by Bonaventura di Siena. It may well have been this version that was known to another Tuscan author of the next generation, Fazio degli Uberti, who in his *Dittamondo* describes both Muhammad's trip and the kind of heaven he found there. Fazio even names the book: "il libro suo che *Scala* ha nome." [16]

Dante's own direct, cited knowledge of some of the Arab philosophers is not extensive. It is limited primarily to passing mention, principally in the *Convivio,* of Avicenna, al-Gazel, Averroes, and others who were far less well known. [17] He was particularly intrigued with Averroes' theory of the "passive intellect," which he developed in his commentary on the *De anima* and which was much disputed by Aquinas and was cited by Dante in both *Convivio* IV, 13, and *Purgatorio* XXV, 62–66. It is clear, in fact, that if one considers only allusions to Arabs in the *Commedia* and the *Convivio* (primarily philosophers, but also other well-known figures, such as ˁAli and Muhammad) that Dante appears to have little knowledge beyond the standard medieval view of Islam and its progeny and certainly very little sympathy for it. Averroes, not surprisingly the most often cited, is mentioned primarily to point up his philosophical errors. And his place in limbo, along with Avicenna and Saladin (as opposed to hell, where Dante will place ˁAli and Muhammad) is perhaps explained by remembering how well known it was that the philosopher had incurred the wrath and condemnation of Islamic religious authorities. Dante may have considered this a mitigating factor, a vaguely redeeming feature of his activities. It may, on the other hand, be merely that Dante felt some compunction about damning the man who had, after all, made Aristotle and Plato available to his generation. All told, what Dante says directly about the Islamic world certainly confirms that he was little interested in it and nonchalant or even negative about its value.

So the question arises: If Dante did know about the *Kitāb al-miʿrāj* through Peter the Venerable's allusions to it or through one of the translations by Bonaventura da Siena (and quite possibly from both in the same manuscript), why and how would he have made any use of this story when he wrote his *Commedia?* How is it possible to assume he would have anything but contempt and condemnation for a story he probably believed to be part of the sacred texts of Islam, the religion whose mosques become the image for Dis itself, the very heart of hell? How could this most Christian of medieval writers, this most conservative defender of the faith, have been in any way influenced by such "scripture"?

But it is these observations themselves, along with a recognition that northern Italy—Tuscany and Bologna in particular—were virtually teeming with Averroist thought and its fruits, that give us part of the answer. It is not unreasonable to assume that some great challenge to the established Christian order must have existed to provoke Dante to write his *Commedia,* so magnificent an apologia for fundamental Christianity. Apologias of a moral or ideological system are rarely written in periods of calm and unquestioned belief. They are more frequently provoked by a serious challenge to the authority of such a system.

Little doubt can exist that there was a serious challenge to Dante's cherished system in his lifetime, a system he defends every step of the way during his journey in the *Commedia,* and he would certainly have identified that challenge, which to him must have seemed an omnipresent danger to many of those he respected and loved most, as Arabic in origin. Whether manifest in the loathsome magic of Michael Scot, in the completely un-Christian poetry of selfish love—poetry coming into Italy from the bastion of Arabism, Sicily, and from foreign courts that were rife with excommunicated monarchs and dangerous heresies—or in the most damaging philosophies of Averroes, that challenge lurked in many places, and it had triumphed in the hearts and minds of many.

What is particularly fascinating about assuming that such a scenario is essential to the motivations and problems of the *Commedia* is that it complements some of that work's most lucid and widely respected readings.[18] Far from contradicting the idea, for example, that Dante saw the *Com-*

media as a poem of conversion that synthesized theology and poetry and was a treatise on ethics meant to inspire people to action, to assert that he may have been creating a countertext to what he may have believed to be the sacred scriptures of a culture that threatened the integrity of Christianity is to reinforce the validity of such a view. It gives Dante's "logology" further meaning to realize that he did not sense *ex nihilo* that a new sacred text was needed to rouse Christians from their fascination with Arabic-Andalusian-Sicilian modes of thought. And it gives greater depth to our knowledge of his vision of paradise as something constructed of immateriality itself to imagine it as a far more redeeming alternative to the Muslim paradise that was, for him, the conceit of knowledge separate from the soul, well represented in the lush Muslim paradise that Peter the Venerable recounts. It is also congruent with my view that the pilgrim's guide is Virgil—the engagé poet of self-abnegation, a poet who represents the native Italian and the Roman heritage at the same time, a poet with a cause—and not Aristotle, for example, who would have better represented Reason. These are choices and developments in the *Commedia* that reflect the poet's championing of what was at the time apparently in danger of being replaced or superseded, his affirming that there was a battle to be fought, just as there was for Virgil.

If we begin rereading the *Inferno* in this context, we note that many of the cantos and characters that have been most fascinating and most problematic for Dante critics appear to address issues that are very much tied to the problems that the Arabic-Andalusian-Sicilian incursions presented for Dante. We may begin to see indications of the nature of the great challenge and danger in the self-centered, deaf literature of unproductive love. It is presented in Canto V, with a Francesca as oblivious to her unnamed lover in hell as any of those voices in the poetic texts described in the previous chapter. The literature of seduction is utterly self-centered, with the power to seduce only itself (Francesca is herself only a creation of Dante's) and having no further end.

The lower part of hell is a city of mosques (not *like* mosques, one notes). It is a part of hell that is ringed and introduced by the circle of heretics, its gateway a circle that itself does not appear to follow conventional Christian classifications of the sin of heresy, and which is not structured similarly to the other circles of hell.[19] It is odd, or so it has appeared, that heresy should play this particular role in Dante's hell. But is it really, if one considers the special threat posed by the special kinds of heresy one sees there? For there, most of all, one encounters the palpable anguish and fear with which Dante hints at Guido Cavalcanti's ruinous Averroism in

Canto X, a preoccupation so great that for one critic it seems to affect the entire structural plan of the *Commedia*.[20] But the spectre of Guido is not all that haunts this city of mosques, nor the only indication that Dante is more than just passingly concerned with the effects of Averroism. For this is the place where Frederick II languishes as an Epicurean, one who does not believe in the afterlife of the soul, a heresy ascribed by fundamentalists to all Averroists. This is also where Farinata degli Uberti, Guido's father-in-law and great-grandfather to Fazio (who would quote the *Scala* in his own work some years later) is enterred with Cavalcante Cavalcanti, Guido's father. In marvelous *contrapasso,* these men, who (for Dante) believed in the primacy of the intellect, are robbed of their intellectual powers, are incapable of understanding what should be elementary. Here, finally, is interwoven Guido's own "Donna me prega," reflecting an Averroist modality of the *dolce stil nuovo.* The issue here, of course, is not the accuracy of any of Dante's judgments or whether Guido really was an Averroist and "Donna me prega" an expression of that new faith in the power of Reason over the old faith. The point is that Dante clearly believed these things to be true and that he is pointing quite clearly at the mortal danger of belief in and admiration for a philosophy and a culture that in his mind (again the question of accuracy is irrelevant) embodied that new and false faith.

Canto XV, the canto of the sodomites, where we see the oedipal struggle with Brunetto Latini, presents the reader with the problem not only of why Brunetto is there—his damnation among the sodomites has long troubled critics—but why sodomy seems to be the sin of professional intellectuals and writers. But Brunetto's sin (and that of his fellows there) is not so different from that of Epicurians and Averroists. Like them, Brunetto, as Dante depicts him, believed that the soul is not immortal. For him, immortality is achieved through letters and learning, and this for Dante is clearly infertile and unnatural—thus the metaphor of sodomy. As with Guido, the sin is to have turned one's back on God and on fundamental Christian belief in the power of God as the only thing that is eternal. As with Guido, it is the sin and the hubris of those who believed that Averroism could supplant and contradict Christianity. It is the mark of the sort of intellectual revolution that swept much of Christendom. It is another of the sins of the city of mosques, the sin of belief in the power of reason over faith, that Averroes and his progeny had brought to Europe in the twelfth century.

Other passages concerning nether hell are further clarified if we recognize Dante's preoccupation with the negative effects of knowledge from and of the Arabic world. Is the image of Michael Scot, for example, condemned with the magicians and soothsayers in Canto XX, as one who "veramente de le magiche frodde seppe il gioco" ("truly knew the game of magical frauds"), simply a literal reference to his reputation as a *mago?* Or is it not more likely that it was also a thinly veiled allusion to the false magic (from a Christian point of view) of the texts he so abundantly translated and in which he apparently believed? Why is Muhammad himself cleft in two as a schismatic, a sower of religious dissent, a categorization that has troubled some critics because it would imply an untypical perception of Islam as a schism rather than a heresy? Can we not more readily understand this if we see that for Dante he *did* symbolize the sowing of internal dissent in the Christian community, the breaking of the body politic, which made his graphic cleavage and dismemberment a punishment that fit his crime? Muhammad is not punished as the prophet of Islam qua distant and little-known faith, but rather as the emblematic prophet and master of the dangerous philosophies and philosophers who, in Dante's own lifetime, were tearing apart the Christian community and who had rent the body politic so savagely that men like Guido, Frederick, and Brunetto are on the other side of the great divide.

This briefest of rereadings has only been able to suggest the sort of additions to our reading and understanding of the *Commedia* that our new vantage point would imply. Dante is, in this view, a true believer and a true defender of the faith. He finds himself in the most embattled position imaginable, that of seeing his most respected elders, the most prestigious intellectuals of the time, and even his own best friends, won over to a philosophical system that, in his own view, can only lead to ultimate perdition. Thus the "Arabic influence" on Dante's work is an overwhelmingly negative one, representing an intellectual and artistic revolution that would undermine everything he believed was important and redeeming in Christian society.[21] In this context, and understanding his belief that he was, as the pilgrim, the model Christian and the scribe of Christ, it is not incongruous to imagine that in setting out to write an apologia he hoped would stem the tide of defections, in making his case for the benefits of fundamental Christianity, he would, consciously or not, have chosen to write a countertext to the *miᶜrāj,* which he believed was part of Islamic sacred writings and which described a sensuous and self-fulfilling paradise in which the prophet of that religion had the mysteries of his faith explained to him by his guide, a text replete with both astonishing similarities to Dante's *Commedia* and, perhaps more significant, important counterpoints.

Dante's own text is in that sense a contrapuntal analogue of Muhammad's otherworld journey (one of several, to be sure, but Dante's literary polysemia is well known and respected). Further, this idea of an analogue is complementary to the concepts of Christian analogues in the *Commedia* that scholars have described. Most of all, if this is what Dante was doing, the *Commedia* is a challenge, a countertext, an anti-*miʿrāj*. Thus it not only negates the value of Islam and its false prophets and teachings, secular as well as religious, it also creates a vision of the rewards of Christianity, which are not as lush as those of Islam but are far superior to them.

It has seemed to some critics that Dante's complete lack of recognition or acknowledgment of any Arabic influence, which is in marked contrast to his continuous recognition of other sources, precludes any assumption of such influences. Clearly, however, the kind of influence I have just described is not the sort that Dante usually cited. Most of what is involved is recognition of what was troubling Dante in the world he saw around him and how he encodes such preoccupations in his text. As for the *miʿrāj*, and any other Arabic texts he may have known and used, they are uncitable, unacknowledgable par excellence.

If there was ever a case where anxiety would have played a role in the suppression or repression of the direct acknowledgment of predecessors, Dante would certainly qualify with regard to Arabic texts. His inimical and powerfully negative relationship with the texts and the intellectual culture with which he was at odds could hardly be more marked. If he is unable to bring himself to deal directly with Guido's seduction, how can we expect him to so honor the seducers? If we are able to recognize that Petrarch's intense rivalry with, envy, and hatred of Dante constitutes a supremely powerful influence marked by his inability even to acknowledge his existence and his outright denial that he had even read the *Commedia,* should it not be even clearer that Dante suffered from similarly powerful and problematc feelings vis-à-vis a culture and an intellectual vogue that threatened the survival not only of the values but also of the souls of the people he held dearest?

And as with Petrarch, the very mention of the enemy, of the sun he is attempting to eclipse, is not just poor rhetorical strategy, since it acknowledges the enemy's power and gives it further life and vitality in one's own text, but it may also be interdicted psychologically. The repression of the influence of the Arab world on the rest of Europe may well be dated to Dante, and, among other things, it may supply part of the answer to the question of why formative influences on the courtly poetry of Provence and Sicily are left conspicuously unaddressed.

Dante fought, and in many ways defeated, the enemies that so threatened him and his view of what was right. He transformed the poetry that presented suffering and denial for the sake of poetry (and of self) into poetry in which a denial of earthly love could serve a higher purpose, the knowledge and love of God. He gave to Christendom, and to a Europe that would quietly assimilate and Graeco-Christianize much of what had been revolutionary and Arabic (and also expel what was not assimilable), a text that did indeed achieve the stature of one of the sacred texts of Christianity. No text other than Scripture itself has been as widely read or as influential in shaping our notions about Christianity as the *Commedia*.

In such a light, the light of triumph that is ultimately his and the *Commedia's*, we should perhaps be able to envision more clearly what Dante perceived as imminent darkness. The threat is long gone, at least in the guise it had in Dante's time, but it might be helpful to try to recapture it. We should not forget what made Michael Scot a "magician" and Frederick II an Epicurean and not euphemise Guido Cavalcanti's intellectual infatuation as "Aristotelianism" or "radical Aristotelianism," obscuring thereby both the direct source and the real philosophical problem at stake: Averroes and Averroism. It can only, I repeat, enrich rather than impoverish our knowledge of *l'altissimo poeta* if we can further explore the possibilities of his psychologically and textually complex relationship with the Arab intellectual culture of his own time and if we accord to that area of possible cultural, historical, and textual interrelationships the possibility of great complexity, veiled neuroses, hidden meanings and allusions, and unwitting intertextuality. This is an important instance in which to give to the European Arab world all of those characteristics, in sum, that we assume as a matter of course as part of his historical and textual relations within the rest of the European framework, that which should no longer be regarded as the only one.

Dante may have won, after all, and in some ways altered history after his time, but he could not change what came before. And is it not further tribute to his triumph to see more clearly what he was battling?

Notes

1. The felicitious image of a crossroads was suggested in Corti 1981. This work is also the source of some of the information given below on the intellectual climate in Bologna at the turn of the fourteenth century. Corti has brought to the attention of many Romanists and Italianists the high degree of Averroist or Averroist-inspired intellectual ferment that characterized the intellectual climate at the time.

2. This is a point that was made above in Chapter 3, and it is agreed on by Frederick's

biographers. Rizzitano (1958) notes that "anche quando il loro [the Arabs'] potere politico non fu più nell'isola altro che un ricordo, da un punto di vista culturale e sociale insieme essi continuarono ad esservi presenti. . . . Nel corso di quei secoli la poesia arabo-sicula non ristagnò . . . e la scarsa documentazione che ne abbiamo oggi è certamente dovuta—come meglio dirò—a difetto di transmissione" (335–36).

See also Gabrieli's important 1950 article on the subject. It is sad to note that his claim is still true that "una storia della poesia araba di Sicilia deve ancor restringersi in gran parte a nudi elenchi di nomi, corredati da magri sagi" (Gabrieli 1950:34). Moreover, as little is known about the subject among Italianists today as when Gabrieli published this study.

3. Ibn Hamdīs, a Sicilian poet who eventually emigrated to Seville, was edited by Schiaparelli in 1887, but as far as I can ascertain, only one poem of his has ever been translated (see Monroe 1974). Nor has al-Ballanūbī been translated, and there is some difficulty in ascertaining much about Arabic editions of his poetry. He is invariably described as an inferior poet.

The earliest notice of the existence of Siculo-Arabic poetry appears in Amari 1933–39. Portions of the lost anthology of Ibn al-Qattāᶜ appear to be preserved in two later Arabic *diwans*. There are the extracts of Ibn as-Sairafi, published with translations in DiMatteo 1935. The extracts of Ibn Aglab, with some translations, are published in Rizzitano 1958, a work clearly intended for the Arabic specialist. There are two further discussions of this poetry by Gabrieli (1950 and 1954a). In his 1950 study he also discusses the possible existence of Sicilian *muwashshahāt* and gives a summary of the known collections of Arabic poetry that include selections of Sicilian poetry. Gabrieli's 1954a essay is a critical review of DiMatteo's edition and translation.

4. Gabrieli 1950 summarizes the dependent relationship that Sicily had to al-Andalus: "La Sicilia insomma . . . non è che una provincia letteraria della Spagna"(35).

5. Rizzitano summarizes his view, after having quoted the translation of the poem cited above: "Di questa e d'altra poesia dello stesso tipo . . . quasi nulla è rimasto nella poesia siciliana" (1971:30). In fact, he clearly thinks that *nulla* (nothing) is more likely the case, for although he goes on to give a clear example of a *strambotto* that appears to incorporate very comparable imagery, in his chapter on the *scuola siciliana* he makes no mention whatsoever of Arabic poetry or the interaction the poets of the *scuola siciliana* may have had with the other cultured men of the court. It is noteworthy to find this kind of dichotomy in a book whose title, foreword, and much of the rest of its content seek to portray the virtually unparalleled syncretism and cultural interaction under Roger and then, especially, under Frederick. As Rizzitano says in the foreword: "L'altro motivo . . . posto in rilievo è quello che il Medioevo siciliano può essere assunto ad esempio della possibilità di convivenza di uomini di razza e di religione diversa: nel Regno, infatti, vissero gli uni accanto agli altri Latini, Saraceni, Greci ed Ebrei, riuscendo a dar vita ad una realtà politico-sociale-culturale" (1971:5). One is left to wonder what happens in the sphere of literature that, to judge from Rizzitano's own description, is completely exceptional, completely removed from this general multilingual, multicultural world. Gabrieli's view, quite the contrary, is seconded by others. See the bibliographical note for the section on Frederick in Chapter 2, above. To that I might add the somewhat surprising (and exceptional) appraisal in Jasinski [1903] 1970. In his preliminary discussion of the origins of the sonnet, Jasinski emphasizes the role of Arabic poetry at Frederick II's court and summarizes: "La poésie arabe a-t-elle agi aussi sensiblement? On sait qu'elle était en faveur auprès de Frédéric . . . et qu'il introduisit même une danse arabe à la cour de Palerme"(11). Wilkins's classic 1915 study also includes a discussion of the possible Arabic origins of the sonnet form, but his assessment is less favorable.

6. See the section of Chapter 2 dedicated to Frederick and his court.

7. Gabrieli (1950:37) discusses what evidence there is for the existence of Sicilian *muwashshahāt*, but two further comments on this subject are needed. First, even though much Siculo-Arabic poetry is clearly lost, perhaps irremediably, that does not allow us to

pretend it did not exist. Second, I cannot help but wonder, especially given the remarkable state of confusion that appears to characterize Sicilian Arabism, whether many such texts are any more "lost" than the *kharjas* once were. It was exceedingly difficult to ascertain even as much as is presented in this chapter about Siculo-Arabic poetry, and it is clear from some of the studies—such as Gabrieli 1950 and 1954a—that quite often the confusion is as great among the handful of Arabists who study Sicilian literary texts (perhaps the poorest of the poor relations of Arabic studies), as it is among Romanists.

8. Even the classicizing poetry (such as the poem cited above) is not to be overlooked altogether or dismissed as a factor in the Sicilian poetic scene. There are many conceits and recondite images that, if we assume literary influence to be something quite far from slavish copying, may well have contributed to the store of imagery of the *scuola siciliana,* as the cited poem indicates. Moreover, as a cultural example it would have played a certain role as well.

9. See Corti 1981, Kristeller 1961 and 1974, and Cerulli 1949 and 1972 for the views on Bologna that follow. Corti summarizes the situation: "il contesto culturale dell'epoca comporta che gli intelletuali bolognesi, e soprattutto i suoi amici medici e filosofi naturali, si siano buttati a pesci nel fiume di notizie che Michele Scoto dopo tanto tradurre aveva pronte per loro" (Corti 1981:22). Corti seconds Kristeller on the same subject: "doveva esistere un gruppo di amici filosofici, letterati e poeti fra Bolgona e Firenze, intelletuali raffinatissimi di aristocratica formazione europea" (25). Corti is perhaps to be taken to task for the use of the adjective "europea" in this context, since it blurs the very point she is making, that what constituted being a *raffinatissimo* intellectual was cognizance of the sort of texts that Michael Scot was making available. I believe these were, indeed, European, for I do not divorce what is Andalusian and Arabic from Europe in that context. I am not sure, however, that most of her readers make this assumption.

10. The original Spanish text is Asín Palacios 1919. The English translation and abridgment of 1926 is useful and often more readily available. For a complete history of the scholarship on the subject since Asín's work, see Cantarino 1965, which provides an analysis of the history of the subject as well as a full bibliography. Monroe 1970:182–85 presents a useful summary of Asín's work, its bases, and its reception in the context of Spanish Arabism. By far the most useful of post-Asín studies are Cerulli 1949 and 1972, which are virtually encyclopedic in their presentation of the versions of the *Libro della scala* known in non-Islamic Europe during the Middle Ages and after. For the less specialized reader, the concluding section of each of the two books is particularly useful. Many of the observations that follow are drawn from Cerulli's work, and I am happy to note that my own conclusion, presented below, that Dante's basic use of the text was to inspire him to write his own countertext, was also Cerulli's conclusion. See also the interesting and complementary work of Lemay 1963b.

11. Monroe also notes that Asín was not, in fact, the first to have noted the parallels. Credit for that is due Blochet (1901).

12. For information on the multilevel, multilingual, and multistage translation system developed at Toledo, see G. Menéndez Pidal 1951 and Procter 1951. For the direct effects this had on the development of Castilian prose, see especially Galmés de Fuentes 1955–56. For the more important indirect shaping effects of the Andalusian presence on the development of Castilian as the prestige standard, see Lloyd (forthcoming). Haskins 1924 indicates that the same system was sometimes used in Sicily, under the influence, no doubt, of the Andalusian translators and scholars Frederick brought there.

13. The question of the impact on Brunetto of his visit to Toledo has not been fully discussed. Carmody 1948 dismisses the affair altogether and assumes that the sojourn was utterly uninfluential and uninformative (xvii), but that view and comparable views implied in most Latini studies are tempered by certain assumptions about the effects of the Arabic or quasi-Arabic world on other Europeans that I believe are erroneous. But see Baldwin 1986, which discusses the possible effect of the Alfonsine translations on Brunetto and provides

further bibliography. More important, such views are also dependent on the assumption that a personal visit to Toledo would be the principal or only source of information about what was transpiring there, or on the sorts of texts being written and translated there.

14. See Chapter 6 for further discussion.

15. For Guido's texts and Dino del Garbo's commentary, see Cavalcanti 1957, which also includes a useful bibliography. See also Quaglio 1964 and Kristeller 1955 for further discussions of Guido's Averroism.

16. For Fazio degli Uberti's poem, see degli Uberti 1952. Book 5, Chapters 10 through 13, of the *Dittamondo* contain descriptions of the *Scala,* as well as other observations on Muhammad and the Koran. The verse cited is verse 94 of Chapter 12. Fazio was apparently believed to be Farinata's grandson (this is discussed below), and it was so reported by Villani, although in degli Uberti 1883 Renier claims that this was in fact a misapprehension concerning the rather complicated degli Uberti family tree.

17. For detailed citation, analysis, and relevant primary bibliography of Dante's allusions to Arabs and Andalusians, see Cerulli 1949:503–14.

18. The views of Freccero, now available in collected form (Freccero 1986) are, for many, among the most convincing and insightful ever voiced on the *Commedia.* I am happy to be able to use (however imperfectly and perhaps erroneously) not only his published work, but notes from one of his brilliant Dante seminars. The work of Singleton (1954 and 1958) is also useful here. Demaray (1974:52–53) has some insights on Dante's view of the Arab world that coincide with my own.

19. See Freccero 1985 and Durling 1981. Durling's discussion of Farinata's heretical views dovetails with my own argument. It is his image that this is the black heart of Dis, part of his analysis of hell as being identifiable in terms of parts of the body—Satan's body.

20. "The question of Guido's salvation or damnation haunts Dante. . . . His preoccupation with it is so intense as to affect the entire structural plan of the *Commedia*" (Durling 1981:25; see note 45 in this source for his further discussion of the subject).

21. This view does not preclude, of course, other kinds of adaptive influence on Dante's part, or further reflections in the *Commedia* of his knowledge of many of the texts that were being translated and studied. There is much in the *Commedia,* of course, that reflects the syncretism of philosophical systems already emerging from the renaissance of the twelfth century, and there are many originally Arabic and Andalusian texts well on their way to being absorbed by Christianity (and thus no longer consciously marked as being Arabic-Andalusian). See especially Cantarino 1968a for a study of the views on light in the *Paradiso* and their mixed philosophical sources. This does mean, however, as I note below, that when they are not yet part of the philosophical system with which Dante was comfortable, the use of such texts and the revelation of such knowledge and sources may be considerably veiled and tempered by Dante's generally reactive attitude. In this sense, perhaps, as in others, Dante represents the very crossroads in the European absorption of and reaction to Arabic factors in the medieval world. What had been accepted and absorbed was now disguised as Christian, its sources no longer acknowledged. What was still clearly marked as Arabic, not fully absorbed or absorbable, was rejected. See Pico della Mirandola's pithy statement of this problem, cited above.

CHAPTER SIX

Other Readers, Other Readings

Recordar la labor realizada por las "Madrasas" árabes, ateneos y escuelas, así como la investigadora llevada a cabo por los Monasterios españoles; la desarrollada por la Escuela de Traductores de Toledo; la fructífera y destacada de nuestras Universidades; y la creada por figuras tan destacadas como Avicena, Averroes, Alfonso X el Sabio, don Raimundo, Mosén ben Hanoc y tantos otros ilustres hombres que destacaron en el siglo XIII, y es entonces cuando, al hacer un sereno análisis de sus obras y compararlas con el panorama intelectual europeo de su tiempo, tendremos que reivindicar su esfuerzo y aportación; darles el mérito y primacía que dentro de la cultura y civilización europea, corresponde a la inmensa obra llevada a cabo por los españoles durante el siglo XIII, para nosotros el verdadero principio de lo que doscientos años después se llamó Renacimiento.

(We should remember the work accomplished by the Arab *madrasas*, atheneums and schools, as well as the research carried out by Spanish monasteries; [we should remember] the work carried out by the School of translators at Toledo; the fertile and distinguished work done at our universities; and the work done by figures as illustrious as Avicenna, Averroes, Alfonso the Wise, Raimundo Llul, Moses ben Hanoc, and so many other distinguished individuals who shone in the thirteenth century. It is then, having made a clear and distinterested analysis of their works and having compared these with the intellectual panorama of Europe in their time, that we would have to demand and recover their effort and their contributions. And we would have to accord them the merit and the primacy within European culture and civilization that is that of the great work carried out by Spaniards of the thirteenth century, for us the true beginning of what two hundred years later would be called the Renaissance.)

—Juan Fuertes Montalbán and Joaquín Gimeno-Besses, *El renacimiento español y el siglo XIII*

There is at least one reader of Dante, Boccaccio, who in his own reworking and interpretation of Dante in the *Decameron* is intrigued by the complexity and problematic nature of literary and philosophical relations with
the European-Arabic world—and by Dante's perceptions of them. It is a
fortunate coincidence that some of the most exciting work currently
being done in Boccaccio scholarship is in the area of its intertextual relations with the *Commedia*.[1] To add to the context of what is already being
done, our perceptions of the influential and, for Dante, menacing Arabic
world could perhaps help to reshape some of these discussions. Those
that come to mind immediately, for example, are stories such as VI, 9,
where the questions of Dante's condemnation of Guido Cavalcanti's Averroism is a central topic, as is the question of interpretation itself, which
Boccaccio weaves into his recounting of how Guido was (mis)understood
by a band of Florentines. The problem of interpretation is not absent
from another story (VIII, 9) that also addresses, apparently, contemporary views of Arabic-derived cultural phenomena. This is one of the
Bruno and Buffalmaco stories, and it incorporates a variety of relevant
characters and prejudices: the doctors, Michael Scot and Avicenna, the
latter being unpronounceable to Bruno:

> —Stanotte fu' io alla brigata, ed essendomi un poco la reina d'Inghilterra
> rincresciuta, mi feci venire la gumedra del gran Can d'Altarisi. Diceva il
> maestro:—Che vuol dir gumedra? Io non gli intendo questi nomi. O maestro
> mio—diceva Bruno—io non me ne maraviglio, ché io ho bene udito dire che
> Porcograsso e Vannacena non ne dicon nulla. Disse il maestro:—Tu vuoi dire
> Ipocrasso e Avicenna! Disse Bruno:—Gnaffe! io non so: io m'intendo cosí
> male de' vostri nomi come voi de' miei; ma la gumedra in quella lingua del
> gran cane vuol tanto dire quanto imperadrice nella nostra.

> ("Last night I was with the company, and since I'm getting a little bored with
> the Queen of England, I had brought to me the *gumedra* of the Khan of Al-
> tarisi." And the doctor said, "What is *gumedra?* I don't understand such names
> [words]." "I'm not surprised, master, since I have heard that neither Por-
> cograsso nor Vannacenna talks about them." "You mean Hippocrates and Avi-
> cenna!" he replied. "What do I know!" said Bruno, "I can't understand your
> words [names] any more than you do mine. But the *gumedra* in that language
> of the Great Khan means what empress does in ours.")

The possible richness of this line of inquiry in the *Decameron* is hardly
limited to Boccaccio's glosses and interpretations of Dante's own knowledge and opinions concerning such forces in their culture. Boccaccio's
own knowledge of and interest in multiple aspects of the Arab world in
Europe, as well as on its own territory (as he conceived it), are consider-

ably more extensive. His attitudes, at least on the surface and given certain readings of his stories, are also considerably more eclectic. In fact, one possible conclusion to draw from tentative readings of the two stories just mentioned would be a certain dissatisfaction with Dante's hasty and not altogether evenhanded judgment of Scot and, especially, of Cavalcanti.

While it has long been known and accepted that a fair number of Boccaccio's sources were "oriental," *Decameron* scholarship, for all its rich multiplicity and wide variation of opinion on the nature of the text and its plausible interpretations, has usually not gone beyond such source studies as far as an Arabic influence is concerned. It has not, in general, explored the possibility that the centrality of the European-Arabic world and its multiple manifestations may be embodied and reflected in that text. The very use of the term "oriental," in fact, obscures even the nature of the sources involved in certain cases.

It is more to the point, and more accurate, to note that such analogs were in many cases Andalusian, texts of which the *Disciplina clericalis* is the best-known source but not the only one. They embody and exemplify the marvelous eclecticism of derivation (traditional Judaic, Arabic adaptations from India and farther east, peninsular, and so forth) and polysemousness (scatological stories in a didactic frame, for example) that are especially apparent in the work of Petrus Alfonsi.[2] A Jew who had been educated in the Arabic tradition as well as in Hebrew and who had converted to Christianity, he wrote his *Disciplina* in Latin, and both he and his work were fêted throughout Europe. But while his narrative material may have entered the West under the guise of instruction for the Christian faithful, it is clearly a product of trireligious Spain and is to be unambiguously understood as such. The synthesis was characteristically Arabic and, for other Europeans, quintessentially Andalusian.[3]

It is misleading, in such a context, to forget that it is al-Andalus and the general Arabic intellectual prominence in Europe that are directly associated with texts such as these. They are the *direct* source, that which brought such stories to the attention of the rest of Europe and with which such a collection would be identified by all other Europeans—Europeans who, unlike the modern scholar, might find it quite difficult to distinguish between the Persian and the Arabic source in such texts and who would distinguish poorly, if at all, between the religious traditions of Maimonides and Avicenna.[4]

The readjustment of our perspectives on the period, in an extension and amplification of the view delineated for Dante, can immediately throw a different light on certain other aspects of the *Decameron*. That certain of its stories derive from the tradition embodied in the *Disciplina clericalis* is a fact recognized as far back in our discipline as the work of Vossler. Obscured and unperceived, however, in the evaluation of such sources, or of the Arabic presence in medieval Europe as peripheral and occasional, marginal and specifically marked, is Boccaccio's own tacit recognition of its centrality, one of the riveting issues during that period of European intellectual and cultural history. More subtle, and perhaps more formative, patterns of a European-Arabic presence may be perceived if we realize how many different kinds of phenomena were associated with the world of "Vanacena": Scot, doctors, Graeco-Arabic learning, Frederick II, the "oriental" setting, and so forth.

It has remained unnoticed that a certain pattern suggests itself for the ninth story of each day. That is the story that is, in certain reckonings, central, since it is told by the respective day's king or queen and is the last of those told on the stated subject of the day. At first glance it would appear that for a number of the days the story is concerned with some feature, problem, or story related in one way or another to Arabic or Arabic-derived cultural and intellectual forces. The two *novelle* mentioned above point the way, and it is no coincidence that the identification with nine in the case of the Cavalcanti story reflects Dante's own numerology in the *Inferno*. The heretics are first seen and identified in IX proper, and the episode with Cavalcanti (the father) follows in X, which is IX of the *Inferno* itself. And just cursorily remembering the settings, stories, and characters of these ninth stories (and engaging in the most elementary and banal identification of what may constitute "Arabic" in such stories) reveals the strong possibility of an interesting pattern: the setting in Cyprus in the first day; in Alexandria on the second; Frederick and the falcon, a seemingly unmistakable reference to Frederick II (best known for his treatise on falconry) in the fifth; on the sixth Cavalcanti; a Greek setting in the seventh (not forgetting that contemporary sources for the knowledge of Greek still came predominantly through Arabic and were associated with it); in the eighth, the Bruno and Buffalmaco story; Salamone on the ninth; Saladin on the tenth. The suggestion here, and it can be no more than that, is that a possible pattern emerges from the relatively simple refocusing of our view, a pattern that is intriguing, worth exploring, and quite possibly rewarding for our understanding of this author, whose artistic richness is no less varied and polyvalent than Dante's but whose ideology and intent in the *Decameron* is much more ambivalent and controversial.

I would add a final suggestion about the changed perspective on

Boccaccio and the *Decameron* that could be facilitated by our wider cognizance and acceptance of the Adalusian texts and traditions he knew. One of the most distinguishing and intriguing features of texts such as the *Disciplina clericalis* and others of the same genre is that they fused what for some might seem dramatically different, even contradictory or irreconcilable, features: the scatological or scandalous story in an avowedly didactic context. Such a fusion is a rhetorical device whose own roots and patterns within the Semitic tradition are less than perfectly understood and certainly less than exhaustively explored. But this feature also immediately invites comparison with a text such as the *Decameron*. This sort of comparative work could well be done, initially at least, by merely assuming that such a comparison is legitimate and leaving genetic questions outside of our immediate focus.

In terms of the current critical emphasis on both the narrative patterns and the meaningful structural complexities of the *Decameron,* a wider field of comparable texts could only yield more cogent and more significant results. It seems wholly appropriate, for textual reasons alone, that texts such as that of Petrus Alfonsi—and others less well known in this context but potentially just as informative, including the *Thousand and One Nights*—should be a part of such a systematic comparative investigation of narrativity in medieval story collections, not just adduced piecemeal for the isolated story that may have been borrowed and recast. Given the well-documented popularity of Petrus's text and the fact that there is no possibility of denying its accessibility, it seems surprising that the *Disciplina* is not regularly adduced in such discussions. Most intriguing and potentially suggestive is the possibility that a comparison with these texts' use of the general structuring narrative to inform (and didacticize) the otherwise moral-less or blasphemous tale within the larger pattern may well add credence and support to the still-revolutionary and (to some) shocking notion that Boccaccio was a fundamentally Christian writer and that his *Decameron* is a Christian, moral book whose lessons are apparent to careful readers, just as the *Disciplina* was and just as its readers must have perceived it.[5]

That his model or models in such a narrative construct, his ways of looking at a text and the ways it might fulfill a didactic, Christian purpose, might be in some measure Arabic or Hebrew in inspiration and/or example would undoubtedly prove to be even more incongruous to some. But is it any more odd or incongruous than that Dante should have relied on Judeo-Arabic astronomical sources for his configurations of time and the stars in the setting of the *Commedia?* And if Boccaccio showed so little squeamishness in his own use and appreciation of texts from that other world, why should we? He knew Fibonacci (whose own name as well as education is a calque from the Arabic "ibn," "son of," nomenclature system, "fi' (glio) Bonacci), for example, and he knew the sort of mathematical and medical work that the likes of the "gran maestro in nigromantia" Michael Scot had translated. I believe he did not expect his perceptive readers to play the role of Bruno and to mispronounce Avicenna's name, to ignore who he was and what he meant in Europe in the twelfth, thirteenth, and fourteenth centuries.

This is only one of many possible future paths for renewed interpretations, new research, readjusted perspectives, and redefined curricula for the medievalist that are implied and facilitated by this tinkering with our view of the Middle Ages. It may be appropriate, in concluding, briefly to suggest what some of those areas are. Many have already been alluded to, but they may be profitably reiterated at this point.

In part because it is one of the requirements of contemporary literary studies, which are reasonable enough in many ways, and in part because of the special problems that exist in this area, theoretical issues are presented here that need further clarification and discussion. It may also be argued that some of these theoretical questions might themselves have been fruitfully explored in this context. Issues of great current import, such as the effects of the ideology of the critic or the reader and how these influence his reading of a text and subsequent writing of literary history, immediately suggest themselves and are central to our concerns. Such problems were discussed, but far from exhausted, in earlier chapters. Discussions of these theoretical issues have generally focused on aspects of the modern period, which to many seems more psychologically and ideologically complex, but it should be clear that the historiographical problems brought into focus by raising such questions are no less critical, no less complex and fascinating, when dealing with the twelfth century than with the twentieth. The complacency that has often dominated our thinking about the medieval period and that has often engendered a supposition of its relative simplicity, is well on its way to being eradicated. I believe the discussion of the complexity of the Arabic component in Europe at that time is an essential part of the reform that scholars are currently undertaking.

Other related theoretical issues are implicit and of direct consequence in this kind of study—that of the relationship between history and the text, for example, and the ancillary conceptual problem of determining where meaning lies, whether it is something created and expressed by writers or is received and more or less recreated by readers, or whether it is more likely to be a complex symbiosis of the two. As with the question of the ideology of the reader/critic, these issues cannot continue to be ignored, as they generally have been in the past, with regard to crucial parts of medieval literary historiography. Clearly, the perceptions of Arabic texts and the conception of the Arabic cultural forces of medieval Europe were critical to the problem of their reception by other Europeans, both then and now. The case made here, that the twelfth-century perspective was radically different from the one adopted in the nineteenth century, may provide an example of just how effective such perceptions are in shaping general views. And if this case shows that a perception or construct of history held a priori is as strong a determinant of perceived meaning as it seems to be, it may prove to be no less compelling an example of how determined meaning shifts hand in hand with the shifts of historical perspective.

The history of medieval literary scholarship over the past century or so and the reception within it of suggestions of the importance of the Arabic world in that context should convince us of the necessity of tackling such questions when embarking on this kind of revisionist work. It is not just that the questions raised are of direct and legitimate importance in attempting to establish that an entire chapter of European literary and intellectual history has been in some measure misrepresented and mis-written. It is even less a question of the current vogue of being cognizant of and raising such theoretical issues. The principal need to raise them derives from the fact that if they are not tackled first, if one does not establish the validity of certain approaches and assumptions, the likelihood of this particular kind of work being ignored is exceptionally high. A medievalist convinced, for whatever reason, of the validity of this different vision of the Middle Ages has a far greater obligation to set out his working assumptions and ground rules than his colleagues. To establish the possible vagaries of intertextuality and the relationship between history and the text is a mere luxury for the scholar who argues that, say, Brunetto Latini in the canto of the sodomites is a reflection of Dante's belief that Brunetto was a sodomite or that Brunetto's *Tresors* is comparable to the *Roman de la Rose* in certain ways. But it is a necessity for the critic who understands sodomy as a metaphor for Brunetto's seduction by the unproductive cult of Arabizing intellectualism or the *Tresors* as inspired by the sort of texts being translated and newly fashioned at the Toledan center of Alfonso the Wise and known not just in Toledo but in virtually every corner of Romance-speaking Europe where learning was prized. Such a requirement is particularly in force if the scholar wishes to have his work read and duly considered by mainstream Dantisti and by students of Brunetto's work.

If innovative interpretations of this period of history are found to be reasonable, then numerous paths for new research and new literary interpretations will be opened up. The expansion of our field of background texts to include those that al-Andalus and her bedfellows (in some cases very Christian courts) were producing and disseminating will certainly make for more promising and more productive genetic and comparative work. In many cases such a broadening of perspectives may shed further light on the nature and structure of a variety of texts that have by and large fallen by the wayside or been classified as *sui generis.*

A poetic-encyclopedic text, for example, such as Brunetto Latini's *Tresors* or Fazio degli Uberti's *Dittamondo,* has clear structural affinities with encyclopedic texts, very much inspired by the Arabic tradition, studied and emulated in Alfonso's Toledo. The possibility that such genres were further adapted and assimilated into non-Arabic traditions (conspicuously the *terza rima* of Fazio's text) is a fascinating one. The complex polymorphism and fusion of different traditions suggested by such possibilities are perhaps ultimately emblematic of the inextricable marriage of initially quite different cultural strands in medieval Europe.

Even more frequently studied works of special generic status, the mixed prose-poetry genre, for example, exemplified by the *Vita nuova* and *Aucassin et Nicolette,* would profit from comparison with texts normally excluded from their study in the past. To adduce Ibn Ḥazm's *Ṭauq al-Ḥamāma* in a study of either one, for example, would bring into focus a text linked to them not just through its relatively simple generic format but in other ways as well. Like the *Vita nuova,* Ibn Ḥazm's work is also an inquiry into the nature of love, and it contrasts that of the courtly tradition with "good" love. No less is true for *Aucassin et Nicolette,* which imaginatively, rather than discursively, contrasts and juxtaposes different theories of love.

Moreover, in the case of the Old French text, our interpretative possibilities are enriched not only by this broadening of our textual horizons but perhaps even more by having a more subtle and complex notion of what the contemporary image may have been of the preeminent Other from the Christian-Latin perspective of the Middle Ages. *Aucassin et Nicolette* is a text whose very title, the names of the two protagonists, juxtaposes and contrasts the two worlds: Aucassin, whose name is clearly meant to seem Arabic, and Nicolette, who is in fact the long-lost daughter of the "King of Carthage" and bears the traditional French name. This work, replete with Arabic images and nomenclature, embodies a general depiction of the Arabic world while telling a story as integrally and characteristically a part of the Semitic story tradition as the related *Floire et Blanchefloire*.

Other such possibilities abound and are too numerous to enumerate. But one other should be mentioned, because it falls somewhat outside the normal bounds of literary studies, though it is nonetheless one of the most striking and potentially significant. It properly lies in the field of linguistic philosophy, not literature per se, but it is a current of thought hardly divorced from those that intrigued writers of fiction in the medieval period and that in some cases dovetailed with their own work. The history of linguistic philosophy is a new field and is almost terra incognita, particularly that of the medieval period. But recent work in this area by a handful of scholars, primarily linguists, who have chosen this as their field of research, has uncovered the existence of a revolutionary school of linguistic theory that began at the end of the eleventh and the beginning of the twelfth centuries and represented the first successful attempt in the history of western Europe to form a fully integrated theory of language.[6]

A major historian of medieval grammar (linguistics) has claimed that developments in grammatical theory between the eleventh and fourteenth centuries possess all the hallmarks of a Kuhnian revolution, but they cannot be fully documented or accounted for, since the linguistic historians working on the problem have no "usable texts of grammatical writing from the period of 1100 to 1260" (Bursill-Hall 1975:181). After 1260 the new approach appears, apparently fully developed, in the writings of certain medieval grammarians in a variety of places in Europe, including the universities of Paris and Bologna. In their analysis of this dramatic revolution—in which the rise of the modistae and of modal grammar suddenly takes place, seemingly from out of nowhere, in twelfth-century Europe—linguistic historians have posited as the most likely intellectual influence the rediscovery of the complete corpus of Aristotle's work on logic. But perhaps it would be best here to listen to the expert's account of this phenomenon:

> Though the influence of the Greek world was not entirely unknown in this period, [i.e., the Middle Ages] . . . it was the fuller incorporation of the complete Aristotelian Organon which was to produce what is often referred to as the "Renaissance of the 12th Century." The 12th century was more a period of assimilation but by 1200 the greater part of Aristotle was available in Latin

translation. The 13th century saw the complete absorption of Aristotelian philosophy and logic as well as the work of his Arab commentators into the teaching of the Trivium; more than any other single factor, this will explain the differences in grammatical thought which characterise the period. The details of the "invasion" of the northern schools of Europe by Aristotle are referred to in a number of studies. The result of the new spirit, as far as grammar was concerned, was that by 1215 the classical authors were absent from the University of Paris and grammar was no longer associated with literary studies but became instead a philosophical, theoretical and speculative discipline.

(Bursill-Hall 1975:198)

It is startling to read, later in the same publication, a flat denial of any connection between this new phenomenon and sources concerned with Arabic and Hebrew linguistic philosophy. By contrast, the passage cited, and many other observations made by the author concerning the historical setting for this revolution in thought, virtually beg for such a comparison.

Like many comparable discussions of the revolutions within the twelfth-century renaissance there is an obscuring through euphemization of the source and direction of the revolutionary thought, the place of origin of the "invasion," and it is essential to point out once again that the translations, as well as the relevant commentaries (which the historian here admits were also absorbed and were very much part of the intellectual upheaval) were an integral part of the long Arabic tradition of the study, translation, and commentary on the Philosopher as the Arabs knew him. In this moment of rediscovery and the upheaval resulting from it, this too was the Aristotle and his meanings that the West knew, that of the Arabic tradition. Suggestive of the pressing need for further work is the fact that the influence of Arabic and Hebrew linguistic philosophy cannot be easily dismissed, since it would have been a fundamental part of the tradition of commentary on, and even the translation of, Aristotle. To suppose a divorce between the philosophy of language and other philosophy is to misunderstand the interdependence of such studies in the tradition of Arabic learning. Moreover, and this certainly would profit from further scrutiny, many essential "revolutionary" features are basic cornerstones of the medieval linguistic philosophy that would have informed all translations of and commentaries on Aristotle or Plato, or other philosophers, for that matter.

One of the principal tenets of the modistae, for example, is the belief that the basis for grammar lies in reality and that language mirrors the reality underlying the phenomena of the physical world. This is also a characteristic premise of much Arabic linguistic philosophy, a linguistic philosophy analyzed by writers who were far from unknown in Europe—al-Ghazhali and the Spaniard Ibn Ḥazm, to name just two. So too is the theory of regents developed by the modistae as part of their analysis of language, a complex, abstract concept of how one word (which may not even be part of the utterance) is able to govern another word and the rest of the sentence. It is a concept of grammatical analysis, incidentally, that was not only revolutionary in terms of twelfth-century Latin-Romance notions of how language operates but bafflingly revolutionary as well for those speakers of English or Romance languages who are learning Arabic even today. It has tormented many a student of Arabic because it is so alien to any mode of linguistic analysis known in the Latin and Romance grammatical traditions in which we have been educated. The modal revolution, in fact, was largely a failure.

But once the veil of Graeco-Christianizing terminology is lifted, the recurring association of the period of greatest flowering and impact of al-Andalus with what Haskins called the renaissance of the twelfth century becomes a persistent presence. This perception crystallizes as the myriad little revolutions that are subsumed under the rubric emerge as predominantly derived from or related to the knowledge and impact of the larger Andalusian world at this critical juncture of European history.[7] Our conviction increases, as we assimilate bits of information previously left segregated, that this renaissance, with all the significance it would have for the development of European intellectual and literary features thereafter, is more fully understood as a reaction to and absorption of the explosive impact of the European Arabic world, one whose own accomplishments and glory were just then reaching their culmination.

To continue our exploration, to expand our knowledge and perceptions of the different moments and instances of this impact, it would be beneficial to fill in the gaps (mostly with facts and tidbits already known to others) in our images of the centers of cultural renascence and upheaval in the twelfth and thirteenth centuries. In addition to those scenarios I have briefly sketched out in Chapter 2, there are undoubtedly others that would likewise be elucidated. To take but one example, it would be revealing to add to our already considerable knowledge of the literary impact of the courts of the daughters of Eleanor of Aquitaine information about non-Latin-based phenomena that were circulating through Europe during the same period, to explore the links between intellectuals such as Andreas Capellanus and his colleagues, who were just beginning to delight in the opening up of whole new schools of thought. Fascinating, too, would it be to consider the extent to which not just a text such as the *Disciplina clericalis* but also the dazzling and alluring world that lay behind it were subjects of interest. And a dazzling world it was, al-Andalus—a golden age, as has been noted by many, not only of things Arabic but of things Jewish as well. Any discussion of Petrus Alfonsi and of the nature and impact of his text suggests the need for further discussion of Jewish culture and intellectual movements in the Middle Ages, particularly because they were so integral a part of Andalusian culture and its subsequent impact on the rest of Europe. Of the many issues barely hinted at in this study, the relative neglect of this one is the most grievous.[8] It is the result of a similar ideologically constrained view of Europe, it results in the training of medievalists whose knowledge of that particular tradition can be quite limited or even nonexistent, and it is certainly no less in need of revision.

Part of our envisioning of a different Middle Ages necessarily involves the role played by the Jews and the Hebraic tradition in a European world so different from our own. One of the essential aspects of that role was that in great measure the destinies of the two Semitic cultures were closely intertwined and identified, often to the point of confusion. The causes of that association are manifold and cannot be addressed here, but it is essential to remember the more extended discussion of the manifold cultural and intellectual strains that were encompassed under the larger rubric and concept of what was Arabic in the medieval period. Certainly, especially here, such a concept was not limited to what was Islamic.

Historians of Judaism have written at great length on the flowering of Jewish culture in al-Andalus, and that flowering is commonly identified as that culture's golden age. In many respects, the flourishing of Jewish culture went hand in hand with the heyday of Arabic, particularly secular Arabic, culture. In great measure, both cultural zeniths were due to the same liberalism and tolerance, and ultimately they would both be destroyed by the same intolerance. Averroes and Maimonides both wrote in Arabic because it was so dominantly the language of prestige, and though in the non-Arabic parts of Europe that received their work they might be distinguished as Muslim and Jew respectively, they were more often seen as bound together as Andalusians—as harbingers of new philosophical and intellectual currents, masters of the language and cultures of a world of myriad riches—than they were seen as divided by any religious doctrine. Both of their religions, in any case, were not Christian, and any further or more enlightened distinction than that was not characteristic or necessary. Both would be avidly and appreciatively read, used, and translated by Frederick II for the benefit of others and for the enlightenment of the rest of Europe. Both Spaniards would suffer exile from their beloved homeland within years of each other, victims of the ravages of the Islamic orthodoxy that had swept the land. Finally, their respective descendants (or what remained of them)[9] were expelled or forced into conversion by the forces of an equally ruthless and intolerant Christianity after the triumph for which 1492 is so haunting a symbol.

Maimonides and Averroes were to remain no less tied to each other thereafter, in history. As Spaniards they were denied their birthright, their nationality, by latter-day Spaniards, for whom Christianity was a requirement for citizenship, even retrospectively. Brilliant, luminous stars in their own lifetimes and in the times and events of Europe for years to come, they were eventually neglected and forgotten (or misnamed) because they did not fit into the established norms of our prestigious European ancestry, an ancestry by and large as cleansed of Jews and Arabs as Spain had tried to be in the sixteenth century. Their restoration to a prominent place in our understanding of medieval cultural and intellectual history will likewise go hand in hand.

These observations lead to the question of why our examination of the role played by al-Andalus in the making of Europe from the twelfth through fourteenth centuries should have so conspicuously neglected, or evoked only briefly and in passing, Spain itself. This study has pointed to al-Andalus, and the rest of Spain, which was tied to it in so many ways, as one of the centers, sometimes *the* center, of medieval Europe. But I have generally avoided that vortex, that eye of the storm of the twelfth-century renaissance, and have only sketched out the most elementary picture of the features and characteristics that made it so stunning and controversial for the rest of Europe, an avant-garde in so many ways. In the large inventory of questions to be pursued as a result of the shift in our focus, revisions and additions to the curriculum of "Hispanic" literature, particularly that of the Middle Ages, would be virtually unending. Yet this facet of our work is passed over here largely in silence.

There are two reasons for such an omission. The first is that part of the work in this area, certainly the background part, has already been done by others. Many logical and obvious suggestions have been made. Tantalizing pictures of Córdoba and its library, its learning, and its songs, have been drawn. Scholars have proposed the startling hypothesis of Spain as a unique cultural mixture, rich not only in the accumulation but in the synthesis of the various features of the Christian, Muslim, and Jewish worlds. There is no scarcity of books, articles, and monographs, each with its own perspective, that would serve as more than ample bases for depicting a world that once flourished, gave of itself generously to others, and then ceased to exist.

But the paradox remains that here—where there are the greatest riches, the most promising possibilities, the most information—the divorce of the Arabic and Latin-Romance worlds is often as pronounced as elsewhere, and the disdain and disparagement of putative Semitic "influences" is often even greater. The hypotheses of this study clearly imply that in our study of the rest of Europe and of authors such as William of Aquitaine and Dante, the world of al-Andalus and her progeny and hand-maidens (Toledo and Palermo, for example) must be considered, because its presence was, for better or worse, imposing and unavoidable. The implication can only be that much stronger that we must see and study Spain itself from such a perspective. This view of Spain, in turn, in which al-Andalus and its culture were of crucial importance to the rest of the peninsula, would be a necessary component of, indeed the very basis for, our broader European reevaluation.

Inevitably, the role of al-Andalus in shaping everything else in Spain—from its "first" literary masterpiece, the *Cantar de Mio Cid,* to Castile's own concept of itself and its literary language—must be tied to such inquiries. Of all the paths for further exploration and revision suggested here, it is the most compelling and potentially the most fruitful. The fact that in this study I have more than once used the terms "Andalusian" and "Spanish" as virtually synonymous reflects the extent to which the two are bound to each other, in my view and in that of others. Is the Toledan translation of an Arabic text Spanish or Andalusian? Is the number system refined in al-Andalus, which we call Arabic, not better designated as Spanish or Andalusian? What are the Mudejares, the Moriscos, the Mozarabs, the Muladíes?[10] What are the Arabic songs sung to troubadours in Catalonian courts? Where, in a world whose cultural borders are so indistinct, is the dividing line between the two?

But this problem evokes the second reason for having bypassed this area and concentrated on the broader European role played by Spain, and it is, all told, no less paradoxical. Many Spaniards, and many Hispanists, following their lead, have wished to view the eight hundred years of Islamic presence as a negative period in their history, a moment of alien intrusion that, if it cannot be erased, can at least be made to disappear in our historiographical fictions. To begin our anthologies of the literature of Spain with the *Cantar de Mio Cid* is commonplace; to believe that "Arab" meant simply the enemy and as such is a simple image that can be dismissed or bypassed is made to seem reasonable;[11] to ignore or marginalize the effects of the literature, philosophy, and other writings in Arabic or Hebrew on the Christian writers of the medieval period is as well; and to accept the notion that the "courtly love" of Spain came solely from Provence and to ignore Ibn Ḥazm, or to admit that perhaps in the popular lyric, but not elsewhere, there might be Arabic influence—all these are common features of Hispanic scholarship.[12]

Perhaps the most commonplace objection and supposed problem raised when one suggests that such features require substantial alteration is that it would also require the learning of Arabic, which is a difficult task, an unreasonable requirement for scholars already overburdened with skills they must have and with two-volume *MLA* bibliographies to peruse. But what is needed first is not to learn Arabic, which is difficult (although arguably this is a matter of attitude and perspective). Why learn a language considered remote from one's interests and needs? What *is* required, however, is considerably more difficult and challenging, the alteration of our attitudes toward European literary history (and thus, in considerable measure, toward ourselves). With this done, and with a vision of Arabic and Hebrew, Morisco and Mozarabic, as central rather than peripheral, the amount of material available even to the scholar with no knowledge of Arabic becomes exceedingly rich, and the number of scholars of future generations who would accept that Arabic and Hebrew are important reading languages for a medievalist with no more protest than they raise over learning Latin, Greek, German, or Anglo-Saxon, would subsequently increase as a matter of course. The standards we have for what languages are necessary, like much of our interpretation of literature, follow rather than precede the Hispanist's and the medievalist's concept of the world and the literature with which he is concerned. The more difficult, and essential, of the tasks is that of considering the validity of the views we hold, understanding their ideological bases, and readjusting them if they are found wanting.

Only in the light of a vision of medieval Spain that does not dismiss a priori its Arabic, Jewish, and mixed cultures as non-Spanish can we rationally examine fascinating new questions, such as whether the works written in Spain in non-Romance languages or in Romance dialects mixed with Arabic or Hebrew are properly a part of the canon of literature of the Iberian peninsula. If they are also part of the canon of a different culture and literature, so what? Was Dante any less part of the canon for Eliot because he was Italian? Is Aristotle not part of the canon of English studies because he is also part of the Greek? Since when does being an essential part of one culture and literature prevent a text or an author from being essential to another?

It is undeniable that Spain's history and its consciousness of itself and what it is have been deeply affected by this period in its history. Whether the impact is seen as one of calques and hybrids, as Américo Castro did, or as a reactive one, as Cantarino does, or even as a highly negative, destructive one, as others have, few would argue that the cultural collision was not an important shaping force. It is equally undeniable that 1492 was a watershed, though whether a positive or negative one is subject to dispute. While many have believed that the victory of Christianity and the expulsion of the Semitic peoples and their culture was Spain's triumph and salvation—its restoration, however belated, to the real Europe and to the Western tradition—other voices have whispered different things. Clearly, for many (including some eminent Spanish Arabists), the "Moors" and Jews, who were never real Spaniards or Europeans in the first place, were banished for the greater good, and Spain is as European as it is today despite their presence and influence. And although most Hispanists—medievalists or not—no longer articulate such views, their behavior as scholars too often ratifies its assumptions.

The irony is a staggering one, for it was precisely when Spain was al-Andalus that Spain was most influential in Europe, most the focus of its interests, most the source for its revolutions. It was a Spaniard, Averroes, whose work in philosophy radically altered the paths of European philosophy; it was to Spain that the great collector of knowledge of his time, Frederick II, sent his savants to study and translate her wealth so that others might profit from it. To talk about Spain's cultural belatedness, due to its not having absorbed the teachings and revolutions of the twelfth-century renaissance, is a reversal and a misconception of egregious proportions.

But if this study has focused on the reasons and ways we can come to see the centrality of al-Andalus in Europe, it is because of a firmly held conviction that only then will what is often the shadow side of medieval Spain, the Andalusian world and its reflections, receive due attention. Only then will Hispanists view this as one of the most glorious periods of Spanish history. Hispanists so often complain, perhaps justifiably, of the backseat they take to French and English literary scholars in preeminence in the profession. They lament the perception that what is Spanish is not as essential for an understanding of European history as what is French or English; that its authors are not as conspicuous on general reading lists as are Balzac and Proust and Joyce and Henry James; that a general medievalist is more likely to have read the *Song of Roland* or the

Divine Comedy than the *Cantar de Mio Cid* or the *Libro de buen amor*. But by ignoring and marginalizing the period and culture of Spain's European preeminence, arguably the greatest and most formative it was to have in terms of European philosophy, sciences, and all manner of intellectual activities, Hispanists have perhaps inadvertently helped to make this so. A recent study on the gaps in the European canon poses the question, in terms of the "poetics of abandonment," of what has become of Aristotle's sister (Lipking 1983). A far less hypothetical question, with a far clearer answer, is why we have abandoned and forgotten Aristotle's faithful keepers, his Spanish brothers Maimonides and Averroes, without whom the course of European Aristotelianism would be far different from what it was and is. A reconstruction of our views and definitions of what constitutes Spanish in this period is clearly as necessary, and potentially as beneficial, as new views and definitions of what is European. These two notions are, indeed, inextricably intertwined. If Hispanists restore a poet such as Ibn al-ʿArabī of Murcia and the Córdobans Ibn Ḥazm, Maimonides, Averroes, and Ibn Quzmān—all stellar Spaniards and Europeans by any measure—to the canon of critical authors in the literary history of medieval Spain, then their importance for the study of medieval Europe will follow.

If Hispanomedievalists shed light on the marvels and glories of al-Andalus, on its uniqueness and its decisive influence over the rest of Europe in this formative period, if they play a role in reminding us just who Aristotle was in the twelfth century, then they will undoubtedly reap the rewards. And if they help to establish that the twelfth, the thirteenth, or the fourteenth centuries and their literatures cannot be fully seen or clearly understood without looking first where others looked, to Spain, then this different kind of Hispanism will certainly be central to European medieval studies. Just as al-Andalus once gave other Europeans so many of the means to decipher and unveil the heavens, such a newly defined Hispanism will uncover a long-obscured constellation of stars that once lit the skies of medieval Europe.

Notes

1. See especially Durling 1983, on Guido Cavalcanti and the metaliterary problem of interpretation in *Decameron* IV, 9. See also Hollander 1981–82.

2. See the bibliography on Petrus Alfonsi and other discussion of his work and its importance in Chapter 2. On the didactic-narrative tradition and its complex origins and peninsular manifestations, see also Kasten 1951, Vernet 1978, Keller 1978, and M. J. Lacarra 1979. For the image of Saladin in medieval literature (and he is an important figure for Boccaccio) see also Richard 1949 and Castro's essay (1977).

3. See the discussion of this issue in Chapter 2.

4. The problem of this kind of obscurantism and of the use of euphemisms is also found in etymological work. See Menocal 1984 for a discussion of this in regard to the etymology of "checkmate" and related words.

5. The major works in this area are Branca 1981, Smarr 1976, Hollander 1977, and Kirkham 1981 and 1985. (Curiously enough, Menéndez Pidal once suggested such a direction for work on Boccaccio and Petrus Alfonsi [1956:24–25].) There is strong resistance among Boccaccisti to the notion that the *Decameron* may have overriding Christian meaning and lessons within which the individual *novelle* are meaningful, even the obscene and blasphemous ones. This tradition of seeing Boccaccio as modern and as writing stories that are just for entertainment is in part a reflection, ironically, of a nonmodern approach to Boccaccio, an assumption of a certain primitiveness. It would be far less likely, for example, to find students of a post-Renaissance text arguing that it cannot be so complex that it combines bawdiness or obscenity with an overriding moral lesson. It is also, perhaps, a reflection of how little other medieval narratives with the same apparently contradictory features are known. The *Disciplina clericalis* is only one of the texts (and is itself part of a tradition of such texts) that reconciles the two elements quite well.

6. For the modistae, see especially Percival 1975, Bursill-Hall 1975, and Joly and Stéfanini 1977. For Arabic linguistic philosophy in general and in al-Andalus in particular, see Asín Palacios 1939, Arnaldez 1956, Chejne 1974, Makdisi 1976, and especially Breva-Claramonte 1977, which includes a very informative bibliography and a lucid presentation of certain of the issues involved. Corti 1981 discusses modal grammatical philosophy and its impact at Bologna, particularly on Dante. Interestingly enough, she traces it not to the Parisian *modistae* but to translated texts coming from Sicily and through Michael Scot.

7. By the "larger Andalusian world" I mean not just al-Andalus as defined by political boundaries, the part of Iberia controlled by descendants of the Arab conquerors, but the world that was in some measure reflective of it, and this includes much (if not all) of Christian Spain as well. See below for a further discussion of this terminological problem.

8. Some bibliography has already been provided in Chapter 2. See especially Stern 1959 and miscellaneous articles and bibliography in Stern 1974, Baer [1961] 1971, Millás y Vallicrosa 1967, Silver 1974, and Cantera 1957 and the revealing response of García Gómez 1957.

9. For the Moriscos, who are also unfortunately neglected in this study, see Burns 1977, Armistead 1978, López-Baralt 1980, López Morillas 1982, and Chejne 1983. All provide bibliographies on Morisco studies and indications of the kind of work that is (and is not) being done.

10. Mudéjares were Muslims living under Christian rule and Moriscos were their "descendants" (i.e., new Christians). Mozarabs were Christians living under Islamic rule and Arabized, whereas Muladíes are new Muslims (i.e., converts to Islam descended from people native to Iberia before the Islamic conquest).

11. M. E. Lacarra 1980 provides a recent example of the extent to which al-Andalus in an analysis of the *Cantar de Mio Cid* can be the Moorish enemy and not much more, even in a study explicitly concerned with "realidad histórica y ideología."

12. Some work done in some of these areas is highly suggestive but far from mainstream. To remark on only one of the various possible areas, see, for example, some of the earlier work on narrative and epic. Hammer-Purgstall 1849, Menéndez y Pelayo 1943, and ʿAbdal Badī 1964, and more recently Galmés de Fuentes 1967, 1975, and 1978. A recent study on Ibn Ḥazm and the theory of love in the *Cárcel de amor* (Benaim de Lasry 1981) is exemplary of the problems involved here. Not least among these is the fact that the author's title clearly reflects a division between, and a juxtaposition of, two entities that, if her study is to have any validity, cannot be said to be legitimate: "A Comparison of 'Courtly Love' in the Sentimental Fiction of Medieval Spain and of Muslim Spain."

Bibliography

ʿAbd al Badīʿ, Luftī. 1964. *La épica árabe y su influencia en la épica castellana.* Santiago de Chile: Instituto Chileno-Árabe de Cultura.

Addison, James Thayer. [1942] 1966. *The Christian Approach to the Moslem: A Historical Study.* New York: AMS Press.

Ahmad, Aziz. 1975. *A History of Islamic Sicily.* Edinburgh: Edinburgh University Press.

Alonso, Dámaso. 1958. *De los siglos oscuros al de oro: Notas y artículos a través de 700 años de letras españolas.* Madrid: Editorial Gredos.

———. 1961. *Primavera temprana de la literatura europea: Lírica, épica, novela.* Madrid: Ediciones Guadarrama.

Alvar, Carlos. 1977. *La poesía trovadoresca en España y Portugal.* Barcelona: Editorial Planeta.

Amari, Michele. 1853. "Questions philosophiques adressées aux savants musulmans par l'Empereur Frédéric II." *Journal Asiatique* 1:240–74.

———. 1883. See Idrisi.

———. 1933–39. *Storia dei Musulmani di Sicilia.* Ed. Carlo Alfonso Nallino. 3 vols. in 5. Catania: R. Prampolini.

———. 1942. *I Musulmani in Sicilia.* Ed. Elio Vittorini. Milano: Bompiani.

Andreas Capellanus. 1941. *The Art of Courtly Love.* Ed. and trans. John Jay Parry. New York: Columbia University Press. Reprint. New York: F. Ungar.

Armistead, Samuel G. 1973. "A Mozarabic *Ḫarǧa* and a Provençal Refrain." *Hispanic Review* 41:416–17.

———. 1978. "¿Existió un romancero de tradición oral entre los moriscos?" In *Actas del Coloquio internacional sobre literatura aljamiada y morisca.* Ed. Álvaro Galmés de Fuentes, 211–36. Madrid: Editorial Gredos.

———. 1980. "Some Recent Developments in *Kharja* Scholarship." *La Corónica* 8:199–203.

———. 1982. "Speed or Bacon? Further Meditations on Professor Alan Jones' 'Sunbeams.'" *La Corónica* 10:148–55.

———. 1986. "Pet Theories and Paper Tigers: Trouble with the *Kharjas*." *La Corónica* 14:55–70.

Armistead, Samuel G., and James T. Monroe. 1983. "*Albas, Mammas,* and Code-Switching in the *Kharjas:* A Reply to Keith Whinnom." *La Corónica* 11:174–207.

———. 1985. "Beached Whales and Roaring Mice: Additional Remarks on Hispano-Arabic Strophic Poetry." *La Córonica* 13:206–42.

Arnaldez, R. 1956. *Grammaire et théologie chez Ibn Ḥazm de Cordoue: Essai sur la structure et les conditions de la pensée musulmane*. Paris: J. Vrin.

Arnold, Thomas, and Alfred Guillaume, eds. [1931] 1974. *The Legacy of Islam*. Reprint. Oxford: Oxford University Press.

Asensio, Eugenio. 1976. *La España imaginada de Américo Castro*. Barcelona: El Albir.

Asín Palacios, Miguel. 1919. *La escatología musulmana en la Divina Comedia.* . . . Madrid: Estanislao Maestre.

———. [1926] 1968. *Islam and the Divine Comedy*. Ed. and trans. Harold Sutherland. Reprint. London: Frank Cass and Company.

———. 1939. "El origen del lenguaje y problemas conexos en Algazel, Ibn Sīda e Ibn Hazm." *Al-Andalus* 4:253–81.

Badel, Pierre-Yves. 1969. *Introduction à la vie littéraire du moyen âge*. Paris: Bordas.

Baer, Yitzhak F. [1961] 1971. *A History of the Jews in Christian Spain*. Trans. Louis Schoffman. 2 vols. Reprint. Philadelphia: Jewish Publication Society of America.

———. 1981. *Historia de los judíos en la España cristiana*. Trans. José Luis Lacave. Madrid: Altalena.

Bakhtin, Mikhail. 1981. *The Dialogic Imagination: Four Essays*. Ed. Michael Holquist, trans. Caryl Emerson and Michael Holquist. Austin: University of Texas Press.

Baldwin, Spurgeon. 1986. "Brunetto Latini's *Tresor:* Approaching the End of an Era." *La Corónica* 14:177–93.

Bate, Walter Jackson. 1983. "To the Editor of *Critical Inquiry.*" *Critical Inquiry* 10:365–70.

Bausani, Alessandro. 1957. "La tradizione arabo-islamica nella cultura europea." *Humanitas* 12:809–28. Reprinted in 1977 in *I Problemi di Ulisse* 14:9–20.

Beard, Michael. 1979. Review of *Orientalism*, by Edward Said. *Diacritics* 9 (Winter).

Beare, William. 1957. *Latin Verse and European Song*. London: Methuen.

Benaim de Lasry, Anita. 1981. "A Comparison of 'Courtly Love' in the Sentimental Fiction of Medieval Spain and of Muslim Spain." *Al-Qantara* 2:129–43.

Benson, R. L., and G. Constable, with Carol D. Lanham, eds. 1982. *Renaissance and Renewal in the Twelfth Century*. Cambridge, Mass.: Harvard University Press.

Bertrand, Louis, and Charles Petrie. 1952. *The History of Spain*. 2d ed. New York: Macmillan.

Bezzola, Reto R. 1940. "Guillaume IX et les origines de l'amour courtois." *Romania* 66:145–237.

Blochet, E. 1901. *Les Sources orientales de la Divine Comédie*. Paris: Maisonneuve.

Bloom, Harold. 1973. *The Anxiety of Influence: A Theory of Poetry*. Oxford: Oxford University Press.

Bloomfield, Morton W. 1979. "Continuities and Discontinuities." *New Literary History* 10:409–16.

Boase, Roger. 1976. *The Origin and Meaning of Courtly Love: A Critical Study of European Scholarship*. Manchester: Manchester University Press.

Bogin, Meg. 1976. *The Women Troubadours*. New York: Paddington Press, Two Continents Publishing Group.

Bonner, Anthony, ed. and trans. 1972. *Songs of the Troubadours*. New York: Schocken Books.

Branca, Vittore. 1981. *Boccaccio medioevale e nuovi studi sul Decameron*. 5th ed. Florence: Sansoni.

Breva-Claramonte, Manuel. 1977. "Sanctius's Antecedents (Part 2)." *Language Sciences* no. 45:6–21.

Broadhurst, J. C. 1952. See Ibn Jubayr 1952.

Brombert, Victor. 1979. Review of *Orientalism*, by Edward Said. *American Scholar* 48:532–42.

Burns, Robert. 1977. "Mudejar History Today: New Directions." *Viator* 8: 127–43.

Bursill-Hall, G. L. 1975. "The Middle Ages." In *Trends in Linguistics* 13, pt. 1:179–230.

Calin, William. 1966. *The Epic Quest: Studies in Four Old French Chansons de geste*. Baltimore: Johns Hopkins University Press.

———. 1983. "Singer's Voice and Audience Response: On the Originality of the Courtly Lyric, or How 'Other' was the Middle Ages and What Should We Do about it?" *L'Esprit Créateur* 23, no. 1:75–90.

Cantarino, Vicente. 1965. "Dante and Islam: History and Analysis of a Controversy." In *A Dante Symposium in Commemoration of the 700th Anniversary of the Poet's Birth (1265–1965)*, ed. William de Sua and Gino Rizzo, 175–98. North Carolina Studies in Romance Languages and Literatures, no. 58. Chapel Hill: University of North Carolina Press.

———. 1968a. "Dante and Islam: Theory of Light in the *Paradiso*." *Kentucky Romance Quarterly* 15:3–35.

———. 1968b. "Sobre los españoles y sobre cómo llegaron a serlo." *Revista Hispánica Moderna* 34:212–26.

———. 1969. "Lyrical Traditions in Andalusian Muwashshahas." *Comparative Literature* 21:213–31.

———. 1974. "The Composition of Andalusian Muwashshahas with a Romance Kharja." *Kentucky Romance Quarterly* 21:447–68.

———. 1978. *Entre monjes y musulmanes: El Conflicto que fue España*. Madrid: Editorial Alhambra.

———. 1980. "The Spanish Reconquest: A Cluniac Holy War against Islam?" In *Islam and the Medieval West*.

Cantera Burgos, Francisco. 1957. *La canción mozárabe*. Publicaciones de la Universidad Internacional "Menéndez Pelayo," no. 7. Santander.

Carmody, Francis. See Latini 1948.

Castro, Américo. 1948. *España en su historia: Cristianos, moros y judíos*. Buenos Aires: Editorial Losada.

———. 1952. "Mozarabic Poetry and Castile: A Rejoinder to Mr. Leo Spitzer." *Comparative Literature* 4:188–89. Response to Spitzer 1952.

———. 1954a. *La realidad histórica de España*. Mexico: Editorial Porrúa. Revision of Castro 1948.

———. 1954b. *The Structure of Spanish History*. Trans. Edmund L. King. Princeton: Princeton University Press. Translation of Castro 1954a.

――――. 1956. *Semblanzas y estudios españoles*. Princeton and Spain: Ediciones Insula. Collection of articles in Spanish written between 1916 and 1954.

――――. 1971. *The Spaniards: An Introduction to Their History*. Trans. Willard F. King and Selma Margaretten. Berkeley: University of California Press.

――――. 1977. *An Idea of History: Selected Essays of Américo Castro*. Ed. and trans. Stephen Gilman and Edmund L. King. Columbus: Ohio State University Press.

Cavalcanti, Guido. 1957. *Le Rime*. Ed. Guido Favati. Milan: Ricciardi.

Cerulli, Enrico. 1949. *Il "Libro della Scala" e la questione delle fonti arabo-spagnole della Divina Commedia*. Vatican City: Biblioteca Apostolica Vaticana.

――――. 1972. *Nuove ricerche sul "Libro della Scala" e la conoscenza dell'Islam in Occidente*. Studi e teste, no. 271. Vatican City: Biblioteca Apostolica Vaticana.

Ceva, Bianca. 1965. *Brunetto Latini: L'uomo e l'opera*. Milan: Ricciardi.

Chejne, Anwar. 1974. *Muslim Spain: Its History and Culture*. Minneapolis: University of Minnesota Press.

――――. 1980. "The Role of Al-Andalus in the Movement of Ideas between Islam and the West." In *Islam and the Medieval West*.

――――. 1983. *Islam and the West: The Moriscos, A Cultural and Social History*. Albany: State University of New York Press.

Clausen, Anna Maria. 1976. *Le origini della poesia lirica in Provenza e in Italia: Un confronto sulla base di alcune osservazioni sociologiche*. Etudes romanes de l'Université de Copenhague. Copenhagen: Academisk Forlag.

Cluzel, Irénée M. 1957. "Jaufré Rudel et *l'amour de lonh*." *Romania* 78:86–97.

――――. 1960a. "A propos des origines de la littérature courtoise en Occident." *Romania* 81:538–55.

――――. 1960b. "Les jarŷas et 'l'amour courtois.'" *Cultura Neolatina* 20:233–50.

――――. 1961. "Quelques reflexions à propos de la poésie lyrique des troubadours." *Cahiers de culture médiévale* 4:179–88.

Contini, Gianfranco, ed. 1960. *Poeti del Duecento*. 2 vols. Milan: Ricciardi.

Corti, Maria. 1979. "Models and Antimodels in Medieval Culture." *New Literary History* 10:339–66.

――――. 1981. *Dante a un nuovo crocevia*. Florence: Sansoni.

――――. 1983. *La felicità mentale: Nuove prospettive per Cavalcanti e Dante*. Torino: Einaudi.

Cremonesi, Carla. 1955. *Lirica francese del Medio Evo*. Milan: Instituto editoriale cisalpino.

Cropp, Glynnis. 1975. *Le Vocabulaire courtois des troubadours à l'époque classique*. Geneva: Droz.

Cummins, John G. 1978. Review of *The Origin and Meaning of Courtly Love: A Critical Study of European Scholarship*, by Roger Boase. *Bulletin of Hispanic Studies*. 55:262.

――――, ed. 1977. *The Spanish Traditional Lyric*. Oxford: Pergamon.

Curtius, Ernst. 1953. *European Literature and the Latin Middle Ages*. Trans. Willard R. Trask. Princeton: Princeton University Press.

D'Alverny, Marie Thérèse. 1982. "Translations and Translators." Benson and Constable, eds., *Renaissance and Renewal in the Twelfth Century*, 421–62. See Benson and Constable 1982.

Daniel, Norman. 1960. *Islam and the West: The Making of an Image.* Edinburgh: Edinburgh University Press.

———. 1975a. *The Arabs and Mediaeval Europe.* London: Longman.

———. 1975b. *The Cultural Barrier: Problems in the Exchange of Ideas.* Edinburgh: Edinburgh University Press.

———. 1979. "The Impact of Islam on the Laity in Europe from Charlemagne to Charles the Bold." In *Islam: Past Influence and Present Challenge,* 105–25.

Defourneaux, Marcelin. 1949. *Les Français en Espagne aux XIe et XIIe siècles.* Paris: Presses Universitaires de France.

Demaray, John G. 1974. *The Invention of Dante's* Commedia. New Haven: Yale University Press.

Denomy, Alexander J. 1944. "An Inquiry into the Origins of Courtly Love." *Mediaeval Studies* 6:175–260.

———. 1945. "*Fin' Amors:* The Pure Love of the Troubadours, Its Amorality, and Possible Source." *Mediaeval Studies* 7:139–207.

———. 1947. *The Heresy of Courtly Love.* New York: Declan X. McMullen.

———. 1949. "*Jovens:* The Notion of Youth among the Troubadours, Its Meaning and Source." *Mediaeval Studies* 11:1–22.

———. 1953. "Concerning the Accessibility of Arabic Influences to the Earliest Provençal Troubadours." *Mediaeval Studies* 15:147–58.

DeStefano, Antonio 1954. *La cultura alla corte di Federico II imperatore.* Bologna: Zanichelli.

DiMatteo, Ignazio. 1935. "Antologia di poeti arabi siciliani estratta da quella di Ibn al Qaṭṭāʿ." *Archivio Storico per la Sicilia* 1:85–133.

Donaldson, E. Talbot 1970. "The Myth of Courtly Love." In *Speaking of Chaucer,* 154–63. New York: Norton.

Dozy, R. P. A. 1861. *Histoire des Musulmans d' Espagne, jusqu'à la conquête de l'Andalousie par les Almoravides.* 3 vols. Leyden: Brill.

———. 1881. *Recherches sur l'histoire et la littérature de l'Espagne pendant le moyen âge.* 3d ed. 2 vols. Paris: Maisonneuve.

———. 1913. *Spanish Islam: A History of the Moslems in Spain.* Trans. Francis G. Stokes. New York: Duffield and Company. Translation of Dozy 1861.

———, ed. and trans. 1856–60. See al-Makkari.

Dronke, Peter. 1965–66. *Medieval Latin and the Rise of European Love-Lyric.* Oxford: Oxford University Press.

———. [1968] 1977. *The Medieval Lyric.* London: Hutchinson University Library.

Dunlop, D. M. 1958. *Arabic Science in the West.* Karachi: Pakistan Historical Society.

Durling, Robert M. 1981. "Farinata and the Body of Christ." *Stanford Italian Review* 2:5–35.

———. 1983. "Boccaccio on Interpretation: Guido's Escape (*Decameron* VI.9)." In *Dante, Petrarch, Boccaccio: Studies in the Italian Tercento in Honor of Charles S. Singleton.* Ed. Aldo S. Bernardo and Anthony L. Pellegrini, 273–304. Medieval and Renaissance Texts and Studies. Binghamton, N.Y.: Center for Medieval and Early Renaissance Studies, State Univeristy of New York at Binghamton.

Dutton, Brian. 1964. "*Lelia Doura, Edoy Lelia Doura:* An Arabic Refrain in a Thirteenth-Century Galician Poem?" *Bulletin of Hispanic Studies* 41:1–9.

————. 1968. "Hurí y Midons: El amor cortés y el paraíso musulmán." *Filología* 13:151–64.

Eliot, T. S., ed. 1972. *Literary Essays of Ezra Pound.* New York: New Directions.

Ellis, John M. 1974. "The Relevant Context of a Literary Text." In *The Theory of Literary Criticism: A Logical Analysis,* 104–54. Berkeley: University of California Press.

Farmer, Henry George. 1926. *The Influence of Music: From Arabic Sources.* London: Reeves.

————. 1930. *Historical Facts for the the Arabian Musical Influence.* London: Reeves.

Fauriel, Claude Charles. [1860] 1966. *History of Provençal Poetry.* Trans. G. J. Adler. Reprint: New York: Haskell House.

Ferrante, Joan. 1975. *Woman as Image in Medieval Literature: From the Twelfth Century to Dante.* New York: Columbia University Press.

————. et al. 1975. *In Pursuit of Perfection: Courtly Love in Medieval Literature.* Port Washington, N.Y.: Kennikat Press.

Finucane, Ronald C. 1983. *Soldiers of the Faith: Crusaders and Moslems at War.* New York: St. Martin's Press.

Fiore, Silvestre. 1964. "Arabic Traditions in the History of the Tuscan Lauda and Ballata." *Revue de Littérature Comparée* 38:5–17.

Fish, Stanley. 1983. "Profession Despise Thyself: Fear and Self-Loathing in Literary Studies." *Critical Inquiry* 10:349–64.

Fish, Compton, Linda. 1976. *Andalusian Lyrical Poetry and Old Spanish Love Songs: The* Muwashshaḥ *and Its* Kharja. New York: New York University Press.

Frank, Grace. 1942. "The Distant Love of Jaufré Rudel." *Modern Language Notes* 57:528–34.

Frank, István. 1952. "'Babariol-Babarian' dans Guillaume IX (Notes de philologie pour l'étude des origines lyriques, I)." *Romania* 73:227–34.

————. 1955a. "Les débuts de la poésie courtoise en Catalogne et le problème des origines lyriques." In *VIIe Congrés International de Linguistique Romane.* Barcelona: Abadía de San Cugat del Vallés.

————. 1955b. "Poésie romane et Minnesang autour de Frédéric II." *Bolletino del Centro di Studi Filologici e Linguistici Siciliani* 3:51–83.

Frappier, Jean. 1959. "Vues sur les conceptions courtoises dans les littératures d'oc et d'oïl au XIIe siècle." *Cahiers de Civilisation Médiévale* 2:135+56.

————. 1972. "Sur un procès fait à l'amour courtois." *Romania* 93:145–93.

Freccero, John. 1986. *Dante: The Poetics of Conversion.* Ed. Rachel Jacoff. Cambridge, Mass.: Harvard University Press.

Frenk-Alatorre, Margit. 1975. *Las jarchas mozárabes y los comienzos de la lírica románica.* Mexico: Colegio de México.

Fuertes Montalban, Juan, and Joaquín Gimeno-Besses. 1954. *El renacimiento español y el siglo XIII.* Madrid: Editorial Alhambra.

Gabrieli, Francesco. 1950. "Arabi di Sicilia e Arabi di Spagna." *Al-Andalus* 15:27–45.

————. 1952. "Federico II e la cultura musulmana." *Revista Storica Italiana* 64:5–18.

————. 1954a. "L'Antologia di Ibn as-Sairafi sui poeti arabo-siciliani." *Bolletino del Centro di Studi Filologici e Linguistici Siciliani* 2:39–51.

———. 1954b. "La poesia araba e le letterature occidentali." *Belfagor* 9:377–86, 510–20.

———. 1957. *La storiografia arabo-islamica in Italia.* Naples: Guida.

———. 1973. *Arabeschi e studi islamici.* Naples: Guida.

———. 177. "Petrarca e gli Arabi." *Al-Andalus* 42:241–48.

Galmés de Fuentes, Alvaro. 1955–56. "Influencias sintácticas y estilísticas del árabe en la prosa medieval castellana." *Boletín de la Real Academia Española* 35:213–75, 415–51; 36:65–131, 255–307.

———. 1967. *El libro de las batallas (Narraciones caballerescas y aljamiado-moriscas).* Oviedo: Universidad de Oviedo.

———. 1972. "'Les nums d'Almace et cels de Durendal' (*Chanson de Roland,* v. 2143): Probable origen árabe del nombre de las dos famosas espadas." In *Studia Hispanica in Honorem R. Lapesa,* 1:229–41. Madrid: Cátedra-Seminario Menéndez Pidal/Gredos.

———. 1975. *El libro de las batallas:* Narraciones épico-caballerescas. 2 vols. Madrid: Gredos.

———. 1978. *Epica árabe y épica castellana.* Barcelona: Ariel.

———. 1985. "Un conte d'al-Ghazālī et le fabliau français *Du vilain asnier.*" *Romance Philology* 39:198–205.

García Gómez, Emilio. 1956. "La lírica hispano-árabe y la aparición de la lírica romanica." *Al-Andalus* 21:303–38.

———. 1957. "Las jaryas mozárabes y los judíos de Al Andalus." *Boletín de la Real Academia Española* 37:337–94.

———, ed. [1965] 1975. *Las jarchas romances de la serie árabe en su marco: Edición en carácteres latinos, versión española en calco rítmico y estudio de 43 moaxajas andaluza.* Madrid: Sociedad de Estudios y Publicaciones. Reprint. Barcelona: Seix Barral.

———. 1983. "En el cincuentenario de la escuela de estudios árabes de Madrid." *Al-Qanṭara* 3:v–xii.

———. 1984. "Arabistas, romanistas y anfibios." *ABC* August 8.

———, ed. and trans. 1952. See Ibn Hazm 1952.

Gibb, Hamilton. 1955. "The Influence of Islamic Culture on Medieval Europe." *Bulletin of the John Rylands Library* 38:82–98.

Giffen, Lois Anita. 1971. *Theory of Profane Love among the Arabs: The Development of the Genre.* New York: New York University Press.

Gittes, Katherine Slater. 1983. "The *Canterbury Tales* and the Arabic Frame Tradition." *PMLA* 98:237–51. Letters on this article in the *PMLA* include those from Charles A. Owen, Jr., 98:902, Ibrahim Dawood, 99:109, and Julie Scott Meisami, 99:109–11.

Glick, Thomas F. 1979. *Islamic and Christian Spain in the Early Middle Ages.* Princeton: Princeton University Press.

Goldin, Frederick, comp. and trans. 1973. *Lyrics of the Troubadours and Trouvères: An Anthology and a History.* New York: Doubleday, Anchor Press.

González Palencia, Angel. 1928. *Historia de la literatura arábigo-española.* Barcelona: Editorial Labor.

———. 1945. *Moros y cristianos en España medieval: Estudios histórico-literarios.* Madrid: Consejo Superior de Investigaciones Científicas, Instituto Antonio de Nebrija.

Gorton, J. T. 1974. "Arabic Influence on the Troubadours: Documents and Directions." *Journal of Arabic Literature* 5:11–16.

———. 1976. "Arabic Words and Refrains in Provençal and Portuguese Poetry." *Medium Aevum* 45:257–64.

Green, Otis H. 1963. *Spain and the Western Tradition.* Vol. 1, *The Castilian Mind in Literature from* El Cid *to* Calderón. Madison: University of Wisconsin Press.

Guidubaldi, Egidio. 1978. *Dal "De Luce" di R. Grossatesta all'Islamico "Libro della Scala": Il Problema delle fonti arabe una volta accettata la mediazione oxfordiana.* Florence: Olschki.

Guiraud, Pierre. 1971. "Les Structures étymologiques du 'Trobar.'" *Poétique* 8:417–26.

———. 1978. *Sémiologie de la sexualité: Essai de glosso-analyse.* Paris: Payot.

Hammer-Purgstall, J. von. 1849. "Sur la chevalerie des Arabes antérieure à celle d'Europe, sur l'influence de la première sur la seconde." *Journal Asiatique* 4:5–14.

Harvey, L. P., ed. See Stern 1974.

———. 1976. "Réplica del Profesor L. P. Harvey." *Al-Andalus* 41:235–37. Reply to Ramírez Calvente 1974.

Haskins, Charles Homer. 1915. *The Normans in European History.* Boston: Houghton Mifflin.

———. 1924. *Studies in the History of Medieval Science.* Cambridge, Mass.: Harvard University Press.

———. 1927. *The Renaissance of the Twelfth Century.* Cambridge, Mass.: Harvard University Press.

Haxen, Ulf. 1982. "Harğas in Hebrew Muwaššaḥas (A Plea for a 'Third Approach')." *Al-Qanṭara* 3:473–82.

Hay, Denys. 1968. *Europe: The Emergence of an Idea.* Rev. ed. Edinburgh: Edinburgh University Press.

Heger, Klaus. 1960. *Die bisher veröffentlichten Harğas und ihre Deutungen.* Tübingen: Max Niemeyer.

Heinisch, Klaus J. 1968. *Kaiser Friedrich II: In Briefen und Berichten seiner Zeit.* Darmstadt: Wissenschaftliche Buchgesellschaft.

Hermes, Eberhard. [1970] 1977. *The 'Disciplina Clericalis' of Petrus Alfonsi.* Berkeley: University of California Press. Reprint. London: Routledge and Kegan Paul.

Hill, R. T., Thomas G. Bergin, et al. 1973. *Anthology of the Provençal Troubadours.* 2d ed. 2 vols. New Haven: Yale University Press.

Hitchcock, Richard. 1977. *The "Kharjas": A Critical Bibliography.* London: Grant and Cutler.

———. 1980. "The 'Kharjas' as Early Romance Lyrics: A Review." *Modern Language Review* 75:481–91.

———. 1984. "The Interpretation of Romance Words in Arabic Texts: Theory and Practice." *La Corónica* 13:243–54.

Hollander, Robert. 1977. *Boccaccio's Two Venuses.* New York: Columbia University Press.

———. 1981–82. "Boccaccio's Dante: Imitative Distance (*Decameron* I 1 and VI 10)." *Studi sul Boccaccio* 13:169–98.

Hornik, M. P., ed. 1965. *Collected Studies in Honour of Américo Castro's Eightieth Year.* Oxford: Lincombe Lodge Research Library.

Ibn Hazm. 1953. *The Ring of The Dove: A Treatise on the Art and Practice of Arab Love.* Trans. A. J. Arberry. London: Luzac.

Ibn Hazm. 1931. *A Book Containing the* Risāla *Known as The Dove's Neck-Ring, about Love and Lovers.* Ed. and trans. A. R. Nykl. Paris: Paul Geunther.

———. 1952. *El collar de la paloma: Tratado sobre el amor y los amantes.* Ed. and trans. Emilio García Gómez. Madrid: Sociedad de Estudios y Publicaciones.

Ibn Jubayr. 1907. *The Travels of Ibn Jubayr.* 2d ed. Ed. and trans. William Wright. Leyden: Brill.

———. 1952. *The Travels of Ibn Jubayr.* . . . Ed. and trans. R. J. C. Broadhurst. London: Jonathan Cape.

Ibn Khaldūn. [1958] 1967. *The Muqaddimah: An Introduction to History.* Trans. Franz Rosenthal. 2d ed. 3 vols. abridged to 1 vol. Reprint. Princeton, N.J.: Princeton University Press, Bollingen Press.

Idrīsī. 1883. *L'Italia descritta nel "Libro del re Ruggero" compilato da Edrisi.* Trans. Michele Amari and C. Schiaparelli. Atti della reale accademia dei Lincei, series 2, vol. 8. Rome: Coi tipi del Salviucci.

Islam and the Medieval West: Aspects of Intercultural Relations. 1980. Albany: State University of New York Press.

Islam: Past Influence and Present Challenge. Ed. Alford T. Welch and Pierre Cachia. Edinburgh: Edinburgh University Press.

Jargy, Simon. 1971. *La Musique arabe.* Paris: Presses Universitaires de France.

Jasinski, Max. [1903] 1970. *Histoire du sonnet en France.* Douai: Brugère. Reprint. Geneva: Slatkine Reprints.

Jauss, Hans Robert. 1979. "The Alterity and Modernity of Medieval Literature." *New Literary History* 10:181–227.

Jeanroy, Alfred. 1934. *La Poésie lyrique des troubadours.* 2 vols. Toulouse: Privat.

Joly, André, and Jean Stéfanini, eds. 1977. *La Grammaire générale des modistes aux idéologues.* Lille: Publications de l'université de Lille.

Jones, Alan. 1980. "Romance Scansion and the *Muwaššaḥāt:* An Emperor's New Clothes?" *Journal of Arabic Literature* 11:36–55.

———. 1981. "Sunbeams from Cucumbers? An Arabist's Assessment of the State of *Kharja* Studies." *La Corónica* 10:38–53.

———. 1983. "*Eppur si muove.*" *La Corónica* 12:45–70.

Jones, Joseph R., and John R. Keller, eds. and trans. 1969. *The Scholar's Guide.* Toronto: Pontifical Institute.

Kantorowicz, Ernst H. 1957. *Frederick the Second, 1194–1250.* Trans. E. O. Lorimer. New York: F. Ungar.

Kasten, Lloyd 1951. "'Poridat de las Poridades': A Spanish Form of the Western Text of the *Secretum secretorum.*" *Romance Philology* 5:180–90.

Kay, Richard. 1978. *Dante's Swift and Strong: Essays on Inferno XV.* Lawrence: Regents Press of Kansas.

Keller, John E. 1978. *Pious Brief Narrative in Medieval Castilian & Galician Verse: From Berceo to Alfonso X.* Lexington: University Press of Kentucky.

Kelly, Amy. 1950. *Eleanor of Aquitaine and the Four Kings.* Cambridge, Mass.: Harvard University Press.

Kelly, H. A. 1979. "Aristotle- Averroes-Alemannus on Tragedy: The Influence of the 'Poetics' on the Latin Middle Ages." *Viator* 10:161–209.

Kenner, Hugh, ed. 1953. *Translations of Ezra Pound.* New York: New Directions.

Kibler, William W., ed. 1976. *Eleanor of Aquitaine: Patron and Politician.* Austin: University of Texas Press.

Kirkham, Victoria. 1981. "Love's Labor Rewarded and Paradise Lost (*Decameron,* III, 10)." *Romanic Review* 72:79–93.

———. 1985. "An Allegorically Tempered *Decameron.*" *Italica* 62:1–23.

Kristeller, Paul Oscar. 1955. "A Philosophical Treatise from Bologna Dedicated to Guido Cavalcanti: Magister Jacopus de Pistorio and His 'Quaestio de felicitate.'" In *Medioevo e Rinascimento: Studi in onore di Bruno Nardi.* 1:425–63. Florence: Sansoni.

———. 1961. *Renaissance Thought: The Classic, Scholastic, and Humanistic Strains.* New York: Harper.

———. 1964. *Eight Philosophers of the Italian Renaissance.* Stanford, Calif.: Stanford University Press.

———. 1974. *Medieval Aspects of Renaissance Learning: Three Essays.* Ed. and trans. Edward P. Mahoney. Durham, N.C.: Duke University Press.

Kritzeck, James. 1964. *Peter the Venerable and Islam.* Princeton: Princeton University Press.

Lacarra, María Eugenia. 1980. *El poema de Mio Cid: Realidad histórica e ideología.* Madrid: J. Porrúa Turanzas.

Lacarra, María Jesús. 1979. *Cuentística medieval en España: Los orígenes.* Saragossa: Departamento de Literatura Española, Universidad de Zaragoza.

———, ed. and trans. 1980. *Disciplina clericalis: Pedro Alfonso.* Saragossa: Guara editorial.

Lasater, Alice E. 1974. *Spain to England: A Comparative Study of Arabic, European, and English Literature of the Middle Ages.* Jackson: University Press of Mississippi.

Latini, Brunetto. 1948. *Li Livres dou Tresor.* Ed. Francis J. Carmody. Berkeley: University of California Press.

Lazar, Moshé. 1964. *Amour courtois et "Fin'amors" dans la littérature du XIIe siècle.* Paris: Librairie C. Klincksieck.

Lehmann, Winfred P. 1968. "Saussure's Dichotomy between Descriptive and Historical Linguistics." In *Directions for Historical Linguistics,* ed. W. P. Lehmann and Y. Malkiel, 3–20. Austin: University of Texas Press.

Lejeune, Rita. 1954. "Rôle littéraire d'Aliénor d'Aquitaine et de sa famille." *Cultura Neolatina* 14:5–57.

———. 1958. "Rôle littéraire de la famille d'Aliénor d'Aquitaine." *Cahiers de Civilisation Médiévale* 1:319–37. Continuation of Lejeune 1954.

Lemay, Richard. 1963a. "Dans l'Espagne du XIIe siècle: Les Traductions de l'arabe au latin." *Annales: Economies, Sociétés, Civilisations* 18:639–65.

———. 1963b. "Le Nemrod de l'‘Enfer' de Dante et le ‘Liber Nemroth.'" *Studi Danteschi* 40:57–128.

———. 1966. "A propos de l'origine arabe de l'art des troubadours." *Annales: Economies, Sociétés, Civilisations* 21:990–1011.

———. 1977. "The Hispanic Origin of Our Present Numerical Forms." *Viator* 8:435–59.

Lerner, Ralph, ed. and trans. 1974. *Averroes on Plato's Republic.* Ithaca, N.Y.: Cornell University Press.

Lévi-Provençal, Évariste. 1948a. *La Civilisation arabe en espagne: Vue générale.* Paris: Maisonneuve.

——. 1948b. *Islam d'Occident: Etudes d'histoire médiévale.* Paris: Maisonneuve.

——. 1951. *Conférences sur l'Espagne musulmane prononcées à la Faculté de lettres en 1947 et 1948.* Publications de la Faculté des lettres de l'Université Farouk Ier d'Alexandrie. Cairo: Impr. nationale.

——. 1954. "Les vers arabes de la chanson V de Guillaume IX d'Aquitaine." *Arabica* 1:208–11. Also in 1951.

——. "Poésie arabe d'Espagne et poésie d'Europe médiévale." In 1948b and 1951.

——. 1955. *La civlización árabe en España.* Madrid: Espasa Calpe. Translation of 1948a.

Lewis, Bernard. 1982. Review of *Orientalism,* by Edward Said. *New York Review of Books* 29, June 24, pp. 49–56.

Lewis, C. S. 1936. *The Allegory of Love: A Study in Medieval Tradition.* Oxford: Oxford University Press, Clarendon Press.

Lida, María Rosa. 1940. "Notas para la interpretación, influencia, fuentes, y texto del *Libro de Buen Amor.*" *Revista de Filología Hispánica* 2:105–50.

——. 1959. "Nuevas notas para la interpretación del *Libro de Buen Amor.*" *Nuevo Revista de Filología Hispánica* 13:17–82.

Lipking, Lawrence. 1983. "Aristotle's Sister: A Poetics of Abandonment." *Critical Inquiry* 10:61–81.

Lloyd, Paul M. forthcoming. "The Constitution of the Castilian Dialect." In *From Latin to Spanish.*

López-Baralt, Luce. 1980. "Crónica de la destrucción de un mundo: La Literatura aljamiado-morisca." *Bulletin Hispanique* 82:16–58.

López Morillas, Consuelo. 1982. *The Qurʾān in Sixteenth-Century Spain: Six Morisco Versions of Sūra 79.* London: Tamesis.

——. 1983. "Las jarchas romances y la crítica árabe moderna." Unpublished paper.

Makdisi, George. 1974. "The Scholastic Method in Medieval Education: An Inquiry into Its Origins in Law and Theology." *Speculum* 49:640–61.

——. 1976. "Interaction between Islam and the West." *Revue des Etudes Islamiques* 44:287–309.

——. 1981. *The Rise of Colleges: Institutions of Learning in Islam and the West.* Edinburgh: Edinburgh University Press.

al-Makkari. 1856–60. *Analectes sur l'histoire et la littérature des Arabes d'Espagne.* Ed. and Trans. R. P. A. Dozy. Leyden: Brill.

Manselli, R. 1979. "La corte di Federico II e Michele Scoto." *L'Averroismo in Italia.* Rome: Atti dei Convegni Lincei 40:63–80.

Manzanares de Cirre, Manuela. n.d. *Arabistas españoles del siglo 19.* Madrid: Instituto Hispano-Arabe de Cultura.

Maravall, José Antonio. 1954. *El concepto de España en la Edad Media.* 2d ed. Madrid: Instituto de Estudios Políticos.

Marks, Claude. 1975. *Pilgrims, Heretics, and Lovers: A Medieval Journey.* New York: Macmillan.

Márquez Villanueva, Antonio. 1977. "La occidentalidad cultural de España." In *Relecciones de literatura medieval*, 135–68. Sevilla: Servicio de publicaciones de la Universidad de Sevilla. Review of *Spain and the Western Tradition*, Vol. 1, *The Castilian Mind in Literature from 'El Cid' to Calderón*, by Otis Green.

Marshall, J. H., ed. and trans. 1972. *The 'Razos de Trobar' of Raimon Vidal and Associated Texts*. Oxford: Oxford University Press.

Martino, Pierre. [1906] 1970. *L'Orient dans la littérature française du XVIIe au XVIIIe siècle*. Paris: Hachette. Reprint. Geneva: Slatkine Reprints.

Mazzeo, Guido Ettore. 1965. *The Abate Juan Andrés: Literary Historian of the XVIII Century*. New York: Hispanic Institute in the United States.

"Medieval Literature and Contemporary Theory." 1979. *New Literary History* 10, no. 2. Special Issue.

Menéndez Pidal, Gonzalo. 1951. "Cómo trabajaron las escuelas alfonsíes." *Nueva Revista de Filología Hispánica* 5:363–80.

Menéndez Pidal, Ramón. 1947. *La España del Cid*. 4th ed. 2 vols. Madrid: Espasa-Calpe.

———. 1955. *Poesía árabe y poesía europea: Con otros estudios de literatura medieval*. 4th ed. Buenos Aires: Espasa-Calpe Argentina.

———. 1956. *España, eslabón entre la Cristiandad y el Islam*. Madrid: Espasa-Calpe.

———. 1961. "Origins of Spanish Literature Considered in Relation to the Origin of Romance Literature." *Cahiers d'Histoire Mondiale* 6:752–70.

Menéndez y Pelayo, Marcelino. 1941. "De las influencias semíticas en la literatura española." In *Estudios y discursos de crítica histórica y literaria*. Santander: Consejo Superior de Investigaciones Científicas.

———. 1943. *Orígenes de la novela*. Vol. 1, *Influencia oriental: Los libros de caballería*. Santander: Sociedad de Artes Gráficas.

Menocal, María Rosa. 1979. "The Singers of Love: Al-Andalus and the Origins of Troubadour Poetry." Ph.D. dissertation, University of Pennsylvania.

———. 1981. "Close Encounters in Medieval Provence: Spain's Role in the Birth of Troubadour Poetry." *Hispanic Review* 49:43–64.

———. 1982. "The Etymology of Old Provençal *trobar, trobador:* A Return to the 'Third Solution.'" *Romance Philology* 36:137–53.

———. 1984. "The Mysteries of the Orient: Special Problems in Romance Etymology." In *Papers from the XIIth Linguistics Symposium on Romance Languages*, 501–15. Amsterdam: John Benjamins.

———. 1985. "Pride and Prejudice in Medieval Studies: European and Oriental." *Hispanic Review* 53:61–78.

Metlitzki, Dorothee. 1977. *The Matter of Araby in Medieval England*. New Haven: Yale University Press.

Millás Vallicrosa, José María. 1920–21. "Influencia de la poesía popular hispanomusulmana en la poesía italiana." *Revista de Archivos, Bibliotecas y Museos* 41:550–64; 42:37–59.

———. 1940. *La poesía sagrada hebráico-española*. Madrid: Consejo Superior de Investigaciones Científicas.

———. 1967. *Literatura hebráicoespañola*. Barcelona: Editorial Labor.

Monroe, James T. 1965. "The Muwashshaḥāt." In *Collected Studies in Honour of*

Américo Castro's Eightieth Year, 335–72. Oxford: Lincombe Lodge Research Library.

———. 1970. *Islam and the Arabs in Spanish Scholarship (Sixteenth Century to the Present)*. Leyden: Brill.

———. 1974. *Hispano-Arabic Poetry: A Student Anthology.* Berkeley: University of California Press.

———. 1975. "Formulaic Diction and the Common Origins of Romance Lyric Traditions." *Hispanic Review* 43:341–50.

———. 1976a. "The Structure of an Arabic *Muwashshaḥ* with a Bilingual *Kharja*." *Edebiyât* 1:113–23.

———. 1976b. "Estudios sobre las jarŷas: Las jarŷas y la poesía amorosa popular norafricana." *Nueva Revista de Filología Hispánica* 25:1–16.

———. 1979. "Kharjas in Arabic and Romance: Popular Poetry in Muslim Spain?" In *Islam: Past Influence and Present Challenge*, 168–87.

———. 1982. "*¿Pedir peras al olmo?* On Medieval Arabs and Modern Arabists." *La Corónica* 10:121–47.

———. 1986. "Poetic Quotation in the *Muwaššaḥa* and Its Implications: Andalusian Strophic Poetry as Sung." *La Corónica* 14:230–50.

Munōz Sendino, José. 1949. *La escala de Mahoma: Traducción del árabe al castellano, latín y frances, ordenada por Alfonso X el Sabio.* Madrid: Ministerio de Asuntos Exteriores.

Murphy, Cullen. 1984. "Nostalgia for the Dark Ages." *Atlantic* May, pp. 12–16.

Nardi, Bruno. 1983. *Dante e la cultura medievale.* Bari, Italy: Laterza.

Newman, F. X., ed. 1968. *The Meaning of Courtly Love: Papers of the First Annual Conference of the Center for Medieval and Early Renaissance Studies, State University of New York at Binghampton, March 17–18, 1967.* Albany: State University of New York Press.

Nichols, Stephen G., Jr. 1983. "Deeper into History." *L'Esprit Créateur* 23, no. 1:91–102.

Nicholson, Reynold A. [1907] 1969. *A Literary History of the Arabs.* Cambridge: Cambridge Univ. Press.

Nolthenius, Hélène. 1968. *Duecento: The Late Middle Ages in Italy.* New York: McGraw-Hill.

Norwich, John Julius. 1970. *The Kingdom in the Sun, 1130–1194.* New York: Harper and Row.

Nykl, A. R. 1931. See Ibn Hazm 1931.

———. 1933. "La poesía a ambos lados del Pirineo hacia el año 1100." *Al-Andalus* 1:357–408. Spanish version of the introduction to Ibn Hazm 1931.

———. 1939. "L'influence arabe-andalouse sur les troubadours." *Bulletin Hispanique* 41:305–15.

———. 1946. *Hispano-Arabic Poetry and its Relations with the Old Provençal Troubadours.* Baltimore: J. H. Furst. Includes an English version of Nykl 1939.

L'Occidente e l'Islam nell'alto medioevo. 1965. 2 vols. Spoleto: Centro Italiano di Studi sull'Alto Medioevo.

O'Donoghue, Bernard, ed. 1982. *The Courtly Love Tradition.* Manchester: Manchester University Press.

Paden, William D., Jr., et al. 1981. "The Poems of the *Trobairitz* Na Castelloza." *Romance Philology* 35:158–82.

Paris, Gaston. 1888. *La Littérature française au moyen âge* (XIe au XIVe siècle). Paris: Librairie Hachette.

———. 1895. "Contes orientaux dans la litterature française au moyen âge." In *La Poésie française du moyen âge*, 2:75–108. Paris: Librairie Hachette.

Parodi, E. G. 1915. "La miscredenza di Guido Cavalcanti e una fonte del Boccaccio." *Bolletino della Società Dantesca* 22:37–47.

Parry, John Jay. See Andreas Capellanus.

Payen, Jean Charles, ed. 1974. *Les Tristan en vers*. Paris: Garnier.

———. 1979. "L'invention idéologique chez Guillaume IX d'Aquitaine." *L'Esprit Créateur* 19, no. 4:95–106.

Percival, Keith. 1975. "The Grammatical Tradition and the Rise of the Vernaculars." In *Trends in Linguistics* 13, pt. 1:231–75.

———. n.d. "Syntax in the Middle Ages." Unpublished paper.

Pérès, Henri. 1953. *La poésie andalouse en arabe classique au XIe siècle: Ses aspects généraux, ses principaux thèmes et sa valeur documentaire*. Publications de l'Institut d'Etudes Orientales, Faculté des Lettres d'Alger. Paris: Adrien-Maisonneuve.

———. 1983. *Esplendor de al-Andalus: La poesía andaluza en árabe clásico en el siglo XI: Sus aspectos generales, sus principales temas y su valor documental*. Trans. Mercedes García Arenal. Madrid: Hiperión.

Pernoud, Régine. 1977. *Pour en finir avec le moyen âge*. Paris: Editions du Seuil.

Peters, F. E. 1968. *Aristotle and the Arabs: The Aristotelian Tradition in Islam*. New York: New York University Press.

Petrus Alfonsi. See Hermes 1977; Jones and Keller 1969; and M. J. Lacarra 1980.

Pirenne, Henri. 1937. *Mahomet et Charlemagne*. Paris: Félix Alcan.

Poirion, Daniel. 1979. "Literary Meaning in the Middle Ages: From a Sociology of Genres to an Anthropology of Works." *New Literary History* 10:401–8.

Press, A. R. 1970. "The Adulterous Nature of *Fin' Amors:* A Re-Examination of the Theory." *Forum for Modern Language Studies* 6:327–41.

Prévost, Claude. 1972. "Littérature et idéologie: Propositions pour une réflexion théorique." *Nouvelle Critique* 57, no. 238:16–23.

Prinz, Joachim. 1966. *Popes from the Ghetto: A View of Medieval Christendom*. New York: Dorset Press.

Procter, Evelyn S. 1951. *Alfonso X of Castile: Patron of Literature and Learning*. Oxford: Oxford University Press, Clarendon Press.

Quaglio, Antonio Enzo. 1964. "Prima fortuna della glossa garbiana a 'Donna me prega' del Cavalcanti." *Giornale Storico della Letteratura Italiana* 141:336–68.

Ramírez Calvente, Angel. 1974. "Jarchas, moaxajas, zéjeles I." *Al-Andalus* 39:273–99.

———. 1976. "Dúplica al Prof. Harvey." *Al-Andalus* 41:237–39.

Reese, Gustave. 1940. *Music in the Middle Ages*. New York: W. W. Norton.

Ribera y Tarragó, Julián. [1896] 1972. *Bibliófilos y bibliotecas en la España musulmana*. Reprint. New York: Burt Franklin.

———. [1927] 1975. *Historia de la música árabe medieval y su influencia en la Española*. Madrid: Editorial Volvontad. Reprint. New York: AMS Press.

———. 1928. *Disertaciones y opúsculos*. 2 vols. Madrid: Estanislao Maestre.

Richard, Jean. 1949. "La *Chanson de Syracon* et la légende de Saladin." *Journal Asiatique* 237:155–58.

————. 1966. "Le Vogue de l'Orient dans la littérature occidentale du moyen âge." Reprinted in *Les Relations entre l'Orient et l'Occident au moyen âge*. London: Variorum Reprints, 1977.

Riquer, Martín de. 1953. "'Hei, ore dolce, qui de France venés.'" *Cultura Neolatina* 13:86–90.

Rizzitano, Umberto. 1958. *Un compendio dell'antologia di poeti arabo-siciliani initolata ad-Durrah al-hatīrah min śufara' al-Gazirah d Ibn al-Quaṭṭa' "il Siciliano" (433–515 Eg.)*. Vol 8, fascicle 5:335–79. Rome: Academia Nazionale dei Lincei.

————. 1975. *Storia e cultura nella Sicilia saracena*. Palermo: Flaccovio.

————. 1977. "La Sicilia e l'Islam." *I Problemi di Ulisse* 14:62–71.

Rizzitano, Umberto, with Francesco Giunta. 1967. *Terra senza crociati*. Palermo: Flaccovio.

Robertson, D. W. 1968. "The Concept of Courtly Love as an Impediment to the Understanding of Medieval Texts." In *The Meaning of Courtly Love*, 1–18. See Newman 1968.

Roncaglia, Aurelio. 1949. "Laisat estar lo gazel (Contributo alla discussione sui rapporti fra lo zagial e la ritmica romanza)." *Cultura Neolatina* 9:67–99.

————. 1952. "'Can la frej' aura venta.'" *Cultura Neolatina* 12:255–64.

————. 1977. "Gli arabi e le origini della lirica neolatina." *I Problemi di Ulisse* 14:72–81.

Rosenthal, Franz. See Ibn Khaldūn [1958] 1967.

Roth, Norman 1985. *Maimonides: Essays and Texts, 850th Anniversary*. Madison, Wis.: Hispanic Seminary.

de Rougemont, Denis. 1956. *Love in the Western World*. Rev. ed. New York: Fawcett.

Rubia Barcia, José, ed. 1976. *Américo Castro and the Meaning of Spanish Civilization*. Berkeley: University of California Press.

Said, Edward W. 1978. *Orientalism*. New York: Pantheon.

————. 1982. "Opponents, Audiences, Constituencies, and Community." *Critical Inquiry* 9:1–26.

————. 1983. "Response to Stanley Fish." *Critical Inquiry* 10:371–73.

Sánchez-Albornoz, Claudio. [1956] 1966. *España, un enigma histórico*. 2 vols. Buenos Aires: Editorial Sudamericana.

————. 1965. *El Islam de España y el Occidente*. Madrid: Espasa Calpe.

————. 1973. *El drama de la formación de España y los españoles: Otra nueva aventura polémica*. Barcelona: EDHASA.

————. 1979. *Estudios polémicos*. Madrid: Espasa Calpe.

Sarton, George. 1927–48. *Introduction to the History of Science*. 3 vols. Baltimore: Published for the Carnegie Institution of Washington by Williams and Wilkins.

————. 1951. *The Incubation of Western Culture in the Middle East*. Washington, D.C.: Library of Congress.

Saville, Jonathan. 1972. *The Medieval Erotic Alba: Structure as Meaning*. New York: Columbia University Press.

Scaglione, Aldo. 1984. "The Mediterranean's Three Spiritual Shores: Images of the Self between Christianity and Islam in the Later Middle Ages." In *The Craft of Fiction: Essays in Medieval Poetics*, ed. Leigh A. Arrathoon, 453–74. Rochester, Mich.: Solaris Press.

Schacht, Joseph, with C. E. Bosworth, eds. 1974. *The Legacy of Islam*. Oxford: Oxford University Press, Clarendon Press.

Schack, Adolf Friedrich graf von. 1865. *Poesía y arte de los árabes en España y Sicilia*. Trans. Juan Valera. Buenos Aires: Editorial el Nilo.

Seay, Albert, 1975. *Music in the Medieval World*. Englewood Cliffs, N.J.: Prentice-Hall.

Silver, Daniel Jeremy. 1974. *A History of Judaism*. Vol. 1, *From Abraham to Maimonides*. New York: Basic Books.

Silverstein, Theodore. 1949. "Andreas, Plato, and the Arabs: Remarks on Some Recent Accounts of Courtly Love." *Modern Philology* 47:117–26.

Singleton, Charles S. 1954. *Dante Studies*. Vol. 1, *Commedia: Elements of Structure*. Cambridge, Mass.: Harvard University Press.

———. 1958. *Journey to Beatrice*. Baltimore: Johns Hopkins University Press.

Smarr, Janet Levarie 1976. "Symmetry and Balance in the *Decameron*." *Mediaevalia* 2:159–87.

Smith, Nathaniel B. 1978. Review of *Le Vocabulaire courtois des troubadours à l'époque classique*, by Glynnis M. Cropp. *Romance Philology* 31:526–33.

Sola-Solé, José María. *Corpus de poesía mozárabe* (Las ḫarǧas andalusies). Barcelona: Ediciones Hispam.

Southern, R. W. 1953. *The Making of the Middle Ages*. New Haven: Yale University Press.

———. 1962. *Western Views of Islam in the Middle Ages*. Cambridge, Mass.: Harvard University Press.

Spitzer, Leo. 1944. *L'Amour lointain de Jaufré Rudel et le sens de la poésie des troubadours*. University of North Carolina Studies in Romance Language and Literature. Chapel Hill: University of North Carolina Press.

———. 1952. "The Mozarabic Lyric and Theodor Frings' Theories." *Comparative Literature* 4:1–22.

Stern, Samuel Miklos. 1948. "Les vers finaux en espagnol dans les muwaššaḥs hispano-hebraiques." *Al-Andalus* 13:299–346.

———. [1953] 1964. *Les chansons mozarabes: Les vers finaux (kharjas) en espagnol dans les muwashshahs arabes et hébreux*. Palermo: U. Manfredi. Reprint. Oxford: Bruno Cassirer.

———. 1959. "The Muwashshaḥas of Abraham Ibn Ezra." In *Hispanic Studies in Honour of I. González Llubera*, ed. Frank W. Pierce, 367–86. Oxford: Dolphin.

———. 1974. *Hispano-Arabic Strophic Poetry: Studies*. Ed. L. P. Harvey. Oxford: Clarendon Press.

Stern, Samuel Miklos, and Edward M. Wilson. 1965. "Mozarabic." In *Eos: An Enquiry into the Theme of Lovers' Meetings and Partings at Dawn in Poetry*, ed. Arthur T. Hatto, 299–303, 322–23. The Hague: Mouton.

Sutherland, D. R. 1956. "The Language of the Troubadours and the Problem of Origins." *French Studies* 10:199–215.

Terrasse, Henri. 1958. *Islam d'Espagne, une rencontre de l'Orient et de l'Occident*. Paris: Plon.

Topsfield, L. T. 1975. *Troubadours and Love*. Cambridge: Cambridge University Press.

degli Uberti, Fazio. 1883. *Liriche edite ed inedite*. Ed. Rodolfo Renier. Florence: Sansoni.

————. 1952. *Il Dittamondo e Le Rime*. Ed. Giuseppe Corsi. 2 vols. Bari, Italy: Laterza.

Vance, Eugene. 1980. "*Aucassin et Nicolette* as a Medieval Comedy of Signification and Exchange." In *The Nature of Medieval Narrative,* ed. Minnette Grunmann-Goudet and Robin F. Jones, 57–76. Lexington, Ky.: French Forum.

Van Cleve, Thomas Curtis. 1972. *The Emperor Frederick II of Hohenstaufen: Immutator Mundi*. Oxford: Oxford University Press, Clarendon Press.

Vernet, Ginés, Juan. 1966. *Literatura árabe*. Barcelona: Editorial Labor.

————. 1978. *La cultura hispanoárabe en Oriente y Occidente*. Barcelona: Ariel.

Von Grunebaum, Gustave E. 1953. 2d ed. *Medieval Islam: A Study in Cultural Orientation*. 2d ed. Chicago: University of Chicago Press.

Walpole, Ronald N. 1960. "Jaufré Rudel—Who Can Open the Book?" *Romance Philology* 13:429–41.

Watt, W. Montgomery. 1972. *The Influence of Islam on Medieval Europe*. Edinburgh: Edinburgh University Press.

————. 1974. "Il contributo arabo alla cultura europea." In *La coscienza dell'altro*. Florence: Cultura.

Watt, W. Montgomery, with Pierre Cachia. 1965. *A History of Islamic Spain*. Edinburgh: Edinburgh University Press.

Whinnom, Keith. 1967. *Spanish Literary Historiography: Three Forms of Distortion*. Exeter, England: University of Exeter Press.

White, Hayden. 1973. *Metahistory: The Historical Imagination in Nineteenth-Century Europe*. Baltimore: Johns Hopkins University Press.

————. 1982. "The Politics of Historical Interpretation: Discipline and De-Sublimation." *Critical Inquiry* 9:113–37.

Wilkins, Ernest H. 1915. "The Invention of the Sonnet." *Modern Philology* 13:463–94.

Wolff, Philippe. 1968. *The Awakening of Europe*. Trans. Anne Carter. Baltimore: Penguin Books.

Wright, William. See Ibn Jubayr 1907.

Zumthor, Paul. 1943. "Notes en marge du traité de l'amour de André le Chapelain." *Zeitschrift für romanische Philologie* 63:178–91.

————. 1954. "Au berceau du lyrisme européen." *Cahiers du Sud* 41, no. 326: 1–61.

————. 1970. "De la circularité du chant à propos des trouvères des XIIe et XIIIe siècles." *Poétique* 2:129–40.

————. 1975. "Autobiographie au Moyen Age?" In *Langue, texte, énigme*, 165–80. Paris: Éditions du Seuil.

Index

University of Pennsylvania Press

Middle Ages Series

Edward Peters, GENERAL EDITOR

Edward Peters, ed. *Christian Society and the Crusades, 1198–1229.* Sources in Translation, including The Capture of Damietta by Oliver of Paderborn. 1971

Edward Peters, ed. *The First Crusade: The Chronicle of Fulcher of Chartres and Other Source Materials.* 1971

Katherine Fischer Drew, trans. *The Burgundian Code: The Book of Constitutions or Law of Gundobad and Additional Enactments.* 1972

G. G. Coulton. *From St. Francis to Dante: Translations from the Chronicle of the Franciscan Salimbene (1221–1288).* 1972

Alan C. Kors and Edward Peters, eds. *Witchcraft in Europe, 1110–1700: A Documentary History.* 1972

Richard C. Dales. *The Scientific Achievement of the Middle Ages.* 1973

Katherine Fischer Drew, trans. *The Lombard Laws.* 1973

Henry Charles Lea. *The Ordeal.* Part III of Superstition and Force. 1973

Henry Charles Lea. *Torture.* Part IV of Superstition and Force. 1973

Henry Charles Lea (Edward Peters, ed.). *The Duel and the Oath.* Parts I and II of Superstition and Force. 1974

Edward Peters, ed. *Monks, Bishops, and Pagans: Christian Culture in Gaul and Italy, 500–700.* 1975

Jeanne Krochalis and Edward Peters, ed. and trans. *The World of Piers Plowman.* 1975

Julius Goebel, Jr. *Felony and Misdemeanor: A Study in the History of Criminal Law.* 1976

Susan Mosher Stuard, ed. *Women in Medieval Society.* 1976

James Muldoon, ed. *The Expansion of Europe: The First Phase.* 1977

Clifford Peterson. *Saint Erkenwald.* 1977

Robert Somerville and Kenneth Pennington, eds. *Law, Church, and Society: Essays in Honor of Stephen Kuttner.* 1977

Donald E. Queller. *The Fourth Crusade: The Conquest of Constantinople, 1201–1204.* 1977

Pierre Riché (Jo Ann McNamara, trans.). *Daily Life in the World of Charlemagne.* 1978

Charles R. Young. *The Royal Forests of Medieval England.* 1979

Edward Peters, ed. *Heresy and Authority in Medieval Europe.* 1980

Suzanne Fonay Wemple. *Women in Frankish Society: Marriage and the Cloister, 500–900.* 1981

R. G. Davies and J. H. Denton, eds. *The English Parliament in the Middle Ages.* 1981

Edward Peters. *The Magician, the Witch, and the Law.* 1982

Barbara H. Rosenwein. *Rhinoceros Bound: Cluny in the Tenth Century.* 1982

Steven D. Sargent, ed. and trans. *On the Threshold of Exact Science: Selected Writings of Anneliese Maier on Late Medieval Natural Philosophy.* 1982

Benedicta Ward. *Miracles and the Medieval Mind: Theory, Record, and Event, 1000–1215.* 1982

Harry Turtledove, trans. *The Chronicle of Theophanes: An English Translation of anni mundi 6095–6305 (A.D. 602–813).* 1982

Leonard Cantor, ed. *The English Medieval Landscape.* 1982

Charles T. Davis. *Dante's Italy and Other Essays.* 1984

George T. Dennis, trans. *Maurice's Strategikon: Handbook of Byzantine Military Strategy.* 1984

Thomas F. X. Noble. *The Republic of St. Peter: The Birth of the Papal State, 680–825.* 1984

Kenneth Pennington. *Pope and Bishops: The Papal Monarchy in the Twelfth and Thirteenth Centuries.* 1984

Patrick J. Geary. *Aristocracy in Provence: The Rhône Basin at the Dawn of the Carolingian Age.* 1985

C. Stephen Jaeger. *The Origins of Courtliness: Civilizing Trends and the Formation of Courtly Ideals, 939–1210.* 1985

J. N. Hillgarth, ed. *Christianity and Paganism, 350–750: The Conversion of Western Europe.* 1986

William Chester Jordan. *From Servitude to Freedom: Manumission in the Sénonais in the Thirteenth Century.* 1986

James William Brodman. *Ransoming Captives in Crusader Spain: The Order of Merced on the Christian-Islamic Frontier.* 1986

Frank Tobin. *Meister Eckhart: Thought and Language.* 1986

Daniel Bornstein, trans. *Dino Compagni's Chronicle of Florence.* 1986

James M. Powell. *Anatomy of a Crusade, 1213–1221.* 1986

Jonathan Riley-Smith. *The First Crusade and the Idea of Crusading.* 1986

Susan Mosher Stuard, ed. *Women in Medieval History and Historiography.* 1987

Avril Henry, ed. *The Mirour of Mans Saluacioune.* 1987

María Menocal. *The Arabic Role in Medieval Literary History.* 1987

Margaret J. Ehrhart. *The Judgment of the Trojan Prince Paris in Medieval Literature.* 1987

Betsy Bowden. *Chaucer Aloud: The Varieties of Textual Interpretation.* 1987

Felipe Fernández-Armesto. *Before Columbus: Exploration and Colonization from the Mediterranean to the Atlantic, 1229–1492.* 1987

Michael Resler, trans. *EREC by Hartmann von Aue.* 1987

Alastair J. Minnis. *Medieval Theory of Authorship.* 1987

Uta-Renate Blumenthal. *The Investiture Controversy: Church and Monarchy from the Ninth to the Twelfth Century.* 1988

Robert Hollander. *Boccaccio's Last Fiction: "Il Corbaccio."* 1988

Ralph Turner. *Men Raised from the Dust: Administrative Service and Upward Mobility in Angevin England.* 1988

David Anderson. *Before the Knight's Tale: Imitation of Classical Epic in Boccaccio's Teseida.* 1988

Charlotte A. Newman. *The Anglo-Norman Nobility in the Reign of Henry I: The Second Generation.* 1988

Joseph F. O'Callaghan. *The Cortes of Castile-León, 1188–1350.* 1989

William D. Paden. *The Voice of the Trobairitz: Essays on the Women Troubadours.* 1989

William Chester Jordan. *The French Monarchy and the Jews: From Philip Augustus to the Last Capetians.* 1989

Edward B. Irving, Jr. *Rereading Beowulf.* 1989

David Burr. *Olivi and Franciscan Poverty: The Origins of the Usus Paper Controversy.* 1989

Willene B. Clark and Meradith T. McMunn, eds. *Beasts and Birds of the Middle Ages: The Bestiary and Its Legacy.* 1989

Richard C. Hoffmann. *Land, Liberties, and Lordship in a Late Medieval Countryside: Agrarian Structures and Change in the Duchy of Wrocław.* 1989

J. M. W. Bean. *From Lord to Patron: Lordship in Late Medieval England.* 1989

Mary F. Wack. *Lovesickness in the Middle Ages: The Viaticum and Its Commentaries.* 1989

Robert I. Burns, S. J., ed. *Emperor of Culture: Alfonso X the Learned of Castile and His Thirteenth-Century Renaissance.* 1990

E. Ann Matter. *The Voice of My Beloved: The Song of Songs in Western Medieval Christianity.* 1990

Patricia Terry. *Poems of the Elder Edda.* 1990

Ronald Surtz. *The Guitar of God: Gender, Power, and Authority in the Visionary World of Mother Juana de la Cruz (1481–1534).* 1990